ADOPTING THE LIBRARY OF CONGRESS CLASSIFICATION SYSTEM

ADOPTING THE LIBRARY OF CONGRESS CLASSIFICATION SYSTEM

A MANUAL OF METHODS AND TECHNIQUES FOR APPLICATION OR CONVERSION

□

by RAIMUND E. MATTHIS
and DESMOND TAYLOR

□

R. R. BOWKER COMPANY, New York & London, 1971

Published by R. R. Bowker Co. (a Xerox company)
1180 Avenue of the Americas, New York, N.Y. 10036
Copyright © 1971 by Xerox Corporation
International Standard Book Number: 0–8352–0493–6
Library of Congress Catalog Card Number: 72–163906
Printed and bound in the United States of America

To Betty
a wife of exceptional forbearance
R.E.M.

For
Erica, Onica, and Ingeborg
D.T.

Contents

Preface

With the appearance of the printed card and more specifically with the availability of the *Catalog of Printed Cards*, the *Author Catalog*, and the *National Union Catalog*, the means for centralized cataloging has arrived. No longer must administrator and librarian tolerate the time-consuming and expensive practices characteristic of the Dewey Decimal Classification system—practices which require local catalogers to do independently, and ofttimes arbitrarily, what is now done centrally.

In 1967 the Council on Library Resources funded our proposal to write a comprehensive manual on the use of the Library of Congress Classification system. The full impact of our presumptuousness in this undertaking became more apparent the further we became involved in the project. After a two-week visit to the Library of Congress in the spring of 1968, it became clear that our original proposal would likely develop into a lifetime project and would have to be more limited in scope. As a result we decided to restrict ourselves to describing the organization of a reclassification project and to discussing some of the more troublesome problems associated with the application of the Library of Congress Classification system.

This manual is designed to make it possible for any library to change efficiently to the Library of Congress Classification system. Detailed procedures are outlined which may serve as exact models or as a series of suggested steps which have proven effective in actual use. Most of the text deals with the necessary criteria for effecting the planning, making the preparations, selecting the tools, and establishing the procedures which are essential for a reclassification project. Beyond this, considerable attention has been given to many of the problem areas of the LC Classification—series, biography, bibliography, law, PZ3 and PZ4. In addition, the literature Tables VIIIa and IXa, two of the most frequently used tables throughout the entire class system, have been thoroughly explained and their application illustrated by a series of comprehensive examples. Since the mechanics, production, and cost of catalog card copy can significantly affect the flow of books to users, a chapter has been devoted to describing the use of Xerox copying machines in library operations. Finally, an annotated bibliography of books and articles judged to be helpful in deciding to reclassify is included for those readers who wish to delve more deeply into the torturous and frustrating 50-year history of the concept of centralized cataloging and classification. The numbers enclosed in parentheses throughout the text refer to sources in the bibliography which relate to or support the arguments being advanced in any particular case.

The letter combination LC is used to refer to the Library of Congress Classification system; L.C. is used to refer to the Library of Congress. The letter combination DC refers, of course, to the Dewey Decimal Classification system.

Naturally, in such a project as this we have come to owe a debt of gratitude to a number of helpful people. We especially thank Mr. Edward D'Arms, Associate Director of the Ford Foundation, for his help in our successful application for a grant from the Council on Library Resources. The cooperation and gracious assistance of the Library of Congress—and particularly of Mr. Robert R. Holms, Assistant Director for Processing Service, and Dr. Charles C. Bead, Chief of the Subject Cataloging Division—are greatly appreciated. Also our grateful thanks go to.Elizabeth B. Lockwood, Assistant Head of the Shelf-listing Section, Subject Cataloging Division, for her valuable editorial comments on the section dealing with the use of Tables VIIIa and IXa in the literature schedules.

Our special thanks also go to Mrs. Betty Matthis for her able assistance in editing the manuscript. All photographs with the exception of Figures 1, 6, and 7 in Chapter 4 were done by Mr. Peter Zoeller of Architectural Graphics (Tacoma, Washington), who interrupted a heavy work schedule of his own to supply us with clear illustrative material. Finally, we owe a special word of appreciation to Mrs. Mildred Fawcett who typed the manuscript with perseverence notwithstanding numerous changes and corrections.

RAIMUND E. MATTHIS
DESMOND TAYLOR

University of Puget Sound
Tacoma, Washington

ADOPTING
THE LIBRARY
OF CONGRESS
CLASSIFICATION
SYSTEM

1

Reclassification

1.1 RATIONALE

The debate on DC versus LC continues. Moreover, this continuing dialogue is now confounded by supporters of UDC (Universal Decimal Classification) with their numerous claims of the perfect or "ideal" hierarchical system completely adaptable to machine searching by virtue of an innate syntactical logic. It is not the purpose of this discussion to deal with the "ideal" or the theoretically perfect classificatory system, but rather to dwell on the practicalities of the present as well as the burdens of the future. Therefore, this discussion will deal with the characteristics of an admittedly imperfect classification system with the purpose of recommending it as the one that best solves the problems of library development. That system, obviously, is the Library of Congress Classification system.

Since the conclusion of World War II, library development and book publishing have entered a period of radical change and extraordinary pressures. The quantity of recorded data has grown so overwhelmingly that librarians generally have been forced to reassess their traditional practices and attitudes. The present interest in reclassification, especially to the LC system, marks a significant acknowledgment of the expanding problems of library classification. The development and application of data processing equipment and computers have also encouraged, if not indeed forced, classification reevaluation. State and federal grants for the purchase of library materials have further served to aggravate the growth problem. As a consequence of the literature explosion and an increasing demand for improved search strategies, we have a cataloging dilemma of considerable proportions. Beyond this there is the not unimportant economic factor of increasing costs for cataloging, for library materials, and, by extension, for the total operation of libraries.

The problem then is how to make our present classification scheme more effective in terms of meeting these contemporary problems. For some it has become a question of reclassification or, in the case of present users of LC, streamlining their cataloging and classification procedures toward the fundamental goal of standardization which is, in effect, the practice of centralized cataloging. It is to those who are so concerned that this manual is directed.

For all practical purposes there are only two library classification systems in use in this country: DC and LC. Both have their faults and advantages—neither is perfect. This discussion however will not deal with classification theory, but rather with a rationale which is based on the concept of centralized cataloging and classification.

If for the sake of argument LC and DC were reversed in terms of support— LC supplied by a satellite "LC Office" and DC devised and advanced by the Library of Congress—then DC might serve as the vehicle for a nationwide centralized cataloging and classification program. In this instance the LC class number printed on the cards would be only a suggested number with no Cutter designation, while the Dewey number would be a complete call number as is currently the case with LC. With this hypothetical reversal of backing, DC would then be promoted by the substantial resources of the world's largest library operation. This is the *main* point. Any reasonably comprehensive classification system developed and maintained by the considerable means of a federally supported agency, that is, the Library of Congress, is the logical classification system for general library use.

As a matter of fact, some maintain that the Dewey Office at L.C. is actually supplying this kind of service. It is claimed that 35 percent or more of printed cards carry a suggested DC class number with the percentage increasing all of the time (16, 17). Nevertheless, one would be hard pressed to consider the work of the Dewey Office as a legitimate manifestation of centralized cataloging and classification. In the first place, no Cuttering is supplied for DC class numbers— a deficiency which involves a time-consuming and costly shelflisting operation; secondly, the DC number is only a suggested number and on older printed cards it may be many editions of Dewey away from the current classificatory usage. With regard to changes in classification the same criticism admittedly has been leveled against LC by Richmond, Perreault, and others, and naturally over the years there have been changes in the LC schedules. Seldom however have these changes resulted in the extraordinary dislocations which so often occur in each new edition of Dewey. In fact in 1964 the Classification Committee of the Resources and Technical Services Division of ALA made this following observation about LC. "It is easy to expand without upsetting classified books. The advantage of a nonlogical classification is apparent in dealing with rapidly advancing subjects, as the sciences, where a major change in thought can throw out a whole branch in a previous arrangement of knowledge. L.C. can interpolate where D.C. must compromise" (16).

Curiously there are those who cavil with the interpolative capabilities of LC and assert that since LC also undergoes revision there is no substantive difference between LC and DC (120). It is our conviction that the continuous revision and interpolative capability of LC represents a strength and not a weakness of the system. It goes without saying that there will always be classification changes and/or amplifications in any system which attempts to cover a growing and expanding collection of materials. The bases for classification changes should always be (1) an acceptable incorporation of new knowledge into a preexistent system, (2) a minimal disjointure of the existing scheme, and (3) an active discouragement of the need for physical reprocessing. With these three criteria in mind one might be inclined to observe that any perfect system is a dead system, and a classification system based on a total view of knowledge is preposterously presumptuous. The Library of Congress Classification system, unconfined by hermetic philosophical assumptions which hold that all knowledge advances in a logical and regular order, can expand to reflect the emergence of the new and accommodate the development of the old with minor dislocations to the existing scheme.

Proponents of Dewey tend to advance what they regard as a telling argument in favor of DC—namely, that DC attempts to group related materials in a more meaningful way than LC. If this is a telling argument, its logic is lost in the face of the real world of library practice. This real world finds special collections of all descriptions (e.g., reference, document, map, phonorecord, microcard, microfilm, oversize, etc.), and, indeed, there is a quality of speciousness about the everything-on-one-subject-in-one-location argument. While genuine reasons exist for attempting to keep related materials together, these reasons cannot be advanced as excuses for ignoring basic problems in the organizing and handling of materials. Ralph Shaw notes that

> [There is] no evidence that the best single classification system, whatever that may mean, is any better than the worst single one for all sizes of universities and all types of materials. While library book classification is supposed to locate a physical object rather than ideas, and bibliographical classification is supposed to be a system for bringing out the ideas in the publications, in both cases their major function is primarily to let one return to something we have recorded as allegedly saying something about the subject we are looking for. (134)

While this statement is quite explicit in its one-classification-system-is-as-good-as-another position, the implicit suggestion seems to be that centralized cataloging and classification *is* the key to library classification problems and not some other system which requires original cataloging on a local or individual basis. Essentially the argument has now moved beyond theoretical discussions of the "best" classification system and settled upon the real issue—the promise and prospect of centralized cataloging and classification. No one classification system will ever solve all of the problems, but the practice of "rugged individualism" in cataloging no longer makes sense and should no longer be tolerated.

For many years the Library of Congress has been a bona fide centralized cataloging operation. By virtue of its immense collection and its extensive acquisition program, the Library of Congress has had to develop a classification system which is rivaled by none in detail or comprehensiveness. Through the cataloging-in-publication program with selected foreign countries and its own activities, the Library of Congress—and, by extension, the LC Classification system—represents a unique opportunity available to all libraries to participate in an authentic nationwide centralized classification and cataloging program. It is apparent that the way is clear; only the impulse is wanting.

As with all things, there will be naysayers among whom, of course, are the information retrieval specialists. These maidens of the machine caution that LC's illogical notation and limited hierarchical capabilities make future machine searching a chancy affair. Perreault's classic paper describes this deficiency (110). But so what? This is but another and newer argument against the use of LC and once again dourly warns us to wait (how many more years?) while shuffling alongside our present outdated Conestoga wagon. Even more interestingly, we are counseled to junk presently used classification schemes and switch to the Universal Decimal Classification system—a system not yet completely developed. This move, however, would mean that we still would continue to catalog locally.

Undoubtedly at some point in the future machine searching for subject relationships will be feasible and maybe even inexpensive. Consequently, it is only right for librarians to be thinking about the implications regarding this kind of technological adjunct to the more traditional library approaches. Even with this eventuality, however, there seems little likelihood that the classification systems now in existence are going to supply the kinds of sophisticated notation necessary for comprehensive machine searching. Regardless of which classification system is generally in use in the future, extensive readjustments and relocations will have to be made to make classification and machine reading systems compatible. Considering the inherent deficiencies of any notational system, one might not inappropriately suggest that machine search strategies in the future will develop on verbal rather than classificatory principles. If one considers for a moment the financial implications of a genuine attempt to utilize computer technology on a wide basis in the library world, one automatically concludes that only the resources of a large and broadly financed organization will be able to cope with such an expensive and experimental project. Would it be presumptuous to assume that the large and broadly financed organization will be the Library of Congress? Moreover, it is farfetched to imagine that experiments with the application of computer technology in libraries will not in some way be related to what already exists at the Library of Congress.

As long as a library is a place where objects such as books are stored for the purpose of education and pleasure and not a place containing shining banks of computer consoles, it will be necessary to utilize some moderately effective organizational scheme which will allow for the retrieval of those objects with a minimum expenditure of time and money. The organizational scheme which at present seems best to fulfill these not too modest demands is the Library of Congress Classification system, which supplies reasonable subject relationships with substantial savings in time and money.

Inasmuch as economy is the basic reason for reclassification, it is important to emphasize that a library adopting, or for that matter using, LC must avoid as much as possible any procedure devised to check whether the Library of Congress is using its own system correctly. With few exceptions (few considering the size of its classification scheme), the call numbers supplied on L.C. printed cards should be accepted. Naturally errors in typography and judgment have occurred in the long history of the L.C. printed card; however, the economic advantage of adopting LC is lost if every call number is verified by each library using the scheme. The relatively few real errors which do occur can be corrected at the time the shelflist cards are filed. A well-trained clerk can spot the obvious errors; smaller errors can be ignored, for they offend no one but the cataloger.

One of the basic problems involved in using or converting to LC is what might be called "the cataloger mystique"—a practice which prompts a Dewey number like 909.09171239206, the suggested Dewey Office class number for *The Dutch Seaborne Empire, 1600–1800* by C. R. Boxer. Was this number constructed for the subject-oriented user or the classification-oriented cataloger? (Incidently, the Library of Congress call number, not class number, for this title is JV2511. B67.) To carry the discussion of notational monstrosities one step further, we might entertain the following UDC class number [73+75]*034(45)*025*:727*7 (729*11). This, if you will, is a class number and not a call number. Now what information does this number supply? It symbolizes "the complex heading sculpture–painting of the Renaissance in Italy–its restoration in the art galleries of Havana" (110). When notation becomes as specific as this, a number of questions come to mind: (1) Do people or computers need this kind of notation? (2) What is accomplished by this kind of specificity? (3) Who is willing or able to pay the cost? Unquestionably UDC demonstrates the niceties of a logical, hierarchical classificatory system, but it also reveals the kinds of gamesmanship catalogers can be drawn into by the systems they use. Inevitably, a book will cover more than one subject, and quixotic attempts to accommodate a multiplicity of subjects within a single classificatory notation seem doomed at the outset.

In view of what has been discussed, it can be said that the primary reason for adopting LC is economy—economy resulting from keying into the world's most extensive library operation. To a large degree the library world has accomplished this already—we accept without question the entries established by LC; we fill our public catalogs with subject headings devised by LC. All of these practices are accepted and done because we recognize that to do them individually would be nonsense. What prideful "hang-up," then, paralyzes the decision to take the next logical step? While it is impossible to give an exact, overall dollars and cents saving for libraries throughout the country, it is possible for each library to assess its own cataloging costs in terms of its salary and wage scales and come up with some rather startling figures. If one examines library literature on cataloging costs, little doubt remains that substantial savings are associated with the adoption of the Library of Congress Classification system.

1.2 POLITICS

It is our position that LC offers a clearly superior system over all others presently in use. Once this thesis is accepted, we firmly believe that LC should be introduced into a given library at the earliest possible time—even if no special funds are available for a reclassification project. Whether one agrees with the "no special funds" position or not, there are staff considerations, human and political, that must be carefully thought out before proposing a change to the LC system.

The initial and most important step is for the chief librarian to inform the professional library staff about the superior efficiency of LC over the presently used classification system. Although not everyone on the staff will agree that reclassification is necessary, professional staff participation in these important decision-making phases is only fair considering the total systems change that will be the inevitable result of reclassification. While it must be remembered that the basic responsibility for a reclassification decision belongs to the chief librarian, it may be extremely useful to appoint a committee of either professional librarians or a mixture of faculty and librarians to investigate the merits of a classification change. It may also be helpful to have professional staff members contact and visit several libraries that have converted to LC for a firsthand report on their experiences. Ultimately, however, committed, firm leadership will be necessary to convince and/or carry any hesitant professional staff member and, for that matter, to push the reclassification project to an orderly and speedy conclusion.

Given the chief librarian's administrative decision, the key person necessary for a successful reclassification project is the librarian in charge of technical services. This individual must be able to use the Library of Congress Classification system, design viable procedures for reclassification, and discard outmoded and clumsy routines. For example, during the first year of reclassification at a Washington state college library, which shall remain nameless, only professional catalogers were involved with LC. Furthermore, the verification and cross-checking of class numbers traditionally associated with the use of Dewey were still in force. All LC class numbers on printed cards were accepted only after careful checking. Due to the use of these anachronistic and cumbersome procedures, particularly in view of the number of professional catalogers and staff involved, the project moved very slowly. In a recent article Robert Rodgers (123) inadvertently implies that a similar situation exists at several midwestern libraries already on LC. The I-can-catalog-better-than-you-can syndrome, it appears, is sadly inadequate to meet the demands of a real centralized cataloging and classification program.

After the staff has been oriented to the LC system and taken any feasible field trips, the final recommendation for reclassification should be presented to the faculty library committee or another appropriate policy-making body for non-library evaluation and support. Faculty members generally view libraries in terms of their own individual disciplines and are concerned with promoting (1) library resources in their own subject areas and (2) better and faster accessibility to those resources. The fact that the major part of a library's acquisitions can be more quickly processed with greater economy is usually a persuasive argument. More expedient cataloging service with greater economy results in a larger number of books being purchased. Beyond these points certain questions from the faculty will arise concerning LC subject distribution. These questions should be resolved. One tool useful in the resolution of these questions is a booklet titled *Outline of the Library of Congress Classification* published by the Library of Congress. This booklet along with copies of the appropriate class schedule for any given subject area should be made available to each faculty member. It is not difficult to demonstrate with the aid of the outline and the various class schedules that respect for subject discipline exists within the framework of LC.

The last phase in the decision to reclassify is the submission of a formal recommendation to the administration of the parent institution. Naturally it is at this stage that the costs of reclassification will be most critically examined. There should be no attempt made to imply to the administration that the reclassification project will not cost money. Three approaches may be suggested as ways to deal with this problem.

1. The first approach emphasizes the need for special and additional funds for a separate reclassification project. A specially funded operation is undoubtedly the fastest and most efficient method of undertaking a reclassification project. However, bear in mind that, if no extra funds are available, administrative approval may be withheld strictly in the basis of "no funds" and not on the merits of the proposed change.

2. The second approach suggests that the project be undertaken as an integrated part of the present technical services operation. This maneuver combines new acquisitions and reclassified materials into one operation. The estimated cost is then projected on an annual basis for which a reasonable timetable for project completion is established and some idea developed concening the needs for staff enlargements as well as equipment and materials requirements. In this estimate it is prudent to overestimate the length of the reclassification project for obvious reasons. This integrated technical services approach assumes a longer project completion period and consequently a smaller initial funding requirement.

3. The third approach is to make it absolutely clear that, while a reclassification project will be an additional expense for a few years, there is at this time no request for special funds. It should be suggested that only the approval of a systems change is at issue and no immediate funding is necessary. The rationale of this posture is, of course, that with smaller institutions, in particular, the sole criteria of approval or denial of the project will rest on budgetary considerations. After an institutional commitment to reclassify has been made, it will be possible later to ask for and receive supplementary funds.

Without question other approaches might be used effectively in attempting to persuade an administration to allow a reclassification project to be undertaken—the three above are only suggestions. Ultimately the approach to use will to a large extent depend upon the librarian's knowledge of his own institution's administrative character and financial situation. The main point to be made is to select the kind of approach that will most likely result in early project approval.

At the University of Puget Sound the administration was well aware of the eventual costs a reclassification project would generate; however, no special funds were requested during the initial phases of the operation. As a consequence, the systems change was approved, and within the next budget year additional funds were available for personnel and materials. In spite of the inauspicious beginnings of the reclassification project at the University of Puget Sound, the project was completed in four and one half years. For statistics relating to this project see Chapter 2 of this manual.

1.3 ADVANTAGES AND DISADVANTAGES

At this point only a brief discussion of the advantages and disadvantages of using LC is necessary. What will be mentioned are only the more important elements in the whole question of reclassification. For a more extended discussion of details and emphasis, it is recommended that the following papers be consulted: Richmond's paper in *The Use of the Library of Congress Classification: Proceedings* (76), Shell's paper in *Reclassification: Rationale and Problems: Proceedings* (22), and the RTSD statement on various classification systems (16). The above including this manual present the most complete and comprehensive statements in the literature on the advantages of using LC.

Undoubtedly for most librarians the principal disadvantage in using LC is the absence of an instruction manual for its application. Consequently, there is no substitute for experience in its use. LC is not a tight, logical classification of knowledge, but rather a system which builds on what has gone before. Precedent, therefore, plays a vital part in its development.

In a recent survey Gaines reported on the most frequently mentioned problems catalogers encounter in the use of LC (46). The following are their difficulties listed in the descending order of frequency in which they were mentioned.

1. Lack of a comprehensive guide to the use of schedules or tables.

2. The LC Cuttering practices and the arrangement of translations in relation to the original work.

3. Difficulties associated with PZ3 and PZ4.

4. The separation of older and newer material because of revisions in the classification schedules.

5. The need to do original classification when LC classifies a monograph as part of a series.

6. Lack of a complete K (law) schedule.

Another disadvantage of changing to LC is the change itself. Naturally a reclassification project has certain automatic problems associated with it (e.g., two separate collections, staff training, public service, space limitations, etc.). Work procedures are inevitably complicated. One immense problem which must be resolved, particularly in large libraries, is the extent to which reclassification will be undertaken; that is, in what subject areas will reclassification be complete and in what subject areas will it be partial. While favoring a change to LC, Dougherty concludes that the principal argument against complete reclassification is its high cost (29). Selective reclassification would, of course, be appropriate in the case of very large collections. The argument may be advanced that since most libraries are collection conglomerates organized by a number of different schemes there is no reason that older and relatively unused portions of the book collection might not remain in Dewey.

One of the most disturbing assertions made concerning LC is that there are extensive classificatory changes which rival those made in Dewey (120). As it has been pointed out, there are changes, but it is our claim that overall these changes are less burdensome and annoying than those made in DC. A recent analysis by Rowell of *LC Additions and Changes* indicates that relocations in LC need not be considered a deterrent to any library using LC (124). This study confirms our position that a change in LC does not necessarily require reclassification to preserve subject relationships. On the contrary, newly classified material "would nearly always remain within the same subject area" and "relocations generally involve single topics rather than entire sections." The most interesting thing discovered by this study is that considering the large number of new subjects introduced into the scheme over the years there have been comparatively few relocations. Furthermore, the Rowell analysis confirms the RTSD statement that "LC can interpolate where DC must compromise." There seems to be a body of research and argument developing which bears out the position that LC is the most useful and desirable system.

The principal advantages of using LC are economy in cataloging, speed in processing, and the benefits realized from tying into a large centralized cataloging operation. It is surprising that a number of libraries refuse to accept LC because some prior brainwashing has convinced them that there is something essentially untrustworthy about the classification system. As Tauber indicated so many years ago, classification is basically a librarian's device, and "the acceptance of one system, preferably one based on a living collection of books, seems the effective procedure for the future (152)." This opinion is supported by Jackson who also contends that since many libraries use LC subject headings the essential value of these subject headings is lost if they do not work in conjunction with the Library of Congress Classification system, and it goes without saying that this value is neither generally appreciated nor even understood (77).

When a library orders or copies an L.C. printed card it is buying a service which is backed by some of the best professionally trained catalogers and subject specialists.

> Furthermore, LC cards give the LC classification which is usually unchanged in the current LC additions and changes. While the DC classification given on the cards is sometimes completely outmoded by complete revisions in later editions, there is a tendency to more frequently shift subjects to other numbers. Therefore, the LC numbers on the cards usually remain useable. (14)

If the cataloging and classifying is professional, and the call numbers supplied conform to what has gone before, what integrity is sacrificed by the acceptance of a structured though nonlogical classification system? It would appear that the hesitancy to reclassify or to change classification systems is for the most part based on fear and misunderstanding. By and large there has been no genuine effort made on the part of the individual librarian to sort out the mental or emotional factors which prompt thousands of libraries to continue their cataloging with Dewey rather than change to LC. The need for a careful rethinking of "What does a library classification system do?" is now.

2

Cost Data

2.1 THE PROBLEM OF ARRIVING AT A COST FIGURE

The costs associated with reclassification are relative and depend upon a number of variables. One such variable is that salary and wage conditions differ from institution to institution depending upon locality; consequently, the possibility of supplying universal cost estimates or final unit figures for a particular project is very small. Two other variables which will largely affect project cost are the nature of cataloging procedures and the characteristics of what are regarded as acceptable cataloging practices in any given library. If no part of the cataloging process in a particular library is adjusted to conform to the bases dictated by the centralized cataloging concept, slight advantage will accrue as a result of reclassification, and reclassification, if undertaken, will prove very costly.

One approach to a cost analysis of reclassification is to use an average time (or time range) base for each standard step involved in a particular repetitive and/or successive procedure. Hitchcock's analysis utilizes this standard time approach (76). Her paper is the best summary of cost data presently available and is a basic contribution to the cost estimate problems associated with reclassification. In her paper Hitchcock rather strongly recommends the reclassification projects undertaken by the University of Rochester (78), the University of South Carolina (62), and State University of Iowa (81) for their production figures and especially their cost figures. Since these projects were initiated in 1932, 1955, and 1952 respectively, she attempts to update them in terms of present costs. Furthermore, she reports on more recent reclassification projects as well as the results of her own 1965–1966 survey of reclassification procedures and costs. On the basis of this information Hitchcock presents average time estimates for the completion of various basic reclassification activities and by extension supplies a fairly acceptable yardstick for estimating what a reclassification project will cost. Using similar techniques, Cox has reported on his experiences at the University of Maryland (24). Even though the Hitchcock and Cox figures

11

will be briefly summarized in this chapter, it is suggested that careful study be made of each of these papers before any attempt is made to estimate what a reclassification project will cost a particular library.

2.2 COST AVERAGES

One of the most time-consuming procedures built into any reclassification project will be the pulling of catalog cards from the public catalog for the purpose of creating new or altered card sets. How expeditiously this procedure will be effected depends upon whether the method of card altering will be done by pulling and changing one card to be used as a master for xerographic duplication or whether the entire old set will be pulled to be altered and refiled after the appropriate book has been changed. According to the information supplied by Hitchcock, it takes on the average 5 minutes to pull a 5-card set (this period includes 1 minute to make a temporary card for the main entry). On the other hand, Cox estimates that it takes an average of 1½ hours to pull 60 main entries with matching shelflist cards. This breaks down to approximately 1½ minutes per title.

An extension of the card pulling process is naturally the preparation of new or altered card sets to replace those pulled from the public catalog. Although Hitchcock briefly describes three procedures for changing call numbers on catalog cards, she provides complete average times for only one procedure which is erasing and typing of new call numbers on a 5-card set, reported to require 16 minutes of preparation. This average time of 16 minutes for a 5-card set would produce catalog cards for approximately four titles an hour. Cox reports that at the University of Maryland new card sets were made on the basis of pulling the old main entry, covering the call number with Snopake, and typing the new call number on this prepared master, after which the card was duplicated on the Xerox 914 in order to produce the number of cards needed to make a new card set. Using this method of card duplication, Cox estimates that the cost of a 6-card set is $.16 (see Sections 4.3 and 4.4).

After main entries have been pulled, the next most time-consuming procedure is a reclassification project is the professional time devoted to original classification in those cases where class numbers are not supplied on L.C. card copy. With experienced catalogers Hitchcock estimates a probable average of 10 minutes per title for original cataloging, although she prefers a somewhat longer period of 15 minutes as a long-term average. For some peculiar reason she estimates an average of 5 minutes per title for an experienced cataloger even with L.C. card copy. Cox found that an experienced cataloger takes almost 2 minutes to assign a call number with L.C. copy. In their estimates, however, both Cox and Hitchcock speak only in terms of professional catalogers. Our experience has been that a well-trained cataloging clerk can handle all materials for which there is L.C. card copy in slightly less than 3 minutes; an experienced cataloger can perform the task in much less than 2 minutes. Cox estimates that an annual cataloger rate of 6000 volumes or roughly 3000 titles is not an unrealistic goal for a professional cataloger. If routines, training, and attitudes are altered to accept the possibility that a large proportion of cataloging can be organized on a semiprofessional level, there is every chance that the output of semiprofessionals may almost match that of professional personnel.

In rounding out the estimates associated with catalog cards, both Hitchcock and Cox report on the staff time involved in catalog card refiling. Since Cox is working with new card sets, he estimates an average of 5 minutes for typing added entries on a 6-card set and a refiling time, which includes alphabetizing and revision, of 1 minute per card. On the other hand, Hitchcock is reporting on the refiling of old card sets which have had the call numbers erased and changed and includes no typing beyond the call number. She estimates a refiling time of 100 cards per hour.

Another procedure for which both Cox and Hitchcock supply some time figures is the changing of call numbers on book spines. For this task Hitchcock estimates roughly 2 minutes with an additional 2 minutes to change all of the internal markings. (This figure of 4 minutes per book includes supervisory as well as revision time.) Cox reports that it took 1 minute to type two spine labels and an average of 10 seconds per volume to change the internal markings. Apparently of these two labels typed, one was for the spine and the other for covering the penciled markings in the book since he indicates there was a production rate of 30 books an hour for the application of these two labels. Obviously, it is very difficult to draw any specific impressions from these two reports because in each instance different aspects of the process of remarking books are being discussed. The only value offered by this type of reporting is that one can gain some modest suggestion of what is implied by various marking procedures.

At this point it may be of interest to mention briefly some of the results of the time and motion study research of Voos (165). By means of the micromotion technique Voos has supplied an even more detailed and painstaking analysis of standard technical services activities. This technique segments the average time periods involved in various repetitive library operations. For example, a stopwatch and a Veedor–Root counter were used to time and count the number of strokes and carriage returns in typing a main entry. The following information about erasures on catalog cards was gathered using the micromotion technique.

call number and subject	89.8 seconds
call number and imprint	319.6 seconds
subject	29.9 seconds
imprint	104.5 seconds
call number	30.9 seconds

As a result of this research, Voos arrived at some general conclusions about library work processes. For example, if the LC card order number is not readily available, it would be cheaper to order cards from the Library of Congress on the basis of author, title, and imprint information than to search for card order numbers before ordering. (Whether this is still true in terms of recent price increases may be questionable.) In regard to a recataloging operation, Voos found it cheaper to retype an entire catalog card if the items for correction took longer than 110 seconds to erase. An even cheaper practice, if it is acceptable, is to cross out unwanted information on catalog cards and then type the revised information above, next to, or below it. Voos also discovered that clerical routines such as typing, pasting, mending, etc., can be done more efficiently by trained personnel who spend all of their time on such activities. In smaller libraries where such work specialization is not possible, these activities should be planned so that enough time can be spent on a specific operation to overcome initial inertia.

As valuable as average time and motion studies appear to be for developing and/or improving procedures, the problem of arriving at an accurate cost analysis, we believe, is more meaningfully resolved by establishing a monthly production capability determined by an analysis of various categories of staff hours worked. In our opinion, it is the annual production rate with x number of personnel processing x number of volumes that seems to be a more relevant means of determining what will be a reasonably accurate cost estimate of reclassification or, for that matter, of technical services processing operations in general. Any great reliance on average performance times for specific procedures can generate a sense of false production capability. For instance, personnel turnover, individual skill variation, intelligence, etc., are relative factors which will play havoc with any exclusive dependence upon average time data or micromotion analysis. Not all typists have the same manual skills, and not all clerks have the same mental skills. Since clerks with better mental skills are often doing work requiring manual skills and vice versa, it is questionable whether this disparity in skill can be resolved except in the broadest terms by a micromotion study. Consequently, the emphasis in this chapter will be on annual production figures using as models (1) reclassification operations that are integrated or combined with new book cataloging and processing, and (2) reclassification operations that are nonintegrated or independent from new book cataloging and processing.

It should be acknowledged that the reclassification of a book requires a more complex set of procedures than processing a new book does. Involved in book reclassification are a number of basic steps which may or may not be modified by the scope of the project. The number of steps and their modification will depend upon the specific situation and needs of a particular library—the financial resources, the quality of past cataloging, the size of the collection, and the procedural considerations established to serve the public while the reclassification project is in progress. The basic steps are these.

Withdrawing the main entry or complete card set for a given title from the public catalog to change the class designation.

Generating the temporary main entry to refile in the public catalog.

Assigning the LC call number.

Typing the call number on catalog cards, whether a main entry is to be used as a master for duplicating or as a complete card set.

Duplicating a card set from the prepared master.

Collecting the book from the shelf.

Checking the book against the card set.

Remarking the book.

Reshelving the book.

Typing added entries on the newly made card set.

Refiling catalog cards.

As any examination of the literature will demonstrate, there are a number of different ways to proceed with each of these steps. The various ways will not be discussed here as they have been covered in Chapter 4, but the main point to remember is that the procedures which are established for the reclassification project will to a very large degree determine its cost. Therefore, is must be carefully established what reclassification is supposed to accomplish and what can be accomplished within the estimated total cost of the project. Naturally throughout the project there will be certain minimum standards which must be observed regardless of the cost.

In outlining his reclassification project, which would cost $.50 per volume (title), Gore ignores a number of crucial decision areas that must be carefully considered when using LC (51). Lapses in a careful decision making arise from failure to consider these questions.

Should the library use PZ3 and PZ4?

Should the library accept series classification as established by the Library of Congress or should monographs in these series be classified as separates?

Should the collection be weeded as reclassification proceeds?

How will missing items be accounted for?

Should old book cards and pockets be reused or should new ones be typed?

Should the entire collection be reclassified?

Should catalog filing rules be changed?

Should the catalog be divided?

Should accession numbers be retained?

All of the above questions and many more must be answered with some understanding of what is implied in terms of the future development of the library, for how these questions are answered will in large measure determine not only the cost, but also the quality of the reclassification project. As a matter of fact, Gaines is one of the few librarians who has raised the question of quality control during reclassification. His paper is one of the best evaluative, no-nonsense approaches to the costs of reclassification and is one of the core resources for anyone planning a reclassification project (45). Other useful materials for project planning are the paper by Elton Shell (135), the article by Edward Holley (72), and the publication of the 1966 Institute on *The Use of the Library of Congress Classification: Proceedings* edited by Schimmelpfeng and Cook (76).

In considering the special costs of reclassification, it is necessary to take into account (1) the method of reproducing the catalog card record and (2) the special L.C. tools and catalogs that must be purchased not only to speedily and accurately process the materials that are to be reclassified, but also to continue to process effectively all new library acquisitions. Insufficient attention has been paid in the literature to these special costs which are intimately involved with the application of the LC Classification system. There are in fact those who may argue that the cost of the Library of Congress author and subject catalogs do not belong in an estimate or reclassification costs. This position appears academic, for, no matter how it is viewed, the cost is there and must be considered in any reclassification planning. Almost without exception these particular costs have not been included in the published reports on various reclassification projects. (See Section 2.4.)

2.3 CATALOG CARD DUPLICATION COSTS

Any model of the Xerox machines listed in Table 2.1 is essential for inexpensive catalog card duplication. For both reclassification and new book cataloging there is no cheaper way at present to produce high quality catalog cards from Library of Congress galleys, printed cards, or typed masters. Any library considering reclassification should plan on the use of one these machines.

TABLE 2.1

XEROX MACHINES FOR CARD DUPLICATION
Monthly Charges

Type	Basic charge (in dollars)	Accessory charge (in dollars)	Minimum charges (in dollars)	
914	25.00	None	52.00	basic
720	24.00	None	150.00	basic
2400	30.00	VWP* 25.00	270.00	basic VWP
3600	50.00	VWP* 25.00	450.00	basic VWP

* *Variable weight paper tray.*

The newer models, the Xerox 2400 and the Xerox 3600, will produce as good a card copy as the older 914 and 720 models. Consequently, the choice of model will largely be made on the basis of a given library budget and the volume of expected use. All models can be used for all-purpose copying as well as card duplication without the need for any special internal adjustments. (See Section 4.3 for detailed operating information.)

Card stock for these machines is available from a number of suppliers in a variety of sizes, weights, and punchings. Several years ago considerable difficulty was experienced with the use of Xerox equipment for catalog card duplication with much of the difficulty undoubtedly associated with the kinds of card stock used. Inasmuch as a certain amount of experimentation will be required to determine which card stock best suits the needs of a particular library, the information in Table 2.2 is offered as descriptive of our own experience with a particular supplier.[1] It might be helpful to know that no duplication problems

---

[1] *While the product of a particular supplier has been described and evaluated, it in no way suggests that there are not other suppliers whose product will be less satisfactory—it is only our own experience which is being reported.*

TABLE 2.2

CARD STOCK

Xerox	Supplier	Type	Stock no.	Cost per 1000*	Description
914	Gaylord Permec	6-up	1413	29.70	Multistrip: perforated, cut, and punched
	Gaylord Permec, 100% rag	6-up	1513	47.40	Same
720	Gaylord Permec	Same	Same	Same	Same
	Gaylord Permec, 100% rag	Same	Same	Same	Same
2400	Gaylord rag	6-up	1508	39.30	Punched
	Gaylord rag	6-up	1509	46.30	Punched and perforated
3600	Gaylord rag	Same	Same	Same	Same
	Gaylord rag	Same	Same	Same	Same

* *The cost is lower, of course, with quantity orders.*

ordinarily arise from using 6-up as opposed to 4-up card stock, but the advantages are obvious in being able to make 6-card sets instead of 4-card sets simultaneously. Since it is more difficult to control the placement of 6 masters on the scanning glass of any of the Xerox machines, it is suggested that a special clear plastic template be purchased to hold the masters in place. (See Section 4.3.2 for the specifications on the template, which has been found to be most useful in our experience.) The type of card stock that should be used with the Xerox 914 or 720 is the multistrip, cut, perforated, and punched style, which will produce the most acceptable quality of card. The type of card stock to be used with the Xerox 2400 or 3600 is plain punched. It is definitely not recommended that the punched and perforated style be used for card duplication with any of the Xerox machines listed in Table 2.2 because of feeding problems that cause fires in the machines. As to the quality of the card stock to be used in any of the Xerox machines, there seems little argument against using the best 100 percent rag available.

2.4 SPECIAL L.C. TOOLS AND CATALOGS

When considering the use of LC, a library should recognize the need for catalogs and/or other tools. Whether these items should be considered a direct cost of a reclassification project may be debated. As a total acquisition these catalogs will represent a sizable investment and if purchased will in all probability have to be acquired over a period of several years. It is our opinion that the Library of Congress catalogs are essential working tools for any library beyond 50,000 volumes, but smaller libraries such as those in newly established junior colleges, special libraries, smaller public libraries, and school libraries will find that they can operate quite well with only the most recent quinquennial cumulation and a subscription to the current *National Union Catalog*. It may even be possible when the collection is very small or the acquisition program restricted to current in-print materials to handle all classification needs by ordering Library of Congress cards using standard acquisition tools like the *CBI, BPR,* and *Publishers' Weekly.*

Other options open to smaller libraries regardless of type may be the use of a commercial cataloging firm or a jointly established centralized technical processing center. While commercial cataloging firms often tend to cut corners on certain aspects of cataloging and processing, it is not impossible to establish specific standards of quality which will be acceptable to both the contracting library and the firm involved. A centralized technical processing center, supported by a number of libraries, is a possible and desirable arrangement, but all participants must realize that the I-can-catalog-better-than-you-can posture is detrimental to the system and must be discarded. At the present one of the most promising and least threatening areas of cooperation among a group of libraries is the production of catalog cards from a central file of Library of Congress proof slips. Working in conjunction with a central file of L.C. proof slips might be the joint acquisition of the necessary book catalogs and other tools necessary for the application of the LC system.

Regardless of how they are acquired, the basic costs of the L.C. tools and catalogs are listed in the two sections that follow.

2.4.1 THE TOOLS

LC Classification schedules	$ 72.80
LC Classification—Additions and Changes	35.70
LC Class KF shelflist (on cards): units 1, 2, 3, and 4 (see Section 3.2.4 for description)	380.00
LC author notation table	free
LC Information Bulletin The weekly staff bulletin available from the L.C. Information Office is an excellent source for news of internal L.C. activities, policies, and the library profession	free
Subject Headings Used in the Dictionary Catalogs of the Library of Congress, 7th ed., 1966	15.00
July 1965–December 1969 cumulations	22.50
1970 quarterly issues—subscription per year	5.00

2.4.2 THE L.C. CATALOGS

The L.C. catalogs represent a major investment amounting to several thousand dollars. Although several firms reprint the L.C. catalogs in cumulated editions, their publishing efforts have unfortunately not been well coordinated. For instance, Gale has announced its cumulated *NUC* for the years 1942–1962. Mansell, of course, is now in the process of reprinting all of the pre-1956 imprints over a ten-year period—a project which will overlap considerably the Gale publication. Shortly after Edwards Brothers brought out the *NUC* Fifth Supplement (1963–1967) in 1969, Rowman and Littlefield announced their *NUC* Twelve-Year Supplement (1956–1967). The question in this case is whether the year's delay in the availability of the *NUC* Twelve-Year Supplement published by Rowman and Littlefield justifies the purchase of the *NUC* Fifth Supplement. For a complete listing of the L.C. catalogs with the addresses of the publishers and other necessary data see Appendix B.

A Catalog of Books Represented by Library of Congress Printed Cards (cards issued August 1898–July 1942)	$1500
———. *Supplement* (August 1942 through December 1947)	395
The Library of Congress Catalog, 1948–1952	275
The National Union Catalog, 1952–1955 (now out of print but due to be reprinted)	420?
The National Union Catalog, 1953–1957	310
The National Union Catalog, 1958–1962	550
LC and National Union Catalog, 1942–1962 (Gale)	2888
The National Union Catalog, 1963–1967	670
The National Union Catalog, Twelve-Year Supplement, 1956–1967	2100
The National Union Catalog, a Cumulated Author List, 1968, 1969	500
The National Union Catalog, 1970	600
The National Union Catalog, Pre-1956 Imprints (Mansell)	9260
LC Catalog—Books: Subjects, 1950–1954	275
LC Catalog—Books: Subjects, 1955–1959	295
LC Catalog—Books: Subjects, 1960–1964	325
LC Catalog—Books: Subjects, 1965–1969	445

2.5 THE INTEGRATED RECLASSIFICATION OPERATION

It is a foregone conclusion that most smaller libraries which decide to reclassify to LC will have to combine current new book processing with the reclassification project itself. The reason for this is, of course, that there will be neither money nor qualified personnel to organize and execute an independent reclassification program. As a result, an "integrated reclassification operation" probably will be necessary, if reclassification is to proceed at all.

When the reclassification project at the University of Puget Sound began in January 1965, little up-to-date information was available in professional literature regarding useful procedures or special equipment needed for a reclassification project. Being uncertain about the kinds of procedures which would be most effective and severely restricted in terms of budget, we were forced to develop procedures which would combine new book cataloging operations with the reclassification project. Under these circumstances it was impossible to isolate the specific costs of every aspect of reclassification, and only general cost determinations could be made.

Some suggestion of staff costs may be supplied by the type of personnel and the number of hours worked on a weekly average during 1968–the peak year for new books cataloged and old books reclassified. The technical services personnel for that year are shown in Table 2.3.

TABLE 2.3

UPS TECHNICAL SERVICES STAFF, 1968

Number and type of personnel	Hours per week
1 Professional cataloger	40
2 Cataloging assistants (clerical)	80
1 Technical services clerk	40
4 Part-time clerks	58
1 Full-time typist	40
1 Three-quarter-time typist	30
Various students	179
Average weekly total	467

Throughout the reclassification period the technical services processing staff remained constant in terms of permanent positions as shown above, while part-time clerks and students were variables during the whole project. One factor that lowered our production rate in the last year of reclassification was the loss of two of our most highly trained cataloging assistants. Over the entire term of the reclassification project there were four replacements in clerical cataloging positions—replacements which naturally affected productivity. Furthermore, it should be pointed out that hourly help, especially student help, played a significant role in the total recataloging operation. Table 2.4 supplies the number of hours of

TABLE 2.4

UPS TECHNICAL SERVICES HOURLY ASSISTANCE
Student and Part-Time Clerical Help

YEAR	STUDENT[*] Annual (hr)	Weekly (hr)	CLERICAL Annual (hr)	Weekly (hr)	TOTAL Annual (hr)	Weekly (hr)
1966	7,332	140	None		7,332	140
1967	10,673	205	636	12	11,309	217
1968	9,317	58	3,103	58	12,330	237
1969	568	11	1,904	36	2,472	47

[*] *Student part-time help.*

student as well as part-time clerical help used from 1966 through the reclassification project which was completed in August of 1969.

Although the figures for a monthly rate of reclassification and cataloging under this "integrated processing system" tended to be uneven for a number of reasons (e.g., card order delays, card duplication problems, procedural experimentation, etc.), the annual figures of volumes classified and reclassified show that a remarkable level of productivity can be achieved with a restricted number of professional personnel (see Tables 2.5 and 2.6). Table 2.6 provides the annual

TABLE 2.5

UPS LC CATALOGING RATE: MONTHLY AVERAGES

Year	New volumes	Reclassified volumes	Total
1965	562.6	946	1508.6
1966	347.8	1848.4	2196.2
1967	782.8	1532.6	2315.4
1968	1591.1	1220.6	2811.7
1969, Total volumes by month			
January	3430	75	3505
February	1757	697	2454
March	772	626	1398
April	551	272	823
May	2510	17	2527
June	750	128	878
July	1061	13	1074
August	3082	26	3108

TABLE 2.6

UPS LC CATALOGING RATE: ANNUAL FIGURES

Year	New volumes	Reclassified volumes	Total
1965	6,752	11,353	18,105
1966	4,172	18,392	26,353
1967	9,194	18,392	27,586
1968	19,094	14,648	33,742
1969 (January– August)	13,913	1,854	15,767
Total	53,125	68,428	121,553

cataloging and classification figures for both new and reclassified books for the entire term of the reclassification period.

Not unassociated with the rate of cataloging and physical processing for both new as well as reclassified volumes is the manner chosen for the production of card copy for all old and new items to be cataloged. In line with this consideration is the need to develop a procedure for card duplication which is rapid and inexpensive. In the first year or so of our own reclassification project there were only unfavorable reports and inaccurate information abroad concerning the use of the Xerox 914 for catalog card duplication. Due to the lack of information, and this misinformation, our attempt to utilize this equipment was delayed for approximately a year and a half. When the manufacturer realized that the area of catalog card duplication was one that needed their serious attention, it was finally possible in 1967 to develop a program of card copying with the Xerox 914 in our own library. The experimentation with catalog card duplication was at times frustrating and maddening. Ultimately, however, it proved successful and we have subsequently moved to the Xerox 720 and finally to the Xerox 2400. Each generation of machine has proven more useful than the previous one, and regardless of which machine is selected the card quality and low cost are recommendations for their use.

During this period the University of Puget Sound reclassification project embraced a number of additional projects: collection inventory, collection weeding, serial records development (none previously existed), collection repair and binding, and the construction of an entirely new public catalog and shelflist. While such projects may not be essential to every reclassification project, they should receive careful consideration on the basis of a library's own special circumstances. What must be determined is the comprehensiveness and quality of the reclassification project under consideration and, then, what realistic adjustments must be made to bring preparations into line with financial support. As much as we might wish that it were, reclassification is not just a matter of slapping a new call number on a book and its catalog cards.

2.6 THE INDEPENDENT RECLASSIFICATION OPERATION

The other method of reclassification is to establish an entirely separate reclassification unit. This reclassification unit would ideally be responsible only for changing the book materials previously cataloged in the former classification scheme. The reclassification project that took place at Antioch College was handled as a completely independent operation with a separate budget.[2] During 1967, the first year of the project, the Antioch staff was composed of the reclassification director, two clerical assistants, two typists, and various students who worked for a total of 19,877 hours.

At the start of the Antioch reclassification project, most of the processing was handled by part-time student workers. During the course of the first year, the difficulty of obtaining reliable and regular student help made it necessary to hire full-time nonstudent clerks. The problem with student help at Antioch was that their working hours were short and they were usually available only for one quarter of the year. Naturally, if a library intends to rely heavily upon student help, it must be prepared for this tedious cycle of rehiring and retraining.

The initial equipment expenditures at Antioch were for such items as four electric typewriters, a Se-lin labeling device, a commercial paper cutter for cutting card stock, a cataloger's camera (available from Polaroid) to produce master cataloging copy from the L.C. printed catalogs, and miscellaneous items such as electric erasers, etc. Although the reclassification unit at Antioch was basically a separate operation, it was found in practice that there were a number of points at which the work of the regular cataloging staff and the reclassification unit overlapped. As a result, some sharing of certain portions of the work seemed obvious for greater efficiency (e.g., pasting of cards and pockets, spine labels), although such sharing tends to make the actual cost of the reclassification operation more difficult to determine.

During the first year of operation the reclassification unit paid all wages for the production of the duplicated catalog cards (about 95% were for reclassified titles), the filing of the subject catalog and all of the filing revision of the author-title catalog (about 85% of the filing and revision was produced by reclassifica-

[2] For the information on the Antioch reclassification we wish to express our gratitude to James E. Gaines, Director of the Reclassification Unit until September 1968, and Sharon Walbridge, the present chief cataloger who directed the reclassification project from September 1968 until its conclusion in June 1969.

tion), the camera costs involved in duplicating master copy from the L.C. printed catalogs, and book repair (about 95% generated by the reclassification project). To keep costs as low as possible, all supplies for regular new book processing and the reclassification project were ordered in bulk lots. Expenditures for the first year of operation are broken down in Table 2.7.

TABLE 2.7

ANTIOCH RECLASSIFICATION UNIT
EXPENDITURES, 1967

(in dollars)

Salaries		16,449.65
Wages		18,300.45
Equipment		6,453.43
Supplies		
Xerox charges		2,006.10
Materials: for the book pocket, card, Se-Lin label, glue including waste		1,392.06
Card stock		1,015.82
Miscellaneous		624.84
	Total	46,242.35

The Antioch reclassification project also included recataloging whenever necessary as well as updating subject headings, series entries, and so forth. The average hourly wage for clerical personnel was about $2.00 per hour, whereas the average figure for students was about $1.65 per hour. The total production figures for 1967 resulted in the following costs per volume and title: 46,402 volumes at $.846 per volume, 37,524 titles at $1.046 per title.

During the fall of 1968 a reduction in personnel seemed appropriate, resulting in a decrease both in monthly production and in the combined salary and wage figures which dropped from $2895.80 to $1990 per month. The reclassification staff was reduced to one professional director, one clerical supervisor, one typist, two half-time clerks, and various part-time students. The number of staff was reduced partly because a more accurate assessment was made of the total number of volumes to be reclassified. This total figure was reduced from the estimated 120,000 volumes to about 100,000 volumes. The final statistics for production and the costs for the entire reclassification project covering January 1967 through June 1969 are listed in Table 2.8.

The total reclassification cost indicates a somewhat higher average per volume cost than that indicated by the first year of operation. This is probably due to costs such as repair and binding as well as more difficult reclassification problems. This is a likely pattern that should be anticipated. The final figures are 93,724 volumes at $1.054 per volume, 70,435 titles at $1.40 per title.

2.7 CONCLUSION

It is not our purpose to claim that the reclassification projects of the University of Puget Sound or Antioch College resulted in the lowest cost per volume reported in the literature. As previously indicated, the single aim of achieving just

TABLE 2.8

ANTIOCH RECLASSIFICATION RATE

Year	Monthly average, volumes		ANNUAL FIGURES	
			Volumes	Costs (in dollars)
1967	3,866		46,402	46,242.35
1968	3,249		38,987	39,436.56
1969	1,392		8,352	13,161.25
		Totals	93,742	98,840.16*

According to Sharon Walbridge, the present Antioch chief cataloger, there is an additional cost factor yet to be computed which will average between 1 and 1½ percent, resulting in an estimated final figure of slightly less than $100,000.

the lowest cost per unit at any price, so to speak, is either to ignore or to be ignorant of the specific problems involved in reclassification to the LC system. We have selected both our own and Antioch's operation because we know that careful and accurate cataloging procedures have been practiced throughout the duration of both projects. Our procedures and statistics are offered with the sincere hope that they can assist and guide those who are convinced, as we are, that the Library of Congress offers the best available and least expensive classification system.

The cost figures and production statistics of this chapter are presented as average indicators of what a library can generally expect to accomplish with x number of personnel. Reclassification is not for the fainthearted. It does, indeed, cost money. For those librarians who decide they must travel this route, it is our hope that their reclassification to LC will be no more expensive or time-consuming or disruptive to public services than absolutely necessary.

3

Cataloging Decisions Prior to Reclassification

Various decisions, both general and special, should be made prior to the actual development of cataloging procedures for a reclassification. While the project is in process, there will undoubtedly be some experimentation with the workability of isolated routines, and without question certain general areas will require careful analysis while other areas, which might be characterized as special problems, will demand early attention. Some will insist that most of the decisions and problems will depend upon the kind and size of library which has opted for reclassification, and to some extent this is true. However, valid generalizations can be made about many aspects of any reclassification project regardless of whether the library is academic, public, special, big, medium or small. The following are these generalizations based on our reclassification experience.

3.1 GENERAL DECISIONS

3.1.1 PRIORITIES

Hopefully, in any reclassification project a series of priorities and procedures can be established which will dislocate as little as possible the public service function of the library. The following suggestions may help in realizing that goal:

1. A decision to reclassify implies that on a certain date all new materials purchased or given to the library will be classified according to the newly adopted classification scheme.[1] While this might appear obvious, professional literature has reported some libraries making reclassification decisions without establishing a specific cutoff date for the old classification scheme's use.

2. Inasmuch as neither staff nor public will have any familiarity with the new scheme, it is recommended that the reference collection be reclassified

---

[1] *For an exception to this general statement, see Section 3.2.4 on Law (Class K).*

first. The fact that most classes will be represented in the reference collection assures a general and progressive familiarization with the new scheme on the part of staff and public. (While the reference collection is being reprocessed, the entire book collection should be compressed into fully filled shelves to make room for the arrangement of the newly adopted system in a single A to Z order. This recommendation is, of course, offered on the assumption that the library does not have a great deal of extra space or a new addition where a separate A to Z grouping can be located.)

3. Since the Library of Congress Classification scheme lacks mnemonic elements, the need for a special reference card catalog will become obvious early in the project. Because the reference staff and the user generally approach the reference collection from a subject and/or title orientation, the expense of constructing a complete card catalog for the reference collection is not justified. A procedure for creating a partial catalog, that is, a subject/ title catalog, can be established prior to the actual reclassification of the first reference title. The method devised for supplying the necessary cards for the reference catalog was to duplicate an extra card for each subject entry and for each title entry. After the new LC notation has been typed on the cards, one complete set will be filed in the public catalog and the extra subject and title cards will be filed in the reference catalog. (It should be remembered that when the main entry is a title main entry it will be necessary to supply an additional title main entry card as well as the additional subject entry cards to fulfill the requirements of a complete subject/title catalog.)

4. Simultaneously with the reclassification of the reference collection, every attempt should be made to reclassify all multivolumed titles into the new scheme. After this has been done, the unreclassified collection can be tightly compressed to supply shelving space for the new LC collection which will be arranged at the beginning of the unreclassified materials. In other words, two separate and complete collections will exist for a period of time because there is no logical way that the two schemes—LC and Dewey—can be meshed. See Table 3.1 for the general DC to LC outline, which will illustrate this point.

5. Following the reclassification of the reference collection and the multivolumed sets, the next kind of material to be dealt with will be current items (those published within the last two decades).
    (a) Since recent materials in most subject areas are generally in great demand, the staff and user will be forced to become gradually familiar with the new scheme.
    (b) As new materials are classified and reclassified, a body of information about L.C. current cataloging practices will accumulate. This body of information will be drawn together and systematized as the library's new LC shelflist grows. Even though it is not recommended that class numbers appearing on printed L.C. cards be verified against the classification schedules, it is important that clerks responsible for shelflist filing be fa-

TABLE 3.1

CONVERSION TABLE: DC TO LC (GENERAL OUTLINE)

DC	LC	DC	LC	DC	LC	DC	LC
000	AC	250	BV	500	Q	750	ND
010	Z	260	BR	510	QA	760	NE
020	Z	270	BR	520	QB	770	TR
030	AE	280	BX	530	QC	780	M
040	AC	290	BL	540	QD	790	GV
050	AP			550	QE		
060	AS	300	H	560	QE	800	PN
070	PN	310	HA	570	GN, QH	810	PS
080	AC	320	J	580	QK	820	PR
090	Z	330	HB	590	QL	830	PT
		340	K			840	PQ
100	B–BJ	350	JF–JS	600	T–TX	850	PQ
110	BD	360	HN, HV	610	R	860	PQ
120	BD	370	L	620	TA	870	PA
130	BF	380	HD	630	S, HD	880	PA
140	B	390	GT	640	TX	890	PK–PL
150	BF			650	HF		
160	BC	400	P	660	TP	900	D
170	BJ	410	P	670	TS, HD	910	G–GF
180	B	420	PE	680	TS, HD	920	CT
190	B	430	PF	690	TH	930	D
		440	PC			940	D, DA–DR
200	BL	450	PC	700	N	950	DS
210	BL	460	PC	710	SB	960	DT
220	BS	470	PA	720	NA	970	E, F
230	BT	480	PA	730	NB	980	F
240	BV	490	PK	740	NC	990	DS, DU

miliar enough with the general structure of the scheme to call attention to gross errors. (See Section 3.1.3 for discussion of class number verification.)

6. No attempt should be made to tie items in circulation into the reclassification project. Library literature has reported that certain reclassification projects have developed elaborate procedures for routing recent titles being returned from circulation to the technical services department. It is better to simply reshelve returning titles into the Dewey collection where they will be reprocessed at the time that particular subject area is being reclassified. Undoubtedly at some point in the project the circulation department will have to become involved in reclassification to a greater or lesser degree; however, during the first year or two, the introduction of another library department into the procedure will only complicate the operation.

7. Although it is recommended that no one class be reclassified as a whole, a glance at the conversion table above will give some clues as to where one might start the project. If the 100's and 200's are to become B–BJ and BL–BX respectively, clearly the physical maneuver of changing from one class scheme to the other is not overwhelming since in either system the books will occupy roughly the same physical location on the shelves. By extension, if the 000's become A and also Z, the head and the tail of the animal you are building is established, and the new arrangement begins with class A at the beginning and class Z at the end. The chart in Figure 3.1 demonstrates that

DC STACKS   LC STACKS

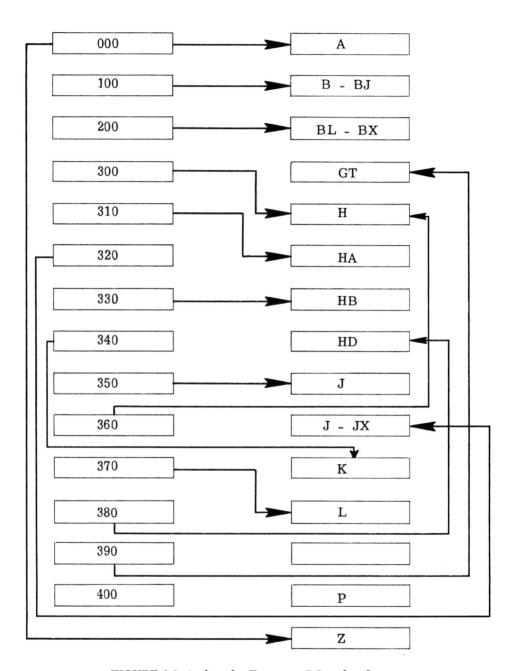

FIGURE 3.1. A chart for Dewey to LC reclassification.

as the old collection is diminished space will become available for the new scheme. Needless to say, as reclassification gains momentum, there will have to be occasional collection shifts to accommodate the movement of materials from the old scheme to the new; however, at the beginning there seems little question but that reclassification must start with the 000's, 100's, 200's, and 300's.

3.1.2 WEEDING AND DISCARDING

The process of weeding and discarding may be obvious, but it bears mentioning regardless. Few will disagree that every library collection contains deadwood which could and should be eliminated; however, in most libraries the need for a consistent and ongoing weeding program is usually ignored or only given lip service when materials that can be discarded clutter almost every subject area. Removal of this clutter is imperative before reclassification begins.

Procedures for this potentially massive kind of weeding program should be carefully worked out in advance of the reclassification. With the initial decision to reclassify, every effort should be made to enlist the cooperation of the teaching faculty in eliminating superseded editions, worn-out copies, and early material which may have been treated better or more comprehensively in recent acquisitions. This faculty aid may effect the removal of a considerable number of titles, and though it is perhaps hard come by, such faculty cooperation is well worth the effort expended to enlist it. If no help is forthcoming from the faculty, then it will be the library director's responsibility to formulate a weeding and discard policy and to delegate responsibility to various staff librarians for effecting the policy. With the aid of current subject bibliographies and the subject competence of librarians, this phase of the reclassification project can be accomplished with fair dispatch.

3.1.3 CLASS NUMBER VERIFICATION

Prior to the actual reclassification project and during the initial decision-making phase, considerable soul-searching must be done with regard to verification of class numbers as shown on printed Library of Congress cards. Needless to say, printers' errors and an occasional cataloging error appear on L.C. cards, and, when discovered, these errors must be corrected. Yet it is neither recommended nor necessary that an extensive verification procedure be established in any class other than personal author names in the various national literatures. The reasons for this decision are amply clear:

1. The very fact that the profession accepts L.C.'s descriptive cataloging and assignment of subject headings implies that L.C.'s classification should also be accepted.

2. The incidence of errors in L.C.'s cataloging and classification is low in terms of the number of titles. Minor errors offend none but the perfect—and who's perfect?

3. Every step built into a routine affects the cost of the overall institutional operation. Centralized cataloging, and that is what is being discussed, represents a move toward economy, and this move should not be vitiated by elaborate verification procedures.

3.1.4 LIBRARY OF CONGRESS CALL NUMBER BREAKDOWN

A glance at any L.C. call number[2] printed on a unit card will reveal that the cataloger must decide how to break down this number when it is used in marking books and when it is typed on catalog cards. This might seem a strange concern, but it is not. There is no universally accepted rule for the subdivision of the L.C. call number.

Initially, it is recommended that the form suggested by Anna C. Laws in *Author Notation in the Library of Congress* not be used. This decision against Laws' form is not caprice, but rather an attempt to devise a spine marking which will allow the call number on the book and on the catalog cards to be broken down in the same way. Such a consideration is not unimportant in an open-stack library where users go directly from the public catalog to the stacks to find their material without using intermediary library clerk or page. One large California university library, having forgotten that notations on catalog cards direct users to physical objects arranged on shelves, shows call numbers in the catalog broken down differently from the call numbers as they appear on the physical books themselves. Obviously, to the user the following forms look quite different:

```
PR6015      PR
E3845C6     6015
            E3845
            C6
```

Our experience with marking 120,000 volumes and typing 600,000 catalog cards has supported the decision to break down the call number in a very specific way. The original questions posed were these: "How will the number be most easily read on the spines of books?" and "How can the number components be arranged so that most elements will be visible as the book stands among the others on the shelf?" With some experimentation it was first determined that placing the alphabetical class or subclass on the first line by itself would make it more easy to read than following it by a succession of digits on the same line. Secondly, it was possible to see that the numerical differentiation within any class or subclass seldom went to more than four digits. (Some run to seven digits plus a decimal—for example, DC166.0623—but the incidence is small.) Regarding decimals in the numerical differentiation of the class, it was decided never to separate the decimals from the whole number:

```
              DC                        DC
always this,   166.0623   never this,   166
                                        .0623
```

In other words, all elements of the numerical differentiation would be on the second line in the breakdown of the class number. By keeping the decimal with the whole number, we found it possible to formulate this general rule for the number breakdown for the entire classification system: each individual element of the call number has a line to itself. The rule applies without exception throughout the system.

---

[2] *The term call number, as used in this section, refers to the entire class number plus the author Cutter.*

Examples 1–8 represent the kinds of number configurations to be expected when applying the rule as formulated previously.

EXAMPLE 1

```
B
133
R16
S3
```

Samartha, S   J   1920–
        Introduction to Radhakrishnan; the man and his thought.
        New York, Association Press [1964]

        127 p. 21 cm.

        1. Radhakrishnan, Sarvepalli, Pres. India, 1888–   I. Title.

        B133.R16S3   181.4   64–11596

        Library of Congress   [5]

EXAMPLE 2

```
BF
173
F85
B75
1968
```

Brome, Vincent, 1910–
        Freud and his early circle. New York, Morrow, 1968
        [°1967]

        xii, 275 p. group port. 22 cm.
        Bibliography : p. 265–268.

        1. Freud, Sigmund, 1856–1939. 2. Psychoanalysis—Hist.   I. Title.

        BF173.F85B75   1968   150.19′52   68–14813

        Library of Congress   [5]

EXAMPLE 3

```
BX
8495
W5
W62
```

Williams, Colin Wilbur, 1921–
        John Wesley's theology today. New York, Abingdon
        Press [1960]

        252 p. 23 cm.
        Bibliography : p. 243–246.

        1. Wesley, John, 1703–1791.   I. Title.

        BX8495.W5W62   230.7   60–5238 rev 2

        Library of Congress   [r67q2]

EXAMPLE 4

E
185.61   Institutional racism in America. Contributors: Owen Blank
I 6   [and others] Edited by Louis L. Knowles and Kenneth
              Prewitt. With an appendix by Harold Baron. Englewood
              Cliffs, N. J., Prentice-Hall [1969]

           xii, 180 p.   22 cm.   (A Spectrum book)   5.95

           Based on working papers prepared for a joint program sponsored
           by the Stanford chapter of the University Christian Movement and
           the Mid-Peninsula Christian Ministry of East Palo Alto, Calif.
           Bibliographical footnotes.

              1. Negroes — Civil rights. 2. Race discrimination — U. S.   I.
           Blank, Owen. II. Knowles, Louis L., ed. III. Prewitt, Kenneth, ed.

           E185.61.I 6   301.451′96′073   78–90975
           SBN 13–467746–3   MARC

           Library of Congress   69 [5]

EXAMPLE 5

HD
9521.5   Burnham, Thomas Hall.
B8   Iron and steel in Britain, 1870–1930. A comparative study
             of the causes which limited the economic development of the
             British iron and steel industry between the years 1870 and
             1930, by T. H. Burnham ... and G. O. Hoskins ... London,
             G. Allen & Unwin ltd [1943]

           352 p. incl. front., tables, diagrs.   21½ cm.

           "First published in 1943."
           Bibliography : p. [345]–346.

              1. Iron industry and trade—Gt. Brit. 2. Steel industry and trade—
           Gt. Brit.   I. Hoskins, George Owen, joint author. II. Title.

           HD9521.5.B8   338.47672   A 44—442

           Harvard Univ. Library   672
           for Library of Congress   [57e½]†   B 9351

EXAMPLE 6

JN
1121   Jackson, Robert J
1968   Rebels and whips: an analysis of dissension, discipline
J32   and cohesion in British political parties [by] Robert J.
             Jackson. London, Melbourne [etc.] Macmillan ; New York,
             St. Martin's P., 1968.

           xii, 346 p.   23 cm.   65/–
                                                         (B 68–19680)
           Bibliography : p. 317–335.

              1. Party discipline—Gt. Brit.   I. Title.

           JN1121 1968.J32   329.9′42   68–19078

           Library of Congress   [2]

EXAMPLE 7

```
JQ
215
1967
P3
```

Park, Richard Leonard.
    India's political system ₍by₎ Richard L. Park. Engle-
wood Cliffs, N. J., Prentice-Hall ₍1967₎

    xi, 116 p. illus., map. 23 cm. (Comparative Asian government series)

    Bibliography: p. 99–101.

    1. India—Pol. & govt.—1947-   2. India—Pol. & govt.
I. Title.

    JQ215 1967.P3   320′.954   67–9655

    Library of Congress   ₍5₎

EXAMPLE 8

```
PR
6003
O6757
A8
1946
```

Bowen, Elizabeth, 1899–
    Anthony Trollope, a new judgement ₍by₎ Elizabeth Bowen.
London, New York ₍etc.₎ G. Cumberlege, Oxford university
press, 1946.

    2 p. l., 22 p., 1 l. pl., port., map, facsim. 19ᶜᵐ.

    "First broadcast by the BBC on 4 May 1945."
    Bibliography: p. 21–22.

    1. Trollope, Anthony, 1815–1882—Drama.

                ₍*Full name:* Elizabeth Dorothea Cole (Bowen) Cameron₎

    PR6003.O6757A8   1946   822.91   46–8478

    Library of Congress   ₍3₎

In training clericals to break numbers, this formula can be used as a simple instructional device:

line one:	all letters
line two:	all numbers
subsequent lines:	letter-number combination, except for the date of year which has a line to itself.

To differentiate between a one and a capital I leave a space between the letter and the following number as shown in Example 4. To differentiate between a zero and a capital O always underline the capital O as shown in Example 8.

One additional decision that remains is what to do with the decimal point separating the class from the special topic and/or author notation. In Examples 1, 2, 3, 4, 5, and 8 note that a decimal point separates the author or special topic Cutter from the class number. While these author and special topic Cutters are decimal numbers, we feel it unnecessary to retain the decimal in marking and on catalog cards. Prompting this decision was the fact that Cutter numbers drawn from the three-figure Cutter table used with the Dewey Classification system are also decimal numbers and appear on books and cards without decimal points; therefore, it does not represent an eccentric approach to ignore the decimal point when it is used in the same manner in the L.C. class system. Furthermore, it was felt that a decimal point in front of a *letter* is more of a hindrance than a help to the library user. Finally, while some problem may occasionally arise for a new shelver or filer (E7 might seem to come before E63), the user will not be more than a book or two away from the one he wants—even if he hasn't read a local handbook which can easily explain the decimal nature of the Cutter lines. In Examples 6 and 7 where year designations are an internal classificatory element, no problem in shelving or shelflisting occurs when the element is regarded as a separate component of the class number and given a line to itself.[3] In Example 8 is the sort of class number to be found throughout the literature schedules for many twentieth-century authors. The four digits following the subclass (i.e., PR, PS, PT, etc.) represent the initial letter of an author's last name, and the numbers following the letter are a decimal device for keeping the author's name arranged alphabetically among other authors of that period and place.

The next to the last element in Example 8 (A8) represents a simple title Cutter to keep the author's works arranged alphabetically by title.

3.1.5 DATES IN CALL NUMBERS

Some thought must be given to the L.C. practice of appending throughout the classification scheme imprint dates to call numbers for every new printing of a title whether or not the edition has been changed in content. Naturally for a "national" library it may be necessary to describe every variant edition of a given title and to supply it with a unique call number; however, there seems to be little advantage for libraries of lesser status to describe completely, with an additional card set each, five different editions of a *Grapes of Wrath* or a *Murder in the Cathedral* if the format of the editions is essentially the same. The point is that if the imprint date of one edition is used in the call number and another copy is received with a different imprint date it is going to be impossible to add the second copy as a copy 2 with an appropriate "imprint varies" note on the shelflist. Therefore, it should be carefully determined whether or not an imprint date will be used in the call number of a given title. There might be an implied question of cataloger integrity here, but dropping the imprint date is worth thinking about. In those instances where it is deemed advisable to carry an imprint date in the call number, remember that it is the imprint date and not the copyright date which is used.

Another kind of date to consider is the date that is an integral part of the class number. Many dates of this type are to be found in the various subclasses of the schedule (see Examples 9 and 10). When a date does appear within a class number and a new edition is published, the date, which is an era or period designation, does not change. Rather than adding another date at the end of the call number to indicate a later edition, the practice is to extend the author Cutter, as illustrated in Examples 11 and 12.

The two titles in Examples 9 and 10 deal with the politics and government of Communist China at the time the books were written; therefore, the dates 1967 and 1968 respectively are part of the classification according to the instruction, by date, in Table 2 of schedule JQ.

---

[3] *When shelving and filing shelflist cards, one should arrange these year numbers chronologically.*

EXAMPLE 9

```
JQ
1509
1967
B3
```
Barnett, A. Doak.
   Cadres, bureaucracy, and political power in Communist China ₍by₎ A. Doak Barnett. With a contribution by Ezra Vogel. New York, Columbia University Press, 1967.

   xxix, 563 p. 24 cm. (Studies of the East Asian Institute, Columbia University)

   1. China (People's Republic of China, 1949–   )—Pol. & govt. I. Vogel, Ezra F. II. Title.   (Series: Columbia University. East Asian Institute. Studies)

   JQ1509 1967.B3   354.51   67–15895

   Library of Congress   ₍7₎

EXAMPLE 10

```
JQ
1509
1968
P9
```
Pye, Lucian W   1921–
   The spirit of Chinese politics; a psychocultural study of the authority crisis in political development ₍by₎ Lucian W. Pye. Cambridge, Mass., M. I. T. Press ₍1968₎

   xxii, 255 p. 21 cm.

   Bibliographical footnotes.

   1. China (People's Republic of China, 1949–   )—Pol. & govt. 2. Authority.   I. Title.

   JQ1509 1968.P9   320.9′51   68–14451

   Library of Congress   ₍3₎

EXAMPLE 11

```
JQ
1509
1967
B312
```
Barnett, A. Doak.
   Cadres, bureaucracy, and political power in Communist China **Rev. & enl. ed.**   With a contribution by Ezra Vogel. New York, Columbia University Press, 1969.

   xxix, 563 p. 24 cm. (Studies of the East Asian Institute, Columbia University)

   1. China (People's Republic of China, 1949–   )—Pol. & govt. I. Vogel, Ezra F. II. Title.   (Series: Columbia University. East Asian Institute. Studies)

   JQ1509 1967.B312   354.51   67–15895

   Library of Congress   ₍7₎

EXAMPLE 12

```
JQ
1509
1968
P92
```
Pye, Lucian W   1921–
   The spirit of Chinese politics; a psychocultural study of the authority crisis in political development. **2d rev. ed.**   Cambridge, Mass., M. I. T. Press [1970]

   xxii, 255 p. 21 cm.

   Bibliographical footnotes.

   1. China (People's Republic of China, 1949–   )—Pol. & govt. 2. Authority.   I. Title.

   JQ1509 1968.P92   320.9′51   68–14451

   Library of Congress   ₍3₎

If a revised edition of either one of the titles were to be published, it would be necessary to extend the author Cutter in one of two possible ways rather than adding a date to the call number to differentiate between editions. See Examples 11 and 12.[4]

3.2 SPECIAL PROBLEMS

3.2.1 SERIES

The question of "How to handle series?" is one which must be resolved early in the use of the Library of Congress Classification system. Whether or not a library chooses to retain the series classification will be determined by how closely the library wants related materials to stand together on the shelf. Certain problems in subject grouping have been created by the very nature of series classification as used by the Library of Congress.

1. Series classification is simply a device to handle large masses of material without much concern for the actual relatedness of the material. The *Transactions* of the American Philosophical Society, for example, are classified in Q 11, which deals with general scientific publications published by American societies. At this point in time, however, the *Transactions* are not chiefly scientific but rather historical, archaeological, and philosophical.

2. The series classification has been used for many university series wherein the subject matter is highly specialized and possibly requires considerable specificity in classification—the series classification groups the material only in the most general way.

3. Many times the Library of Congress has changed its classification of a series to a monographic subject classification in midstream without any indication on a given card set that the monograph in hand was formerly part of a series. This inconsistency on the part of the Library of Congress makes it necessary to have an extensive series check-in file where the particulars of any given series are carefully recorded and controlled.

Of course the LC system cannot be used uncritically. In the following example, the problem of series and PZ3[5] are coupled for the purpose of demonstrating that extraordinary difficulties can arise throughout the entire book collection unless one makes an early decision on how such materials are to be handled.

In the university series published by Wichita State University is a short critical work by Ivey of Gunther Grass's *Blechtrommel*. This series is classified by L.C. in the subclass AS 36 (publications of other individual societies and institutions in the United States). The use of the Library of Congress call numbers for the German edition of *Blechtrommel*, the English edition of *Blechtrommel*, and Ivey's critical work about it would supply the following arrangement.

[4] *Examples 11 and 12 are only illustrative and do not purport to represent actual revised editions.*

[5] *See Section 3.2.5 for discussion of the nonuse of PZ3 and PZ4.*

PT
2613   Grass, Gunther, 1927–
R338   Die Blechtrommel.
B55

PZ
4   Grass, Gunther, 1927–
G774   The tin drum.
Ti

AS
36   Ivey, Frederick M
W62   The Tin drum; or, Retreat to the word.
no. 66

It would seem that this arrangement of materials is no arrangement at all and taxes to the extreme the patience of both user and staff.

By interpolating the English edition and the critical material into the German national literature scheme (a relatively simple matter), the following grouping of materials will result. This arrangement does no violence to the patience, time, or intelligence of user or staff.

PT
2613   Grass, Gunther, 1927–
R338   Die Blechtrommel.
B55

PT
2613   Grass, Gunther, 1927–
R338   The tin drum.
B552

PT
2613   Ivey, Frederick M
R338   The Tin drum; or, Retreat to the word.
B5584

Logic and commonsense are required on these points. Theoretically, L.C. classifies "all" materials for the library that borrows the system; however, individual libraries must not relinquish all responsibility regarding their own collections. This is not an argument for a special practices approach but rather an appeal to allow L.C. to do a large part of the work but not all of the thinking associated with book classification.

The series check-in forms shown in Examples 1–8 have been developed to accommodate the record requirements of series, open entries, and government documents. Notice that the grids on one form are unnumbered to allow indication of special numbering sequences, as in the case of *Transactions* of the American Philosophical Society, or in the case of unnumbered series, such as the Harvard political studies. The adaptability of the forms has proven most gratifying in the maintenance of records for a collection of 125,000 cataloged volumes and 54,000 federal, state, and municipal documents.

In reading the bottom of the check-in card from left to right, one might find the following explanations helpful.

Catalog	This square is reserved for cataloging information, whether it be a specific class number (Examples 1, 3, 6, 8), or instructions such as "document collection" (Example 7), or "catalog as separate" (Examples 2, 4, 5). Special locations are also recorded in this square (Example 3).
Mark	Additional marking information beyond the call number is recorded here, for example, by volume (Example 1 and 3), by year (Example 7), by volume (Examples 1, 3, 6), by volume and part (Example 8).
S.O.	The presence of an "x" indicates that the title or series is a standing order. A series of colored flags is used in the file to indicate with whom the standing order has been placed. A blue flag is used if the standing order has been placed with the publisher as indicated in the publisher square (Examples 1 and 2); a purple flag is used if the standing order has been placed with a particular jobber and a special note is carried on the check-in card (Examples 3 and 8).
Series	An "x" in this square indicates that a series card is made for the public catalog (Example 5).
Add	An "x" in this square indicates that some holdings note has been pencilled on the catalog cards and must be updated when a new item in this title has been received (Example 6).

EXAMPLE 1

✓ 1	11	21	31	41	51	61	71	81	91
✓ 2	12	22	32	42	52	62	72	82	92
✓ 3	13	23	33	43	53	63	73	83	93
✓ 4	14	24	34	44	54	64	74	84	94
✓ 5	15	25	35	45	55	65	75	85	95
✓ 6	16	26	36	46	56	66	76	86	96
✓ 7	17	27	37	47	57	67	77	87	97
8	18	28	38	48	58	68	78	88	98
9	19	29	39	49	59	69	79	89	99
10	20	30	40	50	60	70	80	90	100

Catalog	Mark	S.O.	Series	Add	Chg.	Publisher	LCst	Item No.	Anal.
QD411.A35	v	x			20	Academic Press, 1964–			

Advances in organometallic chemistry.

EXAMPLE 2

v.51	v.52	v.53	v.54	v.55	v.56	v.57	v.58	v.59	v.60
1	1	1	BR 170 M6 1	BX 4813 N 5 1	1	1	1	1	1
2	2	2	R 128 I 7813 2	2	2	2	2	2	2
3	3	3	DA 231 L3 B4 3	DS 53 C4 A5 3	3	3	3	3	3
4	4	4	4	F 273 R 15 4	4	4	4	4	4
JN 2375 G5 5	5	5	5	DD 801 B17 L5 5	5	5	5	5	5
6	6	6	E 302.6 B8795 6	F 1219.1 T27 M82 6	6	6	6	6	6
HE 207 R8 7	7	7	DP 193 J7 P6 7	7	7	7	7	7	7
8	8	8	8	QA 145.8 S565 8	8	8	8	8	8
9	9	9	9	Z 731 K6 9	9	9	9	9	9
10	10	10	10	HD 2346 U52 N43 10	10	10	10	10	10

v.61	v.62	v.63	v.64	v.65	v.66	v.67	v.68	v.69	v.70

* Note: Always put black tape down back of paper cover.
Always supply author and title label for each monograph.

Catalog	Mark	S.O.	Series	Add	S.N.	Publisher	LCat	Item No.	Anal.
as sep.	x*	x				American Phil. Society, 1771-		(Card 2)	

American Philosophical Society. Transactions, new series

Chg[6] A numeric symbol in this square indicates the academic department's library budget to which this title or series is to be charged (Examples 1 and 5).

Publisher The name of the publisher of the series or title is shown in this square (all examples).

[6] *The designation S. N. is no longer used.*

LCst — An "x" here indicates that a standing order for cards has been placed with the Library of Congress for all titles published as of a certain date or number in this series (Example 5).

Item No. — This square carries the item number which controls the receipt of documents on depository status from the U.S. Superintendent of Documents (Example 7).

Anal. — An "x" here indicates that the title or series in question is to be analyzed in the public catalog (Example 6).

The following publishers' series are or have been classified as series by L.C. While there are, of course, others, the items in these series are the ones which we have chosen to classify as separates.

Columbia University studies in law, political sciences, and history.
Everyman's Library.
Harvard classics.
Johns Hopkins studies in history.
Loeb Classical Library.
North Carolina University Publications in Germanic Languages and Literature.
Sacred books of the East.

EXAMPLE 3

✔ 1	11	21	31	41	51	61	71	81	91
✔ 2	12	22	32	42	52	62	72	82	92
✔ 3	13	23	33	43	53	63	73	83	93
✔ 4	14	24	34	44	54	64	74	84	94
5	15	25	35	45	55	65	75	85	95
6	16	26	36	46	56	66	76	86	96
7	17	27	37	47	57	67	77	87	97
8	18	28	38	48	58	68	78	88	98
9	19	29	39	49	59	69	79	89	99
10	20	30	40	50	60	70	80	90	100

* Note: Standing order with T. Front.
    Opera omnia is the title stamped on spine at bindery.

Catalog	Mark	S.O.	Series	Add	S.N.	Publisher	LCst	Item No.	Anal.
M3.G16 Music Dept.	v	x*				American Inst. of Musicology, 1956–		Bindery Color 8848	

Gabrieli, Giovanni. [Works] (Opera omnia) *

EXAMPLE 4

JA84 U5M35								
JC575 L33								
UA42 D46								
JK611 F4								
JA84 U5W67								
F1975 G57								
JK1051 M3								
HX11 I5F3 1966								

* Note: unnumbered series.

Catalog	Mark	S.O.	Series	Add	S.N.	Publisher	LCst	Item No.	Anal.
as sep.						Harvard U. P.			

Harvard political studies.

EXAMPLE 5

1	11	21	PA8577 A24 1963 31	41	51	61	71	81	91
2	12	22	PT2638 N5285 32	42	52	62	72	82	92
3	13	23	PT2528 Z684 33	43	53	63	73	83	93
4	14	24	PT1160 E5T5 34	MLE9 A3L6 44	54	64	74	84	94
5	15	25	35	PT2528 Z684 45	55	65	75	85	95
6	16	26	PN1475 E3 1964 36	Z8794.5 A4 Ref. 46	56	66	76	86	96
7	17	27	PT2528 Z6M3 37	PT150 M3 47	57	67	77	87	97
8	18	28	B3317 I6 38	P26 L3 48	58	68	78	88	98
9	19	29	PT2625 A4W2 39	PT1679 W88 T45 49	59	69	79	89	99
10	20	30	Z8998.95 K5 P65 40	PT175 T45 50	60	70	80	90	100

Catalog	Mark	S.O.	Series	Add	Chg.	Publisher	LCst	Item No.	Anal.
as sep.		x	x		42	U. of North Carolina P.	x		

literatures.
North Carolina. University. Studies in the Germanic languages and

EXAMPLE 6

✓ 1	11	21	31	41	51	61	71	81	91
✓ 2	12	22	32	42	52	62	72	82	92
✓ 3	13	23	33	43	53	63	73	83	93
✓ 4	14	24	34	44	54	64	74	84	94
5	15	25	35	45	55	65	75	85	95
✓ 6	16	26	36	46	56	66	76	86	96
✓ 7	17	27	37	47	57	67	77	87	97
✓ 8	18	28	38	48	58	68	78	88	98
9	19	29	39	49	59	69	79	89	99
10	20	30	40	50	60	70	80	90	100

Catalog	Mark	S.O.	Series	Add	S.N.	Publisher	LCst	Item No.	Anal.
PS3537.T323 A6	v			x		Yale U. P., 1951-58.			x

Gertrude Stein.
Stein, Gertrude. The Yale edition of the unpublished writing of

EXAMPLE 7

1	11	21	31	41	1951	1961	71	81	91
2	12	22	32	1942	1952	1962	72	82	92
3	13	23	33	1943	1953	1963	73	83	93
4	14	24	34	1944	1954	1964	74	84	94
5	15	25	35	1945	1955	1965	75	85	95
6	16	26	36	1946	1956	1966	76	86	96
7	17	27	37	1947	1957	1967	77	87	97
8	18	28	38	1948	1958	1968	78	88	98
9	19	29	39	1949	1959	69	79	89	99
10	20	30	40	1950	1960	70	80	90	100

Catalog	Mark	S.O.	Series	Add	S.N.	Publisher	LCst	Item No.	Anal.
Document Collection	yr					GPO, 1865/66-		785	

U. S. Library of Congress. Report of the Librarian of Congress.

EXAMPLE 8

✓1	11	21	31	41	51	61	71	81	91
✓2 (pt.1)	12	22	32	42	52	62	72	82	92
✓3 (pt.2)	13	23	33	43	53	63	73	83	93
4	14	24	34	44	54	64	74	84	94
✓5	15	25	35	45	55	65	75	85	95
✓6 (pt.1)	16	26	36	46	56	66	76	86	96
7	✓17	27	37	47	57	67	77	87	97
✓8	18	28	38	48	58	68	78	88	98
9	✓19	29	39	49	59	69	79	89	99
✓10 (pt.1)	✓20	30	40	50	60	70	80	90	100

* Note: Standing order with Stechert.

Catalog	Mark	S.O.	Series	Add	S.N.	Publisher	LCst	Item No.	Anal.
PQ8549.B3 1951	v & pt	v*				Caracas, Ministerio de Educacion, 1951–			

Bello, Andres. Obras completas.

3.2.2 BIOGRAPHY (SUBCLASS CT)

Biography has been treated in two ways by L.C. First, where no specific subject relationship exists, general biography—both collective and individual—is classed in the subclass CT. Second, where biography is regarded as germane to the understanding of a subject (e.g., history, mathematics, law, etc.), the material is placed with the subject. While L.C. does supply an alternative scheme which would place all biography in CT with biography by subject at the end of the subclass, it is not recommended that it be used because this alternative scheme would again represent one of those marvelous local arrangements that would undercut the overall objective of uniform centralized cataloging.

The following table is recommended for the arrangement of works by and/or about individuals for whom no other table has been specifically indicated in the classification schedule.

INDIVIDUAL BIOGRAPHY

.x	= Cutter number for the individual
.xA2	= Collected works
.xA3	= Autobiography, diary, etc.
.xA4	= Letters
.xA41–49	= Letters to particular individuals, A–Z, by correspondent
.xA5	= Speeches, etc.
.xA6–Z	= Works by other persons about the individual

Selections, excerpts, and the like may be put with .xA2, usually as .xA25–29, so that room for expansion of collected works is left between .xA2 and .xA24. Indexes, concordances, and the like are put in .xA6–Z. This table may be used with all schedules in classes which mean individual biography, except when other provisions are inserted in the schedule.

This table is reproduced from Robert R. Holmes' "Assignment of Author Numbers" in *The Use of the Library of Congress Classification: Proceedings* (76).

3.2.3 BIBLIOGRAPHY (CLASS Z)

With a few exceptions, notably music in ML and law in K, bibliography is classified in class Z. One might be inclined instead to place subject bibliography with the subject literature; however, this practice is not recommended for the simple reason that here again would be a case of "special local practices" which would undercut the whole concept of centralized classification. If we must have "special local practices" let them do more than would be accomplished in this particular instance. In most cases, the Z classification represents an advantage since it supplies a unified bibliographic collection, an advantage most evident in those instances where bibliography is considered a special area of acquisition and is regarded as an adjunct to reference. Furthermore, the Z class is arranged in an alphabetical sequence by large subjects and is not difficult to use. Any difficulties encountered in attempting to locate subtopics—for example, detective stories are classed in Z5917.D5 (see Figure 3.2)—the public catalog will resolve. It is important to remember that persons treated as subjects of bibliography have a specially numbered scheme beginning with Z8001. This arrangement is alphabetical without regard to period, nationality, or field (see Figure 3.3).

> NOTE: When this particular special problem is being considered and if bibliography has not been regarded as essentially a reference and/or acquisition tool in a given library, it would be well to rethink what has gone before and possibly decide that all bibliographies will henceforth be reference materials.

3.2.4 LAW BOOKS (CLASS K)

At present no complete classification schedule has been developed for law materials. While this does represent a problem in terms of current acquisitions, it does not greatly affect a reclassification project. It is possible to reprocess the entire Dewey collection leaving law materials until the last, at which time, it is hoped, Class K will have been developed and be available. In any reclassification project, therefore, the best method of handling most law materials is to leave them in Dewey and catalog new law materials on a demand basis only. New law titles can be supplied with provisional numbers or classified into Dewey, but in either case they will ultimately have to be reclassified.[7]

While the complete Class K is being awaited, a partial solution to the problem of law books can be applied, since current acquisitions in American law are being classified by L.C. in the KF subclass. As an aid to the local cataloger, L.C. is now publishing its own KF shelflist in a 3 by 5 card format and as of this date has put out four sets of KF shelflists.[8] In purchasing these L.C. shelflist records and checking your own public catalog against this file, you can begin to reprocess American law materials and at the same time build a central core of L.C. law classification.

At whatever point law materials are reprocessed, a word of caution should be directed toward class numbers assigned to some legal materials prior to 1969. For many years legal aspects of subjects were classified with the subject, for example, in classes H, J, L, and R. Therefore, an effort must be made to determine whether or not those legal aspects will remain with the subject or be moved

---

[7] *While this situation represents an inconvenience, it is no argument against conversion to LC as its advantages outweigh this particular defect.*

[8] *The purchase information on the four KF shelflist files will be found on page 55.*

to Class K. For example, if a subject heading assigned to a title reflects some legal aspect of the subject, such as Education—Law and Legislation—U.S., it would be wise to check the index of the KF subclass to determine whether this material belongs with law or with the subject.

NOTE: Congressional hearings, whether joint, Senate or House, are classified by L.C. into KF25, KF26, and KF27. While every effort should generally be made not

---

Z	SUBJECT BIBLIOGRAPHY	Z

Botany.

5358	Local, A–Z—Continued.	
	.F8	France.
	.G3	Germany.
	.G7	Great Britain.
	.I8	Italy.
	.K6	Korea.
		Melanesia, *see* .O3.
	.M6	Mexico.
		Micronesia, *see* .O3.
	.N86	North America.
	.N88	Norway.
	.O3	Oceania.
		Micronesia, Melanesia, **Polynesia.**
	.P65	Poland.
		Polynesia, *see* .O3.
	.R9	Russia.
	.S5	South America.
	.S7	Spain.
	.S9	Sweden.
	.S92	Switzerland.
	.U4	Ukraine.
		United States.
	.U49	General.
	.U5	Local, A–Z.
5360	Catalogs.	

Canals.

5451	General bibliography.	

Erotic literature, facetiae, curiosa, etc.

Ethnology, *see* Z 5111–5119.

5877	**Etiquette.**	
5883	**Exhibitions.**	
5885	**Explosives.**	
5896	**Fables.**	
	Cf. Z 5981–5988, Folklore.	
	Z 8018, Aesop.	
5906	**Fencing and dueling.**	

Fiction.

General and general special, only.
Individual countries, *see* National bibliography.
    e. g. Z 1231.F4, American fiction.
Cf. Z 5896, Fables.
    Z 5981–5985, Folklore.
    Z 6878.G5, Ghosts.

5916	General bibliography.	
5917	Special topics, A–Z.	
	.D5	Detective stories.
	.F3	Fantastic fiction.
	.H6	Historical fiction.

FIGURE 3.2

to change class numbers assigned by L.C., there may be real arguments for putting this material into its appropriate subject area rather than into such a general classification that may work very well for a closed-stack library such as L.C. but not well for academic or public libraries.

A synopsis of the Class K outline scheme is given on the next eight pages. The pages are reproduced from *L.C. Classification—Additions and Changes. List 157* dated January–March 1970.

Z	PERSONAL BIBLIOGRAPHY		Z
	G	8349.55	Godoy Alcayaga, Lucila.
8319.8	Gacon, François.	8349.6	Godwin, William.
8320	Gaddesden, John of.	8349.7	Gökalp, Ziya.
8320.7	Galiani, Ferdinando.	8349.85	Goes, Damião de.
8321	Galilei, Galileo.	8350	Goethe, J. W. von.
8321.18	Galindo y Villa, Jesús.	8351	Gogh, Vincent van.
8321.32	Gallardo, B. J.	8351.7	Gogol', N. V.
8321.45	Galsworthy, John.	8351.8	Golding-Bird, C. H.
8322	Gama, Vasco da.	8352	Goldoni, Carlo.
8322.7	Gandhi, M. K.	8353	Goldsmith, Oliver.
8323.5	García Icazbalceta, Joaquín.	8353.5	Goldziher, Ignác.
		8353.75	Gómara, F. L. de.
8324	Gardiner, S. R.	8353.9	Gomes Coelho, J. G.
8324.13	Gardner, E. G.	8354	Gómez de Avellaneda y Arteaga, Gertrudis.
8324.2	Garibaldi, Giuseppe.		
	Garrett, J. B. da Silva Leitão de Almeida, *see* Z 8028.8.	8354.2	Gonçalves Dias, Antonio.
		8354.3	Goncharov, I. A.
8324.45	Garrick, David.	8354.8	Góngora y Argote, Luis de.
8324.48	Garufi, C. A.	8355.15	Gonzaga, T. A.
8324.52	Gascoigne, George.	8355.2	González Alcorta, Leandro.
8324.6	Gaskell, E. C. (Stevenson).	8355.25	González de Mendoza, Juan, bp.
8324.7	Gaskell, William.		
8325.5	Gassendi, Pierre.	8355.3	González del Valle y Ramírez, Francisco.
8326	Gastaldo, Jacopo.		
8328	Gaudin, M. A. A.	8356.1	Gordon, A. C.
8341.3	Gibbon, Edward.	8362	Gould, John.
8341.6	Gide, A. P. G.	8362.3	Gourmont, Remy de.
8342.2	Gill, Eric.	8362.4	Goya y Lucientes, F. J. de.
8342.4	Gilliéron, J. L.	8362.5	Gozzi, Carlo, conte.
8342.52	Ginsburg, S. M.	8364	Grabar', I. É.
8342.57	Ginzberg, Louis.	8365	Graham, R. B. C.
8342.6	Gioberti, Vincenzo.	8365.5	Grandmaison, Charles de.
8343	Giordani, Pietro.	8366.5	Grassi, Carmelo.
8343.3	Giotto di Bondone.	8368.9	Gray, Thomas.
8344	Girard, Charles.	8368.988	Greene, Robert.
8344.17	Girard, J. B.	8369	Greenlaw, E. A.
8344.7	Giraudoux, Jean.	8369.08	Gregor, Joseph.
8345.9	Giry, Arthur.	8369.1	Gregorio, Antonio de, marchese.
8346.2	Gistel, Johannes von Nepomuk Franz Xaver.		
		8369.19	Gregorius I, the Great, Saint, pope.
8346.8	Gjorgjević, Bartholomaeus.		
		8369.2	Gregory, J. W.
8347	Gladstone, W. E.	8369.26	Greve, Karl.
8347.3	Glaser, J. A.	8369.263	Grey, Sir George.
8348	Glendower, Owen.	8369.264	Griboedov, A. S.
8348.3	Glinka, M. I.	8369.265	Griffith, Arthur.
8349.48	Gode, P. K.	8369.268	Grigorovich, V. I.

FIGURE 3.3. Figure 3.2 and Figure 3.3 are reprinted from the U.S. Library of Congress. Subject Cataloging Division. Classification. Class Z: Bibliography and Library Science. 4th ed., with supplementary pages. Washington, D.C., U.S. Government Printing Office, 1965.

Supplementary K entries

CLASS K OUTLINE SCHEME
(SYNOPSIS)

The following synopsis of the Outline Scheme is being
published in response to inquiries regarding the future
arrangement of the sub-classes of Class K. The notation
in this Outline is limited to those jurisdictions or groups
of jurisdictions which are to be represented by combinations
of 2 or 3 letters. The assignment of the numerical notation
must await the development of the classification for the
individual jurisdictions. In the meantime the letters may
serve the purpose of a provisional shelf arrangement for the
publications to be classed in Class K, in order to facilitate
the use of the collections during the completion of this
schedule. The letter notation indicated in the Outline will
not appear on LC catalog cards until the schedule, or parts
of the schedule, have been completed.

K	Generalia: Periodicals. Philosophy of law. Jurisprudence. Comparative law. International legislation
KBB	Ancient law
KBD	Roman law
	Theocratic legal systems
	Christian
KBG	Canon
KBH	Orthodox
KBJ	Other Christian
KBL	Islamic
KBM	Jewish
KBP	Other
KD	United Kingdom. Anglo-American law
	General
	Including British Commonwealth in general
	England and Wales
	Scotland. Scots law
	Northern Ireland
	Isle of Man
	Channel Islands
	Eire (Ireland)

CLASS K OUTLINE SCHEME
(SYNOPSIS)

KE	Canada
KEZ	St. Pierre and Miquelon
	Greenland
KF	United States
	Latin America
KG	General
KGC	Mexico
KGE	Central America
	General
	British Honduras
	Guatemala
	El Salvador
	Honduras
	Nicaragua
	Costa Rica
	Panama
	Canal Zone
KGG	West Indies
	General. Regional organization
	Colonial and former colonial jurisdictions
	British West Indies
	French West Indies
	Netherland Antilles
	Individual islands and jurisdictions
	South America
KH	General
	Colonial jurisdictions
KHA	Argentina
KHB	Bolivia
	Brazil
KHC	Chile
	Colombia
KHE	Ecuador
KHF	French Guiana
KHG	Guyana
KHP	Paraguay
	Peru
KHS	Surinam
KHU	Uruguay
KHV	Venezuela
KHX	South Pacific Islands
	South Atlantic Islands

```
                    CLASS K OUTLINE SCHEME
                       (SYNOPSIS)


                    Europe
KJ                     General
                          Cf. K, Comparative law
                       Regional federations
                       Western Europe
                         General
                         Regional federations
KJB                      Portugal
KJD                      Spain
                         Andorra
                         Gibraltar
                         Malta
KJF                      Italy
                         San Marino
                         Vatican City
KJJ                      France.  The French Community (General)
                         Monaco
                         The Low Countries.  Luxembourg
KJM                        General
                           Luxembourg
                           Belgium
KJN                        The Netherlands
                       Central Europe
KK                       General
KKC                      Germany.  German Federal Republic
                            German Democratic Republic
KKH                        Switzerland
                           Liechtenstein
KKL                        Austria
KKN                        Hungary
KKP                        Czechoslovakia
KKR                        Poland
                       Southeastern Europe
KL                       General
KLC                      Yugoslavia
KLE                      Albania
KLG                      Greece
KLK                      Bulgaria
KLM                      Rumania
KLP                    Northern Europe.   Scandinavia
                         General
                         Denmark
                         Norway
                         Sweden
```

CLASS K OUTLINE SCHEME
(SYNOPSIS)

	Europe
KLP	Northern Europe. Scandinavia - Continued.
	Finland
	Iceland
KM	Soviet Union
	Asia
KP	General
	Southwestern Asia. The Near East
KPA	General
	Historic countries
	Cyprus
	Turkey
	Iraq. Mesopotamia
	Lebanon
	Syria
KPD	Israel. Palestine
KPF	Jordan. Transjordania
	Saudi Arabia
	Kuwait
	Persian Gulf States
	General. Federation
	Bahrain. Qatar. Trucial States
	Muscat and Oman
	Yemen
	Southern Yemen
	Iran (Persia)
	Southern Asia
KPK	General
	Afghanistan
KPL	Pakistan
KPN	India
	Nepal
	Sikkim
	Bhután
	Ceylon
	Maldive Islands
	Southeastern Asia. The Far East
KQ	General
	Southeastern Asia
	The Far East
KQB	Burma
	Thailand
	Malaysia

CLASS K OUTLINE SCHEME
(SYNOPSIS)

Asia
  Southeastern Asia. The Far East - Continued.
KQB   Singapore
          Indochina (1899-1946)
          Cambodia
          Laos
          Vietnam
KQE   Indonesia
KQH   Portuguese Timor
          Cocos (Keeling) Islands
          Christmas Island
          Ashmore and Cartier Islands
          Philippines
KQK   China. People's Republic of China
            Taiwan
KQP   Japan
KQS   Korea
            North Korea
            South Korea
  Africa
KR   General
        Regional organizations
KRB   North Africa
          General
          Egypt. United Arab Republic
          Former Barbary States
          Libya
          Tunisia
          Algeria
          Morocco
          Spanish West Africa
KRD   Eastern Africa
          General
          Sudan
          Ethiopia
          Eritrea
          Afars and Issars
          Somali Republic
KRG   Western Africa
          General
          French West Africa (1854/93-1960)
          British West Africa (1787/1896-1957/1961)
          Mauritania

CLASS K OUTLINE SCHEME
(SYNOPSIS)

	Africa
KRG	Western Africa - Continued
	Senegal
	Mali
	Gambia
	Portuguese Guinea
	Guinea
	Sierra Leone
	Liberia
	Ivory Coast
	Ghana
	Upper Volta
	Togo
	Dahomey
	Niger
	Nigeria
KRK	Central Africa
	General
	French Equatorial Africa (1884-1960)
	Chad
	Central African Republic
	Cameroun
	Equatorial Guinea
	Gabon
	Republic of the Congo (Brazzaville)
	Democratic Republic of the Congo (Kinshasa)
	British East Africa (1890/1920-1962/1964)
	East African Community
	Uganda
	Kenya
	Rwanda
	Burundi
	Tanzania
	Tanganyika
	Zanzibar and Pemba
	Malawi
	Angola (Portuguese West Africa)
	Zambia
	Southern Africa
KRL	General
	Mozambique
	Rhodesia (Southern Rhodesia)

CLASS K OUTLINE SCHEME
(SYNOPSIS)

	Africa
KRL	Southern Africa - Continued
	Botswana
KRM	Republic of South Africa
	South West Africa
KRQ	Swaziland
	Lesotho
	Malagasy Republic
	Islands in the Atlantic
	Islands in the Indian Ocean
	Madagascar (Malagasy Republic), <u>see</u> supra
	Australia. New Zealand. Oceania. Antarctica
KTA	Australia
KTC	New Zealand
KTF	Oceania
	Melanesia
	Nauru
	Micronesia
	Trust Territory of the Pacific Islands
	Guam
	Gilbert and Ellice Islands
	Polynesia
	French Polynesia
	American Samoa
	Western Samoa
KTJ	Antarctica
(KX)	Optional notation for public international law

* * * * * *

Since the numbers K1-30 are being used on L. C.
cards, the development on the next page is
being printed at this time. The remainder of
the K schedule will be printed at a later time.

* * * * * *

CLASS K

K

Periodicals

Class here all legal periodicals regardless
of subject matter and jurisdiction.
The book number, derived from the main entry
is determined by the letters following the
letter for which the class number stands.

1	A.
2	B.
3	C.
4	D.
5	E.
6	F.
7	G.
8	H.
9	I.
10	J.
11	K.
12	L.
13	M.
14	N.
15	O.
16	P.
17	Q.
18	R-Reu.
19	Revista ...

    The book number is determined by the second
word of the main entry.

20	Revj-Revt.
21	Revue ...

    To be cuttered as 19 above.

22	Rew-Rz.
23	S.
24	T.
25	U.
26	V.
27	W.
28	X.
29	Y.
30	Z.

L. C. Classification--Additions and Changes. List 157   43

Class KF Shelflist

A fourth segment of the Class KF Shelflist, resulting from
the retrospective classification of holdings of the Law Library
in the field of United States law (i.e. publications cataloged
before March 1967), is now available to libraries desiring to assign Library of Congress call numbers to their collections.
This portion of the KF Shelflist consists of electrostatic positive prints on 3x5-inch cards, with call numbers written in the
upper left hand corner. It represents chiefly treatises and monographs entered under headings beginning with the letters R to
Z which were classified and shelflisted between May 1 and December 31, 1969. The price for each set of 2541 cards is $95 for
prints on 28-pound ledger stock and $120 for prints on high-qual-
ity durable card stock.

Inquiries should be addressed to the Photoduplication Service, Department C-132, Library of Congress, Washington, D. C.
20540. Orders should specify which set (or sets) is desired of
the following four sets now available, as well as the type of
card stock desired.

Set I--1,326 cards (legal periodicals classed K 1-30, mul-
ti-volume monographs, and monographs and treatises entered
under headings beginning with the letter A). $50 a set
on 28-pound ledger stock and $60 a set on high-quality
durable card stock.

Set II--2,415 cards (treatises and)
monographs entered under headings)
beginning with the letters B to H)) Sets II-IV
) each at $95
Set III--2,576 cards (treatises and) a set on 28-
monographs entered under headings) pound ledger
beginning with the letters I to Q)) stock and
) $120 on high-
Set IV--2,541 cards (treatises and) quality durable
monographs entered under headings) card stock.
beginning with the letters Q to Z))

Orders should be accompanied by checks or money orders
made payable to the Chief, Photoduplication Service, or may be
charged to deposit accounts with the Photoduplication Service.

3.2.5 NONUSE OF PZ1, PZ3, AND PZ4

One of the problems associated with the Library of Congress Classification system is the use by L.C. of the dump numbers PZ1, PZ3, and, more recently, PZ4, which are special collection designations for standard and current fiction including English translations of foreign authors. The classification schedule itself characterizes these numbers as special collection designations that do not purport to be a class. Needless to say, this approach to fiction for a college or university library will create havoc in the location of materials in all language studies. In fact, conversations with staff members at the Library of Congress revealed that if given a second chance L.C. probably would not use the PZ3 and PZ4 locators at all.

An example in point might be that a well-known author such as Dickens has his works separated on the shelves by the PZ3 device. A complete edition of his works would be classified in PR4450 (a class for English authors of the nineteenth century), a special edition of *Great Expectations* would fall in PR4560, an ordinary reprint of *Great Expectations* would be located in PZ3, and critical material about *Great Expectations* would fall in PR4560. Obviously, it is necessary to bring some sort of logical resolution to bear upon a scheme which may work well enough in an immense closed-stack library such as the Library of Congress but not well in open-stack university libraries. That logical resolution is to classify works of fiction into their appropriate national literatures.

The simplest problem to resolve is that of PZ1, which the Library of Congress has used for collections of short stories in English and in English translations. Collections of short stories restricted to authors of one nationality may be classified in the appropriate national literature subclass.

> American short stories, PS643 or PS645
> British short stories, PRI283 or PRI285
> French short stories, in English, PQ1278; in French, PQ1274
> German short stories, in English, PTI308; in German, PTI338
> Russian short stories, in English, PG3286; in Russian, PG3280
> Etc.

Collections of short stories by authors of various nationalities will have to be kept in PZ1, or a count will have to be made of the greatest number of authors of any one nationality represented and the collection put into that national literature number. The most expedient method has been to retain the PZ1 designation for collections of short stories by authors of more than one nationality for the simple reason that any other location will tend to be arbitrary and imprecise. An argument may be advanced for the placement of PZ1 materials, where more than one national literature is involved, in PN6014 for British and American authors or PN6019, which would place English translations of short stories by authors of different nationality in a sequence of numbers designed for collections of general literature in English. However, inasmuch as short story collections not specifically restricted to one national literature tend toward wide national representation, an attempt to classify this type of collection in PN6014 or PN6019 would appear to be quixotic.

The recommended way to resolve the stickier problem of PZ3 illustrated by the Dickens work above—and by extension all such difficulties—would be as illustrated in the four cards[9] shown here.

```
PR
4550    Dickens, Charles, 1812-1870.
E79         Works of Charles Dickens.  Globe edition.  Illustrated
         from designs by Darley and Gilbert ...  Boston, Houghton,
         Osgood and company, 1879.
            15 v. fronts., plates, port.  18 cm.
               CONTENTS.—[v. 1] Oliver Twist.  Great expectations.—[v. 2] Christ-
            mas stories.  Pictures from Italy.  American notes.—[v. 3] Old curi-
            osity shop.  Sketches, pt. I.—[v. 4] Barnaby Rudge.  Sketches, pt. II.—
            [v. 5] Little Dorrit.—[v. 6] David Copperfield.—[v. 7] Martin Chuzzle-
            wit.—[v. 8] A tale of two cities.  Hard times.—[v. 9] Our mutual
            friend.—[v. 10] Nicolas Nickleby.—[v. 11] Dombey and son.—[v. 12]
            The Pickwick papers.—[v. 13] The uncommercial traveller.  [New]
            Christmas stories.  Master Humphrey's clock.—[v. 14] Bleak house.—
            [v. 15] The mystery of Edwin Drood.

                                                              A 40—151

            Cincinnati.  Univ.  Libr.     [ PR4550 .E79]
            for Library of Congress         [2]
```

```
PR
4560    Dickens, Charles, 1812-1870.
A1          Great  expectations.   By  Charles  Dickens.   ("Boz.")
1861     Printed  from  the  manuscript  and  early  proof-sheets  pur-
         chased  from  the  author ...  Philadelphia.  T. B. Peterson &
         brothers [c1861]
            168  p.  incl.  front. (port.)   25cm.   (Peterson's  uniform  edition  of
         Dickens' works)


            I. Title.
                                                              14-21532

            Library of Congress          PR4560.A1   1861
                                         [a38b1]
```

```
PR
4560    Dickens, Charles, 1812-1870.
A1          Great expectations.  Illustrated by Edward Ardizzone.
1962     New York, Heritage Press [1962, c1939]
            457 p.  illus. (part col.)  24 cm.




            I. Title.

            PZ3.D55Gr 50                                      62-51709

            Library of Congress           [5]
```

[9] *The E79 in the call number for the complete edition comes from the instruction in Table II for editions of complete works for authors assigned 48 numbers (see Figure 3.5). E79 stands for 1879, which is the publication date of the edition cited.*

CRITICAL WORK

PR
4560   **Lettis, Richard,** *ed.*
L4   Assessing Great expectations, materials for analysis, se-
          lected and edited by Richard Lettis and William E. Morris.
          San Francisco, Chandler Pub. Co. [ᶜ1960]
              230 p.   23 cm.

              1. Dickens, Charles.   Great expectations.   ɪ. Morris, William E.,
          joint ed.   ɪɪ. Title.

          PR4560.L4   823.8   63–9889 ‡

          Library of Congress   [3]

A look at the instructions from the schedule, as shown in Figure 3.4, will indicate how this sequence of numbers was determined. (Notice that some individual titles have special numbers assigned to them.) The Roman numeral following Dickens' name indicates that Table II, partially reproduced in Figure 3.5 is to be used in the arrangement of books by and about him. The instruction given in Table II for separate works which have been assigned a special number in the schedule is to use Table X for subarrangement of editions, translations, and criticism of and about that work (see Figure 3.6). Notice that there are two Table X's and that Table Xa is used for works written after 1600 A.D. Therefore, line 1 in Table Xa supplies the A1 plus date designation which produces the complete call number for the two editions of *Great Expectations* shown previously. Subsequently, line 8 of Table Xa produces the L4 author Cutter for the critical work *Assessing Great Expectations* edited by Lettis.

While the above is only the most cursory discussion of a table as used in one of the national literature schedules, it indicates that the genuine classification of fiction in English is not an impossible chore and that with some diligence it can be accomplished. These cautionary remarks are, of course, not to be construed as arguments against using the L.C. system. They are, rather, a warning against

PR   ENGLISH LITERATURE   **PR**

4550–4598   **Dickens, Charles (II).**
                       Separate works.
              4555   Barnaby Rudge.
              4556   Bleak House.
              4557   Christmas books and Christmas stories.
          → 4558   David Copperfield.
              4559   Dombey and son.
              4560   Great expectations.
              4561   Hard times.
              4562   Little Dorrit.
              4563   Martin Chuzzlewit.
              4564   Mystery of Edwin Drood.

FIGURE 3.4. Figures 3.4, 3.5, 3.6, 3.7 are reprinted from U.S. Library of Congress. Subject Cataloging Division. Classification. Class P, subclasses, PN, PR, PS, PZ: Literature (general), English and American literatures, fiction in English, juvenile literature, with supplementary pages. Washington, D.C., U.S. Government Printing Office, 1964.

TABLE OF SUBDIVISIONS UNDER INDIVIDUAL AUTHORS.

May be modified in application to specific cases whenever it seems desirable.

I (98 nos.)	II (48 nos.)		Authors with forty-eight or ninety-eight numbers.
			Collected works.
0	0 or	50	Original editions, and reprints. By date.
			To 1500: A00–A99.
			1500–1599: B00–B99.
			1600–1699: C00–C99.
			1700–1799: D00–D99.
			1800–1899: E00–E99.
			1900–1999: F00–F99.
1	1	51	Editions with commentary etc. By editor, A–Z.
2	2	52	Selected works. Minor works. Inedited works, fragments, etc.
3	3	53	Selections. Anthologies. Extracts.
4	4	54	Translations. By language; subarranged by translator.
			.F5, French.
			.G5, German.
			.I5, Italian.
			.S5, Spanish.
			.Z5, Other, A–Z.
5–40	5–22	55–72	Separate works, alphabetically by title.
			(Only the more important have a special number or numbers assigned to them, the lesser works are to have Cutter numbers.)
			For subdivisions where one number is assigned to a work use Table X. For Cutter numbers, use Table XI.
			Under each:

		0	Texts.
0	0		By date.
1	1		By editor.
2	2		Selections.

FIGURE 3.5

those who would counsel using the PZ3 and PZ4 numbers and allowing materials to fall in whatever manner they may. Lack of an intelligent appraisal of the class system one adopts creates extraordinary problems for both user and staff.

How does one get around the PZ3 mountain? A few basic guides are all that are necessary to smooth over what can be a rough road. In the first place, most authors have been assigned national literature numbers, as any reference to the schedules will testify. Even though the non-English literature schedules

X (1 no.)	X* (1 no.)	Separate works with one number. Use Table X* for works after 1600.
		Texts.
.A1	.A1	By date.
.A11–2	.A2A–Z	By editor.
	.A3	School texts.
		Translations.
.A21–39		Modern versions of medieval works.
.A4–49	.A4–49	French.
.A5–59	.A5–59	German.
.A6–69	.A6–69	Other languages. By language.
.A7–Z	.A7–Z	Criticism.

FIGURE 3.6

have not been supplied with indexes, it is not difficult to locate authors' names within the body of the schedules themselves. Also, one can always consult the *National Union Catalog,* which supplies author numbers in many instances. The basic requirement in working with the literature schedules is that each time a personal author number is found it should be entered in the appropriate schedule and index, if available, so that an ever-expanding file of personal author numbers assigned by L.C. is at hand for that time when the local cataloger will interpolate an author number into the scheme. (For a sample of index and schedule additions in the PR and PS subclasses, see Figures 3.7 and 3.8.)

An additional aid has been supplied by the Library of Congress, for as of November 1, 1968 all fiction in English cataloged after that date has alternative personal author numbers printed on L.C. cards. It is well to realize that these numbers are only author numbers and not complete call numbers; it is necessary to add a title notation to form a unique call number for specific titles (see Examples 1 and 2). Notice that the title notation for the Montherlant book is taken from the original French title, *Les jeunes filles,* which would be J4 to which is added a 2 to make the notation J42.[10] This device places the English edition next

```
PQ
2625                                                          EXAMPLE 1
O45
J42       Montherlant, Henry de, 1896–
               The girls; a tetralogy of novels.  Translated from the
          French by Terence Kilmartin.  Introd. by Peter Quennell.
          [1st U. S. ed.]  New York, Harper & Row [1968]

              639 p.  22 cm.  8.95

              Translation of Les jeunes filles.

              CONTENTS.—The girls.—Pity for women.—The hippogriff.—The
          lepers.


              I. Title.

          PZ3.M7683Gi 3              843'.9'12              68–28224
          [PQ2625.O45J43]
          Library of Congress          [7]
```

[10] *A locally devised method for handling translations of foreign fiction is to add a 2 for English or a 3 for French or a 4 for German to the call number of the title in the original language.*

EXAMPLE 2

```
PR
6063   Murdoch, Iris.
U7          Bruno's dream.  New York, Viking Press [1969]
B7
            311 p.  22 cm.  $5.75
            SBN 670-19268-6




         I. Title.
         PZ4.M974Br              823'.9'14              69-11725
         [PR6063.U7 B7]

         Library of Congress          [3]
```

to the French edition, if and when the French edition is received. The Murdoch title requires a simple title notation from *Bruno's Dream.*

The following steps are recommended for developing controls over the assignment of personal author numbers.

1. Always search the classification schedules to determine whether or not the author in question has had a literature number assigned.

2. If no number is found in the classification schedules, search the *National Union Catalog* to see whether a national literature number has been assigned to the author. Remember that the PZ3 and PZ4 numbers are assigned only to novels written in or translated into English; therefore, if the author in question has written a book of poems or a play or has had one of his novels translated into a foreign language, he will have had a national literature number assigned to him. Also check in the *Books: Subjects* for works about the author.

3. Always record in the appropriate schedule and index, if available, an author number which is found in the *National Union Catalog* or which appears on a printed card set.

4. In those cases where no author number has been assigned by L.C. and it is necessary to assign one at a local level, be sure to record the fact that it is a local creation by marking the name in the schedule with a check. With each future acquisition of that author's work or a work about him, verify the number to make certain that no conflict has developed between a locally assigned number and an L.C. number. The need to verify personal author numbers as listed in your own schedule is clearly demonstrated when one realizes that the Library of Congress has itself changed author numbers, as, for example, in the case of John Updike, whose number PS3541.P47 has been changed to PS3571.P4. Remember that one checks personal author numbers against the schedules not only for books by a particular author, but also for books about a particular author. When a personal author number found on a printed card does not correspond to the personal author number in your annotated schedule, every effort must be made to make your number conform to the number on the printed card. This naturally requires remarking books and altering the appropriate catalog cards.

ADDITIONS AND CHANGES TO MARCH 1963

PR

6045	W—Continued.		
.I55	Williamson, Henry.		
.I73	Winter, John Keith.		
.O53	Wodehouse, Pelham Grenville.		
*6047	Y.		
	Yates, Peter, *pseud.*, *see* Long, William, PR 6023.O44.		
.E35	Yeats-Brown, Francis Charles Claypon.		
.O46	Young, Andrew.		
.O47	Young. Francis Brett.		

1961–

Here are usually to be classified authors beginning to publish about 1950, flourishing after 1960.

The author number is determined by the second letter of the name.

Works of fiction (except limited editions and works in the Rare Book Collection) are classified in PZ 4.

6050	Anonymous works (XIII).		
	Individual authors.		
6051	A.		
6052	B.	6052. R 583	Brophy, Brigid
6053	C.	6053. O7	Cornwell, David John Moore ✓
6054	D.	6053. R8	Cruise O'Brien, Conor
		6054. Y4	Dyer, Charles
6055	E.		
6056	F.	6056. L4	Fleming, Ian
6057	G.	6057. A4	Gainham, Sarah ✓
6058	H.		
6059	I.		
6060	J.		
6061	K.		
6062	L.	6062. U4	Luke, Peter
6063	M.	6063. O7	Mortimer, Penelope
		6063. U7	Murdoch, Iris
6064	N.	6064. G8	Ngugi, James
6065	O.		
6066	P.	6066. I53	Pinter, Harold
6067	Q.		
6068	R.		
6069	S.	6069. A5	Sanders, Joan ✓
6070	T.	6070. H6	Thorn, Ronald Scott
6071	U.	6070. R3	Tracy, Honor Lilbush Wingfield ✓
6072	V.		
6073	W.		
6074	X.		
6075	Y.		
6076	Z.		

FIGURE 3.7. The check mark following the names of Cornwell, Gainham, Sanders, and Tracy indicates that as of the last title of each of these authors cataloged into the University of Puget Sound library collection no personal author numbers had been assigned to them by the Library of Congress. The personal author numbers as shown for these writers were assigned locally.

ADDITIONS AND CHANGES TO JUNE 1955

INDEX

Wright, Frances: PR 4525.D35.
Wright, Richard: PS 3545.R815.
Wright, Willard Huntington: *Wright, Sydney F.*
PS 3545.R846.   *PR 6045. P45*
Wurdemann, Audrey: PS 3545.U7.   *Wyatt, Edith*
Wylie, Elinor (Hoyt): PS 3545.Y45. *PS 3545. Y3*
                                  Wylie, Philip
                                  PS 3545.Y5

Y

Yates, Peter, *pseud.*: PR 6023.O44.
Yeats-Brown, Francis Charles Clay-
pon: PR 6047.E35.
Yiddish theater: PN 3035.
Yiddish wit and humor, *see* Jewish wit
and humor.
Yordan, Philip: PS 3547.O37.
Young, Andrew: PR 6047.O46.
Young, Francis Brett: PR 6047.O47   *Young, Samuel*
Young, Stanley: PS 3547.O59.   *PS 3547. Q58*
Young, Stark: PS 3547.O6.
Young people's letters: PN 6140.Y6.
Ywain (Medieval legends): PN 686.Y8.

Z

Zaturenska, Marya: PS 3549.A77.   *Zugsmith, Leane*
Zukor, Adolph: PN 1998.A3Z8.   *PS 3549. U5*

FIGURE 3.8. An index page from the *Additions and Changes to June 1955* of the 1956 reprint of the PN–PZ schedule has been used to supply an example of how personal author names and numbers should be added to the schedule index. These numbers have been recorded as a result of appearing on printed cards, of searching in the *National Union Catalog*, or of being interpolated into the schedule locally.

This short discussion of the PZ3 and PZ4 problem clearly demonstrates the need for carefully designed procedures in working with the L.C. system and gives the lie to the blasé counsels of those who would have you use all numbers as shown on printed cards without some evaluation of the nature of the subject area concerned. The burden of learning to work with all of the subclasses lies with the professional cataloger, and, on the basis of his experience with any subject area, determination must be made whether or not call numbers printed on L.C. cards can be accepted without a thought.

3.2.6 EXPLANATION OF CAPTIONS IN TABLES VIIIa AND IXa

While the comprehensive example developed at the end of this chapter will be for Table IXa, the caption analysis as outlined below applies to both Tables VIIIa and IXa. When a particular literature, generally a non-Western European literature, does not have a Table IXa printed in its schedule, the practice is to use Table IXa as it appears in the PN–PZ classification schedule. There are presently no variations in Tables VIIIa and IXa from one national literature to another. Works by and about Paul Claudel have been used for the development of a comprehensive example which will illustrate the application of Table IXa. It is hoped that the explication of captions along with the example will serve as a guide for interpreting all VIIIa and IXa tables throughout the literature classes.

> NOTE: The literature schedules indicate that when possible Tables VIIIa and IXa are to be used. In Tables IX, IXa, and IXb, the .x equals the Cutter number. In the following examples, the Cutter number for twentieth-century authors is taken from the second letter of the author's last name.[11]

EXAMPLES

PQ

2603		B
	.E5875	Bernanos, Georges, 1888–1948.
	.E6	Bernard, Tristan, 1866–1947.
	.E65	Bernstein, Henry, 1876–1953.
	.U73	Butor, Michel.
2605		C
	.A3734	Camus, Albert, 1913–1960.
	.E55	Cendrars, Blaise, 1887–1961.
	.L2	Claudel, Paul, 1868–1955.[12]
	.O15	Cocteau, Jean, 1889–1963.

VIIIa   IXa
(1 no.) (Cutter no.)

Collected works   Means complete editions of an author's works. In the language of the original.

.A1   .x   By date   Means that the imprint date of the complete edition is added to the .A1 designation for authors with one number (Table VIIIa) or to the personal name Cutter for those authors with a Cutter number (Table IXa). In case of multiple volume editions where the imprint dates cover more than one year, use the earliest date in the class number. (See comprehensive example PQ2605.L2 1950, Section 3.2.7.)

.A11–13   .xA11–13   By editor   Means that complete editions of an author's works in the language of the original can be arranged alphabetically by editor using the successive Cutter numbers .A11–13 (Table VIIIa) or .xA11–13 (Table IXa). This provision for arranging complete editions is used only infrequently. Inasmuch as .A11–13 (VIIIa) and .xA11–13 (IXa) are used so seldomly, it is necessary to refer to another section of the table to demonstrate what a successive Cutter number is and how it is developed. An instance of successive Cutter number development is supplied by the PQ2605.L2Z544 to PQ2605.L2Z98 section of the comprehensive example on Paul Claudel (see pp. 98–108).

---

[11] *This Cuttering practice is not true of Dutch, Scandinavian, South American literatures, etc., prior to 1960. Where it is true, it is explained in each schedule (e.g., American literature, PS3501–3576; English literature, PR6001–6076, etc.).*

[12] *Works by and about Paul Claudel have been used to develop a comprehensive example of the application of Table IXa.*

.A14   .xA14   **Uncataloged materials**   Designed as a "dump" number before the collection was fully cataloged. This number is not now used.

.A15   .xA15   **Collected novels**   Means a collection of novels, novellas or short stories which have been chosen at random from an author's works. Different editions are differentiated by the imprint date of the edition in hand. In the language of the original.

.A16   .xA16   **Collected essays, etc.**   Means a collection of various essays, papers, lectures, etc., collected at random from an author's works. Different editions are differentiated by the imprint date of the edition in hand. In the language of the original.

.A17   .xA17   **Collected poems**   Means a group of poems selected at random by a publisher but not a group of poems written and published as an integrated whole. A group of poems published as a unit would be regarded as a separate work and fall in the .A61–Z49 (Table VIIIa) or .xA61–Z49 (Table IXa) section of the table. Different editions of collected poems are differentiated by the imprint date of the edition in hand. In the language of the original.

.A19   .xA19   **Collected plays**   Means a group of plays selected at random and published as a collection. Different editions of collected plays are differentiated by the imprint date of the edition in hand. In the language of the original.

NOTE: Where an author is known almost exclusively as a poet or a playwright or a novelist or an essayist, a collection of his poems or plays or novels or essays would be regarded as a collected work and would be designated .A1 plus imprint date (VIIIa) or .x (i.e., author Cutter) plus imprint date (IXa). See the Robert Frost example. It should be remarked that this interpretation has not always been applied at the Library of Congress and that printed cards can be found which will indicate the .A16–19 (VIIIa) or .xA16–19 (IXa) Cuttering for complete works of a poet or playwright, etc. No attempt should be made to alter class numbers on older printed cards where the Cuttering does not conform to current interpretations of this part of Tables XIIIa and IXa.

```
PS
3511      Frost, Robert, 1874-1963.
R94          Complete poems [by] Robert Frost.  London, Cape, 1967.
1967            504 p.  20 cm.  (Jonathan Cape paperback, JCD 52)  18/-
                                                          (B 67-12109)



         PS3511.R94   1967        811'.5'2            67-111042

         Library of Congress      [2]
```

Translations (Collected) Means <u>any group of collected works in translation</u>. There is no literary form grouping, that is, for novels, essays, poems, or plays used in this part of the table. For example, a collection of plays by Bertolt Brecht in English translation would fall in the .xA2–29 section of the table. Similarly a group of poems by Brecht in English translation would fall in the .xA2–29 section of the table, as the following examples show.

PT
2603
R397
A24
1959

Brecht, Bertolt, 1898–1956.
  Selected poems. Translation and introd. by H. R. Hays.
New York, Grove Press ₍1959₎

  179 p. 22 cm.

  German and English.

  PT2603.R397A24 1959   831.912   59—13887 ‡

  Library of Congress   ₍a65d₄₎

PT
2603
R397
A27

Brecht, Bertolt, 1898–1956.
  Plays. London, Methuen ₍1960–

  v. 21 cm.

  CONTENTS.—v. 1. The Caucasian chalk circle, translated by J. and T. Stern, with W. H. Auden. The threepenny opera, translated by D. I. Vesey and E. Bentley. The trial of Lucullus, translated by H. R. Hays. The life of Galileo, translated by D. I. Vesey.

  Full name: Bertolt Eugen Friedrich Brecht.

  PT2603.R397A27   832.912   61–1061 ‡

  Library of Congress ₍5₎

.A2–29 .xA2–29 English. By Translator Means that <u>collected translations of an author's works into English are arranged alphabetically by translator</u> by the use of successive Cutter numbers within the number span .A2–29 (VIIIa) or .xA2–29 (IXa).

.A3–39 .xA3–39 French. By Translator Means that collected translations of an author's works into French are arranged alphabetically by translator by the use of successive Cutter numbers within the number span .A3–39 (Table VIIIa) or .xA3–39 (Table IXa).

.A4–49 .xA4–49 German. By Translator Means that collected translations of an author's works into German are arranged alphabetically by translator by the use of successive Cutter numbers within the number span .A4–49 (Table VIIIa) or .xA4–49 (Table IXa).

.A5–59   .xA5–59   Other. By language   Means that collected translations into languages other than the above, that is, English, French, or German, are arranged alphabetically by language within the number span .A5–59 (Table VIIIa) or .xA5–59 (Table IXa) through the use of successive Cutter numbers. The current Cuttering for "other" languages at the Library of Congress is as follows.

.A54   Hebrew
.A55   Italian
.A56   Norwegian
.A57   Russian
.A58   Spanish
.A59   Swedish

To be adjusted as necessary. The principle has generally been applied, but not these exact numbers, in the case of each language. (For an example of the arrangement of translations of collections into languages other than English, French, or German, see Brecht example on pp. 108–110.)

NOTE: Translations of individually titled works (i.e., separate works) are classified to stand on the shelf after the original language edition. The arrangement of the translations is alphabetical by language; that is, a French translation precedes a Russian translation which precedes a Spanish translation. This convention is applied at L.C. in all cases except translations of fiction into English which are classed in PZ3 and PZ4. For arguments against using this practice, see Section 3.2.5 on the use and nonuse of PZ3 and PZ4. That part of the table designed to handle separate works is designated .A61–Z49 (Table VIIIa) and .xA61–Z49 (Table IXa) and will be discussed below.

.A6   .xA6   Selections   Means that random collections of works or extracts from whole works of mixed literary form (e.g., novels, poems, lectures, etc.) published in the original language are Cuttered .A6 (Table VIIIa) or .xA6 (Table IXa). Different editions of selected works are differentiated by imprint date of the edition in hand.

.A61–Z49   .xA61–Z49[13]   Separate works   Means an integral work of any literary form originally published under a title unique to the work. This may be a cyclic novel, such as Proust's *A la recherche du temps perdu;* a group of poems always published under one title, such as John Updike's *The Carpentered Hen;* as well as any individually titled novel, poem or play. Remember that the number span for individual works of an author has specific alphameric limitations imposed by the table. An example on both ends of the alphabet is supplied by the following two titles. Hemingway's *Across the River and into the Trees* is assigned the book number PS3515.E37A7 and not PS3515.E37A25 as might be expected on the basis of the author numbers table (see Section 3.3) because of the .xA61–Z49 limitation imposed by Table IXa. Similarly, *Zuleika Dobson* by Max Beerbohm is assigned the book number PR6003.E4Z3 and not PR6003.E4Z8 as might be expected on the basis of the author numbers table, because of the .xA61–Z49 limitation imposed by Table IXa. If the Hemingway were title Cuttered .A25, the number would place this separate title among books which are collected

---

[13] *This table change is based on personal correspondence with Elizabeth Lockwood, Assistant Head, Shelflisting Section, Library of Congress Subject Cataloging Division.*

translations into English arranged by translator. If the Beerbohm book were title Cuttered .Z8, the book would fall among books written about Beerbohm rather than books written by Beerbohm.

NOTE: Inasmuch as the notation for biography and criticism in Table VIIIa is different from the notation for biography and criticism in Table IXa, each table will be discussed separately.

VIIIa
(1 no.)

.Z5A–Z   **Biography and criticism**   Means a work which is biographical or critical or any combination of these two approaches. No attempt is made in Table VIIIa to separate biography from criticism. Notice that in this case a concordance of the poems of Emily Dickinson has been put on .Z49 which would place it at the end of editions of separate works by Emily Dickinson and before autobiography, diaries, and letters. Autobiography, diaries, letters, etc., are grouped at the beginning of the .Z5A–Z sequence in the number span .Z5A3–A5. Works by other persons about the author are arranged alphabetically within the alphameric span .A6–Z8. See the sequence of book numbers in the Emily Dickinson examples.

```
PS
1541      Rosenbaum, Stanford Patrick.
Z49            A concordance to the poems of Emily Dickinson, edited
R6         by S. P. Rosenbaum.   Ithaca, N. Y., Cornell University
           Press [1964]
               xxii, 899 p.   25 cm.   (The Cornell concordances)




               1. Dickinson, Emily, 1830–1886—Concordances.    I. Title.
           (Series)

               PS1541.Z49R6             811.4                64–25335

               Library of Congress        [5]
```

```
PS
1541      Dickinson, Emily, 1830–1886.
Z5             ·Letters.  Edited by Mabel Loomis Todd.  With an introd.
A3         by Mark Van Doren.  London, Gollancz, 1951.
1951a          xxiv, 389 p.  port., facsims.  22 cm.




               PS1541.Z5A3   1951a          928.1              52–42389

               Library of Congress         [1]
```

```
PS
1541      Dickinson, Emily, 1830–1886.
Z5              Letters to Dr. and Mrs. Josiah Gilbert Holland; edited
A36        by their granddaughter, Theodora Van Wagenen Ward.
           Cambridge, Harvard University Press, 1951.

               vii, 252 p.  illus., ports., facsims.  22 cm.




               I. Holland, Josiah Gilbert, 1819–1881.  II. Holland, Elizabeth Luna
           (Chapin) 1823–     III. Ward, Theodora (Van Wagenen) ed.

               PS1541.Z5A36              928.1                 51—10236

               Library of Congress              ₍70o1₎
```

```
PS
1541      Amherst College.
Z5              Emily Dickinson: three views ₍by₎ Archibald MacLeish,
A6         Louise Bogan ₍and₎ Richard Wilbur.  Papers delivered at
           Amherst College as part of its observance of the bicentennial
           celebration of the town of Amherst, Massachusetts, on Octo-
           ber 23, 1959.  Amherst, Amherst College Press ₍1960₎

               46 p.  24 cm.




               1. Dickinson, Emily, 1830–1886.    I. MacLeish, Archibald, 1892–

               PS1541.Z5A6              811.4                 60–14002

               Library of Congress              ₍5₎
```

```
PS
1541      Anderson, Charles Roberts, 1902–
Z5              Emily Dickinson's poetry; stairway of surprise.  ₍1st ed.₎
A63        New York, Holt, Rinehart and Winston ₍1960₎

               334 p.  22 cm.





               1. Dickinson, Emily, 1830–1886.

               PS1541.Z5A63              811.4                 60–9546 ↕

               Library of Congress              ₍20₎
```

```
PS
1541      Blake, Caesar Robert, 1925–      ed.
Z5              The recognition of Emily Dickinson, selected criticism
B55        since 1890.    Edited by Caesar R. Blake and Carlton F.
           Wells.  Ann Arbor, University of Michigan Press ₍1964₎

               xvi, 314 p.  port.  24 cm.




               1. Dickinson, Emily, 1830–1886.    I. Wells, Carlton Frank, 1898–
           joint ed.  II. Title.

               PS1541.Z5B55              811.4                 64—10612

               Library of Congress              ₍69f2₎
```

PS
1541
Z5
G7

Griffith, Clark.
 The long shadow; Emily Dickinson's tragic poetry. Princeton, N. J., Princeton University Press, 1964.

 viii, 308 p. 23 cm.

1. Dickinson, Emily, 1830–1886. I. Title. II. Title: Emily Dickinson's tragic poetry.

PS1541.Z5G7   811.4   63–16234

Library of Congress   ₍5₎

PS
1541
Z5
L4

Leyda, Jay, 1910–
 The years and hours of Emily Dickinson. New Haven, Yale University Press, 1960.

 2 v. illus., ports., facsims. 24 cm.

 "Variety of juxtaposed documents, transcribed and extracted from manuscript and printed sources, ordered and dominated by a single chronology."
 "The sources": v. 2, p. 485–488. "Locations of manuscripts, illustrations, memorabilia": v. 2, p. 489–508.

1. Dickinson, Emily, 1830–1886. I. Title.

PS1541.Z5L4   928.1   60—11132

Library of Congress   ₍564d²⁹₎

PS
1541
Z5
S4

Sewall, Richard Benson, *ed.*
 Emily Dickinson, a collection of critical essays. Englewood Cliffs, N. J., Prentice-Hall ₍1963₎

 183 p. 22 cm. (A Spectrum book: Twentieth century views, S–TC–28)

 Includes bibliography.

1. Dickinson, Emily, 1830–1886.

PS1541.Z5S4   811.4   63—9307 ↕

Library of Congress   ₍6Sq14₎

PS
1541
Z5
T8

Tusiani, Joseph, 1924–
 La poesia amorosa di Emily Dickinson. New York, Venetian Press ₍1950₎

 35 p. 22 cm.

 Bibliography: p. 35.

1. Dickinson, Emily, 1830–1886. I. Title.

PS1541.Z5T8   811.49   51–15946 rev

Library of Congress   ₍r62b½₎

```
PS
1541     Ward, Theodora (Van Wagenen) 1890–
Z5           The capsule of the mind; chapters in the life of Emily
W3       Dickinson.  Cambridge, Mass., Belknap Press, 1961.
             205 p.  22 cm.




             1. Dickinson, Emily, 1830–1886.   I. Title.

         PS1541.Z5W3            928.1           61—13746 ‡

         Library of Congress        ₍a62q5₎
```

Critical works about a certain title are Cuttered to follow translations of the
original language edition of that title in the .A61–Z49 section of Table VIIIa.

IXa
(Cutter no.)

.xZ5–99   **Biography and criticism**   Means a work which is biographical or
critical or any combination of these two approaches. No attempt is made in
Table IXa to separate biography and criticism. Autobiography, diaries, letters, etc., are grouped at the beginning of the sequence in the number span
.xZ5–Z53 plus. Notice that the entire arrangement of biography and criticism
in the case of Paul Claudel must be effected by the use of successive Cutter
numbers within the number span .xZ554–Z99. This pattern will hold in its
essentials, though not in its specific numbers, throughout all literature where
there are authors who have been assigned Cutter numbers. Critical works
about a particular title are Cuttered to follow translations of the original
language edition of that title in the .xA61–Z49 section of Table IXa. This
practice is illustrated in the comprehensive example developed for separate
works by Paul Claudel, pp. 78–95.

3.2.7 EXAMPLE OF THE APPLICATION OF TABLE IXa TO WORKS BY AND ABOUT CLAUDEL

COLLECTED WORKS   By date   .x

```
PQ
2605     Claudel, Paul, 1868–
L2           Œuvres complètes.  ₍Paris₎ Gallimard ₍1950–
1950         v.  port.  24 cm.
         CONTENTS.—t. 1. Poésie.




             Full name: Paul Louis Charles Marie Claudel.

         PQ2605.L2   1950        840.81          51–3924

         Library of Congress        ₍2₎
```

A complete edition in the original language of the works of Paul Claudel which was begun in 1950. Notice that the edition is an open entry. The date 1950 will be part of the call number regardless of how many volumes are ultimately needed to finish the edition and regardless of the year in which subsequent volumes are published.

COLLECTED WORKS   By editor   .xA11–13

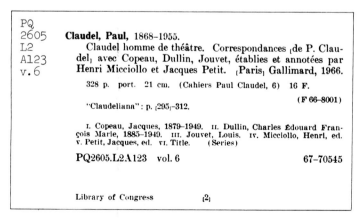

```
PQ
2605     Cahiers Paul Claudel.  1–
L2       1959–
A123     ₁Paris₁ Gallimard.

              v.  ports.  21 cm.




         I. Claudel, Paul, 1868 1955.
         PQ2605.L2A123                              A 59—8758

         Illinois.  Univ.  Library
         for Library of Congress        ₁G5rG4e¼₁†
```

Cahiers or notebooks in the original language are usually Cuttered in the .xA11–13 section of the table. Sometimes, however, a notebook is autobiographical which would place it in .xZ5–52. A prose notebook will go in .xA16 plus date if it is a collection of essays. Inasmuch as .xA11–13 is for collections arranged by editor and there is no editor indicated, the successive Cutter number was devised on the basis of the title.

```
PQ
2605     Claudel, Paul, 1868-1955.
L2            Claudel homme de théâtre.  Correspondances ₁de P. Clau-
A123     del₁ avec Copeau, Dullin, Jouvet, établies et annotées par
v. 6     Henri Micciollo et Jacques Petit.  ₁Paris₁ Gallimard, 1966.
              328 p.  port.  21 cm.  (Cahiers Paul Claudel, 6)   16 F.
                                                          (F 66–8001)
              "Claudeliana": p. ₁295₁–312.

              I. Copeau, Jacques, 1879-1949.  II. Dullin, Charles Édouard Fran-
         çois Marie, 1885–1949.  III. Jouvet, Louis.  IV. Micciollo, Henri, ed.
         V. Petit, Jacques, ed.  VI. Title.   (Series)

         PQ2605.L2A123   vol. 6                          67-70545

         Library of Congress        ₁2₁
```

An analytic for volume 6 of *Cahiers Paul Claudel.*

```
PQ
2605        La Figure d'Israël.   Paris, Gallimard, 1968.
L2
A123           429 p.  plate.  21 cm.  (Cahiers Paul Claudel, 7)  25 F
v. 7                                                                    (F***)
               "Claudeliana" : p. [419]–423.
               Bibliographical footnotes.




               1. Claudel, Paul, 1868–1955.  2. Jews in literature.   (Series)

               PQ2605.L2A123   vol. 7          848'.9'1209        68–118419


               Library of Congress              [13]
```

An analytic volume 7 of *Cahiers Paul Claudel.*

```
PQ
2605        Gadoffre, Gilbert.
L2             Claudel et l'univers chinois.  [Paris,] Gallimard, 1968.
A123           399 p.  maps, port.  21 cm.  (Cahiers Paul Claudel, 8)  26.00  F***
v. 8           Bibliography : p. [363]–380.




               1. Claudel, Paul, 1868–1955.  2. China—Foreign relations—France.
               3. France—Foreign relations—China.   I. Title.   (Series)

               PQ2605.L2A123   vol. 8                             70–379968


               Library of Congress              69 [2]
```

An analytic for volume 8 of *Cahiers Paul Claudel.*

```
PQ
2605        Claudel, Paul, 1868–1955.
L2             Oeuvres en prose.  Préf. par Gaëtan Picon.   Textes
A13         établis et annotés par Jacques Petit et Charles Galpérine.
            [Paris, Gallimard, 1965]
               xlvii, 1627 p.  18 cm.  (Bibliothèque de la Pléiade, 179)




               I. Petit, Jacques, ed.  II. Galpérine, Charles, ed.

               PQ2605.L2A13                                   66—36104

               Library of Congress              [67b1]
```

A complete edition in the original language of the prose works of Paul
Claudel. Subarrangement of successive Cutter number is by editor.

COLLECTED POEMS   .xA17

```
PQ
2605     Claudel, Paul, 1868–1955.
L2            Œuvre poétique.  Introd. par Stanislas Fumet.  [Paris,
A17      Gallimard, 1957]
1957          xxxviii, 993 p.  18 cm.  (Bibliothèque de la Pléiade, 125)




                                                       A 58–4106

         Oregon.  Univ.  Libr.
         for Library of Congress          [2]
```

An edition of collected poems in the original language. Different editions of collected poems are differentiated by imprint date.

```
PQ
2605     Claudel, Paul, 1868–1955.
L2            Œuvre poétique.  Introduction par Stanislas Fumet.
A17      Textes établis et annotés par Jacques Petit.  Paris, Galli-
1967     mard, 1967.
              lviii, 1246 p.  illus.  18 cm.  (Bibliothèque de la Pléiade, 25)
         50 F

                                                            (F•••)

         Bibliographical references included in "Notes": p. [1015]–1208.




         PQ2605.L2A17  1967                         68–108587

         Library of Congress          [18]
```

COLLECTED PLAYS   .xA19

```
PQ
2605     Claudel, Paul, 1868–1955.
L2            ... Théâtre (première série) ...  Paris, Mercure de France,
A19      1910–12.
1910          4 v.  18½ cm.

              CONTENTS.—I. Tête d'Or (première et seconde versions)  1911.—
         II. La ville (première et seconde versions)  1911.—III. La jeune fille
         Violaine.  L'échange.  1910.—IV. Le repos du septième jour.  L'Aga-
         memnon d'Eschlye.  Vers d'exil.  1912.



                     Full name: Paul Louis Charles Marie Claudel.

         PQ2605.L2A19  1910                         A 13—1109

         Harvard Univ.  Library
         for Library of Congress          [a59r45m½]†
```

An edition of collected plays in the original language. Different editions of collected plays are differentiated by imprint date. The earliest imprint date in this edition is 1910 as indicated in the contents note for volume 3. Notice that with an open entry the earliest imprint date is picked up as an element in the call number.

```
PQ
2605      Claudel, Paul, 1868–1955.
L2              Théâtre.  Tête d'or.  Partage de midi.  L'Annonce faite
A19         à Marie.  L'Otage.  Le Soulier de satin.  Avec 32 illustra-
1966        tions par André Masson, Lucien Coutaud, Félix Labisse.
            ₍Paris,₎ Gallimard, 1966.
                707 p.  col. plates.  23 cm.  65 F.
                                                        (F 67–2344)
                Illustrated cover.


                I. Title.
                PQ2605.L2A19   1966        842′.9′12        67–111565


            Library of Congress          ₍2₎
```

An edition of collected plays in the original language. Different editions of collected plays are differentiated by date.

NOTE: The principles of subarrangement demonstrated by the German language translations of Claudel's works shown in the following examples would be applied also to English translations when appropriate. It is important to remember that collected works in translation are arranged ·by translator among other translations in that language. In other words, collected works and selections are not separated but are organized by translator using successive Cutter numbers.

TRANSLATIONS. GERMAN   By translator   .xA4–49

```
PQ
2605      Claudel, Paul, 1868–1955.
L2              Paul Claudel: Auswahl aus den frühen Dichtungen; über-
A43         tragen und kommentiert von Klara Marie Fassbinder und
1955        Franz Fassbinder.  Paderborn, F. Schöningh, 1955 ₍i. e. 1954₎
                142 p.  port.  20 cm.
                "Eine erweiterte und veränderte Neuauflage des ... Werkes, Der
                Schrei aus der Tiefe."

                I. Fassbinder, Klara Marie, 1890–     ed. and tr.  II. Fassbinder,
                Franz, 1886–    ed. and tr.
                            Full name: Paul Louis Charles Marie Claudel.
                PQ2605.L2A43   1955                          55–25945


            Library of Congress          ₍3₎
```

A German translation by Fassbinder of the early poetry of Paul Claudel. Collected poems in German translation are arranged alphabetically by translator among other collections of German translations of Claudel's works without regard to literary form. The alphabetical sequence by translator is effected by the use of successive Cutter ·numbers within the number span .xA4–49. The imprint date in the call number results from this title being a new and expanded edition of *Der Schrei aus der Tiefe*.

```
PQ
2605    Claudel, Paul, 1868–1955.
L2            Gedanken zur Dichtung.  Auswahl, Übertragung und
A44      Nachwort von Edwin Maria Landau.  (Müchen, Wien)
         Langen/Müller (1967).

              398 p.  23 cm.  26.50                      GDB 68–A26–131
              Bibliography: p. 393–[399]




              I. Landau, Edwin Maria, 1904–     ed.  II. Title.

         PQ2605.L2A44                                    70–396724

         Library of Congress          69 [18]
```

A selection and translation by Landau of Paul Claudel's observations on
poetry. The arrangement is again alphabetically by translator within the
number span .xA4–49.

```
PQ
2605    Claudel, Paul, 1868-1955.
L2            Gesammelte Werke.  [Herausgeber...
A445    Edwin Maria Landau.  Heidelberg, F. H.
1958    Kerle, 1958-63, v.1. c1963]

              6 v.

              Each vol. has special t.p.; general
         title from spine.

              CONTENTS. - Bd. 1. Gedichte [von Hans
         Urs von Balthasar besorgt] - Bd. 2-3.
         Dramen. - Bd. 4. Länder und Welton. -
         Bd. 5. Kritische Schriften. - Bd. 6.
         Religion.
              I. Landau,      Edwin Maria, 1904-
         ed.             [PQ2605.L2A445  1958]
```

A German edition of the collected works of Claudel edited by Landau.
Translations into German are arranged by translator regardless of whether
they are collected works or selections. If there is more than one translation
by the same translator, the successive Cutter number is expanded to allow
for a further subarrangement by title. If no translator is identified, the Cuttering is on the basis of editor. If no editor is identified, the Cuttering is on
the basis of the publisher. (This call number was assigned locally.)

```
PQ
2605    Claudel, Paul, 1868–1955.
L2            Häusliches  Paradies.   [Essays.]   (Übertragen von
A45      Rudolf Nikolaus Maier.  Zürich,) Sanssouci (Verlag, 1967).
1967          96 p.  illus.  16 cm.  (Sanssouci-souvenirs)  sfr 6.80

                                             (Sw 67–A–4586)




              I. Title.
         PQ2605.L2A45  1967                           68–87430



         Library of Congress          [18]
```

A German translation of some of Claudel's essays, translated by Maier. Notice that among the German translations represented by the last four titles in this comprehensive example no attempt is made to group by literary form. This convention obtains in all cases throughout Tables VIIIa and IXa.

TRANSLATIONS. OTHER   By language   .x5–59

(For an example of arrangement of translations of collections into languages other than English, French, or German, see Brecht example on pp. 108–110.)

SELECTIONS   .xA6

```
PQ
2605     Claudel, Paul, 1868–
L2           … Morceaux choisis, avec un portrait et un autographe de
A6       l'auteur.  Paris, Nouvelle revue française ₁ᶜ1925₁
1925
            2 p. l., ₁9₁–251 p.  front. (port.) facsim.  19ᶜᵐ.
            "Bibliographie": p. ₁245₁–248.



         I. Title.
                              ₁Full name: Paul Louis Charles Marie Claudel₁
                                                26—7791
         Library of Congress          PQ2605.L2M6  1925
                                   ₁44c1₁
```

An edition in the original language of selected works by Claudel. Notice that the book number assigned by L.C. in 1925 does not conform to current practices. As a selection of works in the original language, it would now be Cuttered .xA6 and differentiated by imprint date.

```
PQ
2605     Claudel, Paul, 1868–1955.
L2           Paul Claudel, une étude, un choix de poèmes par Louis
A6       Perche, une bibliographie d'après un travail de René Lacote,
1948     des inédits et des portraits.  ₁Paris₁ P. Seghers ₁1948₁
            215 p.  ports., facsims.  16 cm.  (Poètes d'aujourd'hui, 10)



         I. Perche, Louis, ed.     (Series)
         PQ2605.L2A6  1948
                                                48—25347*


         Library of Congress          ₁a67c₁₁
```

A selection in the original language of poems and previously unpublished materials. Differentiated by imprint date.

```
PQ
2605      Claudel, Paul, 1868-1955.
L2             Morceaux choisis, réunis par Robert Mallet.   Paris, Galli-
A6         mard [1956]
1956          413 p.  illus.  21 cm.




          PQ2605.L2A6   1956                          56—41602 ‡

          Library of Congress            [a66c]
```

A selection in the original language of various works of Claudel. Differentiated by imprint date.

SEPARATE WORKS   .xA61–Z49

```
PQ
2605      Claudel, Paul, 1868-1955.
L2             Accompagnements.  [Essais.  Paris] Gallimard [1949]
A65           312 p.  19 cm.




              I. Title.
                           Full name: Paul Louis Charles Marie Claudel.

          PQ2605.L2A65            848.91            49—26313*

          Library of Congress         [a55i½]
```

Notice that even though the word *accompagnements* files very close to the beginning of the A's the Cuttering is .A65 within the .xA61–Z49 range. The next three examples demonstrate the title Cuttering practices with an author's work when the initial words in the titles begin with the same letter. The principle demonstrated by the examples is common throughout the scheme. Remember, no given letter has a fixed number value but rather only an approximate value. The L.C. Cuttering method is marvelously elastic.

```
PQ
2605      Claudel, Paul, 1868-
L2             ... Ainsi donc encore une fois...   Paris, Gallimard [1940]
A67           62 p., 1 l.  19ᵐ.  (On cover: Collection catholique; dirigée par André
1940       David)

              CONTENTS.—Ainsi donc encore une fois.—Derrière eux.—Aux morts des
          armées de la république. — La Vierge à midi.—Le précieux sang. — La
          grande attente.—Ce n'est point de nous seulement.—Si pourtant.—Pater
          Noster.—Sainte Geneviève.—Saint Martin.—Aux martyrs espagnols.—A
          travers la France en auto par une nuit de pleine lune.—Sainte Catherine.—
          Adresse au peuple allemand.—Ballade.—Envoi.

              I. Title.
                             [Full name: Paul Louis Charles Marie Claudel]
                                                                   40—31553
              Library of Congress         PQ2605.L2A67   1940
              Copyright  A—Foreign        46294
                                          [2]                        848.91
```

A group of essays which are always published under the title *Ainsi donc encore une fois*. The title Cuttering falls within the Cutter sequence .xA61–Z49.

```
PQ
2605      Claudel, Paul, 1868–
L2            ... L'annonce faite à Marie, mystère en quatre actes et un
A8        prologue. Paris, Éditions de la Nouvelle revue française,
1912      M. Rivière & cie, 1912.
              3 p. l., ₍9₎–210 p., 1 l.  19½ᶜᵐ.




             I. Title.
                        ₍Full name: Paul Louis Charles Marie Claudel₎
                                               15—22990
             Library of Congress          PQ2605.L2A8  1912
                                          ₍a31d1₎
```

A play published as a separate work. The title Cuttering falls within the Cutter sequence .xA61–Z49.

```
PQ
2605      Claudel, Paul, 1868–1955.
L2            The tidings brought to Mary; a mystery, by Paul
A82       Claudel; tr. from the French by Louise Morgan Sill.  New
1916      Haven, Conn., Yale university press, 1916.
              2 p. l., 171 p.  21½ cm.



             I. Sill, Louise Morgan (Smith) tr.  II. Title.
                        Full name: Paul Louis Charles Marie Claudel.
             PQ2605.L2A82   1916                      16—15748


             Library of Congress          ₍a63r26g½₎
```

An English translation of *L'annonce faite à Marie*. Notice that a 2 has been added to the French title Cutter to produce the notation .A82. This device will place the English translation of this work next to the French original when the book is shelved. Imprint date has been added to book number. (See Section 3.1.5 on dates in call numbers.)

```
PQ
2605      Claudel, Paul, 1868–
L2            The tidings brought to Mary : a mystery : by Paul Claudel :
A82       translated from the French by Louise Morgan Sill.  New
1927      Haven, Conn., Yale university press, 1916 ₍i. e. 1927₎
              2 p. l., 171 p.  21½ cm.
              "First published, June, 1916 ...  Third printing, November, 1927."


             I. Sill, Louise Morgan (Smith) tr.  II. Title.
                        Full name: Paul Louis Charles Marie Claudel.
             PQ2605.L2A82   1927           842.91          36—1331

             Library of Congress          ₍a62b½₎
```

This is also an English translation of *L'annonce faite à Marie*. Notice that the translator is the same, the publisher is the same, and the paging is the same, but L.C. has added an imprint date to the book number to differentiate this particular edition. In a case like this, it is necessary to decide whether or not the book should be cataloged as a new title or whether this edition could not be added as a copy 2 with an imprint varies note on the shelflist. (See Section 3.1.5 on dates in call numbers.)

```
PQ
2605      Boly, Joseph.
L2            L'annonce faite à Marie ₍par₎ Paul Claudel; étude et
A8215     analyse. Paris, Éditions de l'École ₍1957₎

              140 p.   illus., port., map, table.   17 cm.   (Collection "Pierres
          d'angle")

              Bibliography: p. 137–140.




              1. Claudel, Paul, 1868–1955.  L'annonce faite à Marie.

          PQ2605.L2A8215                                     59–28458

          Library of Congress              ₍³₎
```

A critical work on *L'annonce faite à Marie*. Critical material about a particular work is Cuttered to stand on the shelf after all original language editions and all translations regardless of language.

(For an extended example of the arrangement of different language translations of and critical materials about a separate work, see the Joyce example on pp. 110–120.)

```
PQ
2605      Claudel, Paul, 1868–
L2            ... Art poétique: Connaissance du temps.  Traité de la con-
A85       naissance au monde et de soi-même.  Développement de
1929      l'église ...  11. éd.  Paris, Mercvre de France, 1929.
              221, ₍3₎ p.  18½ cm.
              "La Connaissance du temps a été imprimée pour la première fois ...
          en 1904 (chez la veuve Rosario, Foutcheou, 1904) tiré à 150 ex., hors
          commerce.  Il a été réédité avec les deux autres traités par le Marcvre
          de France en 1907.  Le texte de la présente réimpression est celui de
          cette édition avec quelques corrections et adjonctions."—"Notice biblio-
          graphique" dated "novembre 1913."
              I. Title.
                              Full name: Paul Louis Charles Marie Claudel.
          PQ2605.L2A85   1929                              39—6089



          Library of Congress
```

Three treatises in the original language which are published under the unique title *Art poétique*. Notice that the title Cuttering leaves room for the insertion of another title between this one and the preceding critical work on *L'annonce faite à Marie*.

```
PQ
2605      Claudel, Paul, 1868–1955.
L2            Poetic art; tr. by Renee Spodheim.  New York, Philo-
A852      sophical Library ₁1948₎

              150 p.  23 cm.

              CONTENTS.—Knowledge of time.—Discourse on the affinity with the
          world and on oneself.—Development of the church.




              I. Spodheim, Renee, tr.  II. Title.

              PQ2605.L2A852              844.91                 48—9279*

              Library of Congress        ₁a67n½₎
```

An English translation of *Art poétique*. Notice that a 2 has been added to the call number of the original language edition to place the English edition after the French edition.

```
PQ
2605      Claudel, Paul, 1868–1955.
L2            Au milieu des vitraux de l'Apocalypse; dialogues et
A865      lettres accompagnés d'une glose.  Éd. établie par Pierre
1966      Claudel et Jacques Petit.  ₁Paris₎ Gallimard ₁1966₎

              426 p.  21 cm.

              Bibliographical references included in "Notes et glose" (p. ₁321₎–
          ₁405₎)


              I. Title.

              PQ2605.L2A865   1966                           67–33774



              Library of Congress        ₁2₎
```

Notice the ease with which the title Cutter can be advanced. Always remember to leave room to expand the Cutter to retain an alphabetical order within a given group of titles.

```
PQ
2605      Claudel, Paul, 1868–
L2            ... Les aventures de Sophie.  Paris, Gallimard ₁1937₎
A9
1937          2 p. l., ₁7₎–222 p., 1 l.  18½ᶜᵐ.

              "La Sagesse de Dieu ... qui est en grec Sophia."—p. 11.

              CONTENTS.—Judith.—Le livre d'Esther.—Le livre de Tobie.—Les dix
          commandements de Dieu.—Commentaire sur le Psaume XXVIII.—Com-
          mentaire sur le Psaume CXLVII.—Deux discours: I. La science chrétienne.
          II. Non impedias musicam.

              I. Title.
                              ₁Full name: Paul Louis Charles Marie Claudel₎

                                                              37–14271
              Library of Congress        PQ2605.L2A9  1937

              Copyright  A—Foreign        35463

                              ₁2₎                              844.91
```

A separate work in the language of the original titled *Les Adventures de*

Sophie. Even though the title Cuttering in this case is .A9, there is still room to expand the Cutter number to accommodate translations into other languages, critical works, and other titles which might possibly fall after it alphabetically. Ordinarily, L.C. attempts to avoid the use of the numerals 1 and 9 in Cuttering because to a very large degree the Cuttering options are reduced significantly.

PQ
2605
L2
C3
1931

Claudel, Paul, 1868–

   ... La cantate à trois voix, suivie de Sous le rempart d'Athènes, et de traductions diverses. Nouv. éd. Paris, Gallimard, Éditions de la Nouvelle revue française [1931]

   4 p. l., [11]–176 p., 4 l. 19ᵐ.

   CONTENTS.—La cantate à trois voix.—Sous le rempart d'Athènes.—Traductions: Coventry Patmore. Francis Thompson. Thomas Lowell Beddoes.—Abeille.

   I. Title. II. Title: Sous le rempart d'Athènes.

                   [*Full name:* Paul Louis Charles Marie Claudel]

                                    31—20357

Library of Congress	PQ2605.L2C3 1931	
Copyright A—Foreign	12142	
	[39c1]	842.91

A separate work in the language of the original. Notice that there are two separate works as well as miscellaneous translations of Claudel included in this edition. The title Cuttering is taken from the title of the first work cited *La cantate à trois voix.*

PQ
2605
L2
C5
1913

Claudel, Paul, 1868–

   ... Cinq grandes odes, suivies d'un processional pour saluer le siècle nouveau. Paris, Éditions de la Nouvelle revue française, 1913.

   3 p. l., [9]–204, [2] p., 1 l. 19½ᶜᵐ.

   On cover: Nouv. éd., augm. d'arguments.

   CONTENTS.—Les muses.—L'esprit et l'eau.—Magnificat.—La muse qui est la Grâce.—La maison fermée.—Processional.

   I. Title.

              [*Full name:* Paul Louis Charles Marie Claudel]

                                  15—8115

| Library of Congress | PQ2605.L2C5   1913 | |
| | [42r80g1] | |

A separate work in the language of the original titled *Cinq grandes odes,* followed by a shorter work called *Processional pour saluer le siècle nouveau.* When two separate works are included in the same edition, the title Cutter is taken from the first work cited on the title page.

```
PQ
2605      Claudel, Paul, 1868-1955.
L2            Cinq grandes odes, suivies d'un Processionnal pour saluer
C5        le siècle nouveau.  La Cantate à trois voix.  Préface de Jean
1966      Grosjean.  ₍Paris₎ Gallimard, 1966.

              192 p.  16 cm.  (Collection Poésie)  3.50 F.
                                                                  (F 66-7676)
              Cover illustrated in color.



                  I. Title.  II. Title: Processional pour saluer le siècle nouveau.
              III. Title: La Cantate à trois voix.

              PQ2605.L2C5   1966                          67-94124

              Library of Congress              ₍2₎
```

Another edition of *Cinq grandes odes* in the language of the original followed by two shorter works called *Processional pour saluer le siècle nouveau* and *La cantate à trois voix*. The need to differentiate this edition from the preceding one is clear because the contents of the two editions are different.

```
PQ
2605      Claudel, Paul, 1868-1955.
L2            Five great odes; translated from the French by Edward
C513      Lucie-Smith.  London, Rapp & Carroll, 1967.

              ₍5₎, 88 p.  22½ cm.  25/-
                                                                  (B 67-19816)
              Originally published as Cinq grandes odes.  Paris, 1913.




                  I. Lucie-Smith, Edward, tr.  II. Title.

              PQ2605.L2C513              841'.9'12              67—108498

              Library of Congress              ₍69c2₎
```

An English translation of *Cinq grandes odes*. Notice that in this instance the numerals 13 have been added to the title Cutter of the French language edition so that the English translation will be placed next to it on the shelf. Remember that, while the convention may often be to add the numeral 2 to the title Cutter of a foreign language edition to indicate an English translation, this is only a convention and not a hard and fast rule.

```
PQ
2605      Maurocordato, Alexandre.
L2            L'ode de Paul Claudel; essai de phénoménologie littéraire.
C545      Genève, E. Droz, 1955.

              232 p.  facsims.  25 cm.

              Errata slip inserted.
              Bibliography: p. ₍221₎-226.




                  1. Claudel, Paul, 1868-1955.  Cinq grandes odes.   I. Title.

                                                                  A 56-3335

              Vassar College.  Library
              for Library of Congress              ₍2₎
```

A critical work by Maurocordato about Claudel's *Cinq grandes odes*. This call number was devised locally on the basis of other call numbers assigned to works about *Cinq grandes odes* by L.C. When attempting to interpolate into a successive Cutter number sequence, it is recommended that all editions and supplements of the *Library of Congress Catalog—Books: Subjects* be searched carefully to maintain an alphabetical order of authors writing about the given title. Remember that locally assigned call numbers are always at the mercy of L.C. shelflisting and must with few exceptions be adjusted to conform to L.C. call numbers.

```
PQ
2605      Claudel, Paul, 1868–1955.
L2            ... Connaissance de l'Est.  3. éd.  Paris, Mercvre de France,
C6        1913.
1913
                261, ₁1₁ p.  18¼ cm.

              CONTENTS.—1895–1900.—1900–1905.




          1. East (Far East)     I. Title.

                             Full name: Paul Louis Charles Marie Claudel.

          PQ2605.L2C6   1913                                   15—6662

          Library of Congress            ₁a58r36f¾₁
```

A separate title in the language of the original called *Connaissance de l'Est*. Differentiated by imprint date.

```
PQ
2605      Claudel, Paul, 1868–1955.
L2            Connaissance de l'Est; précédé de Premiers vers et de
C6        Vers d'exil.  ₁Paris₁ Mercure de France, 1960.
1960          258 p.  20 cm.




          I. Title.  II. Title: Premier vers.  III. Title: Vers d'exil.

                             Full name: Paul Louis Charles Marie Claudel.

          [PQ2605.L2C     ]                              A 61–1879

          Illinois.  Univ.  Library
          for Library of Congress          ₁⅜₁
```

The same title as above plus two shorter works called *Premiers vers* and *Ver d'exil*. Notice that the call number as printed on the card is enclosed in brackets. An incomplete bracketed call number indicates that L.C. holds another edition of the title. Any incompleted bracketed call number must be extended to place the book on the shelves in proper order. In the example at hand the call number will be PQ2605.L2C6 1960 which will put it next to the 1913 edition cited above.

```
PQ
2605      Claudel, Paul, 1868-1955.
L2            The East I know, by Paul Claudel ... tr. by Teresa Frances
C62        and William Rose Benét. New Haven, Yale university
1914       press; [etc., etc.] 1914.

              xiii p., 1 l., 199 p.   21 cm.


              1. East (Far East)      I. Benét, Teresa Frances (Thompson) 1881-
           1919, tr.   II. Benét, William Rose, 1886-    joint tr.   III. Title.
                        Full name: Paul Louis Charles Marie Claudel.

           PQ2605.L2C62   1914                              14—22601


           Library of Congress              [a57j½]
```

An English translation of *Connaissance de l'Est*. The numeral 2 is added to the title Cutter of the French language edition. Differentiated by imprint date.

```
PQ
2605      Claudel, Paul, 1868-1955.
L2            Conoscenza dell'Est, nella versione
C65        di Gian Felice Ponti.  [Milano]
           Schwarz [1958]

              145 p.  (Dialoghi col poeta, 45)




           [PQ2605.L2C65]
```

An Italian translation of *Connaissance de l'Est*. (Refer to p. 67, part .A5–59 and .xA5–59, for number values assigned by L.C. to languages other than English, French, and German.) Notice that the terminal numbers in the numerical sequence referred to can serve as a rough guide when organizing translations by language, even when dealing with separate works. The call number for this edition was locally assigned to place the Italian translation alphabetically by language among other translations of the work.

```
PQ
2605      Claudel, Paul, 1868-
L2            ... Le livre de Christophe Colomb.   Paris, Gallimard
L5         [1935]
1935          3 p. l., 9-247, [2] p., 2 l.   19 cm.
              First published in English, 1930 (New Haven, Yale university
           press)
              Music for "Le livre de Christophe Colomb" and "L'homme et son
           désir" was composed by Darius Milhaud.
              CONTENTS.—Le drame et la musique.—Le livre de Christophe Co-
           lomb.—L'homme et son désir, scénario de ballet.—La femme et son
           ombre, scénario pour un mimodrame.—La parabole du festin (pro-
           gramme pour un oratorio)—Pan et Syrinx, cantate pour Darius
           Milhaud.
              1. Colombo, Cristoforo—Drama.      I. Milhaud, Darius, 1892-
           II. Title.


           PQ2605.L2L5   1935          842.91                35—19435

           Library of Congress              [a69d½]
```

A play in the language of the original titled *Le Livre de Christophe Colomb*.

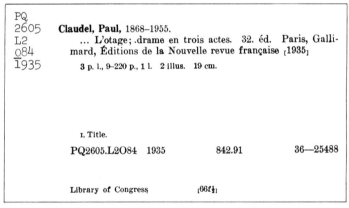

PQ
2605
L2
M6
1925

Claudel, Paul, 1868–

... Morceaux choisis, avec un portrait et un autographe de
l'auteur.   Paris, Nouvelle revue française ₍ᶜ1925₎

2 p. l., ₍9₎–251 p.   front. (port.) facsim.   19ᶜᵐ.

"Bibliographie": p. ₍245₎–248.

ɪ. Title.

₍*Full name*: Paul Louis Charles Marie Claudel₎

26—7791

Library of Congress   PQ2605.L2M6   1925

₍44c1₎

The call number printed on the L.C. card for this title would no longer be
used. This is a random selection of works by Claudel in the language of the
original and would be assigned the Cutter .A6 plus date. (See the example
PQ2605.L2A6 1925 p. 77).

PQ
2605
L2
O84
1935

Claudel, Paul, 1868–1955.
          ... L'otage; .drame en trois actes.   32. éd.   Paris, Galli-
mard, Éditions de la Nouvelle revue française ₍1935₎

3 p. l., 9–220 p., 1 l.   2 illus.   19 cm.

ɪ. Title.

PQ2605.L2O84   1935   842.91   36—25488

Library of Congress   ₍66f1₎

A play in the language of the original titled *L'otage.*

PQ
2605
L2
O85

Claudel, Paul, 1868–1955.
          The hostage, a drama, by Paul Claudel, tr. from the
French, with an introduction by Pierre Chavannes.   New
Haven, Yale university press; ₍etc., etc.₎ 1917.

2 p. l., 167 p.   21½ cm.

ɪ. Chavannes, Pierre, tr.   ɪɪ. Title.

PQ2605.L2O85   17—29252

Library of Congress   ₍a680½₎

An English translation of *L'otage.* Notice that translations of *L'otage* into
languages which would fall alphabetically after English will have to fall

within the number span .085 plus and .0859 because the critical work by Avré on *L'otage* (example following) has been given the call number PQ2605.L20859.

Other language translations might be developed as follows.

.08523   German translation
.08524   Hebrew translation
.08525   Italian translation
.08526   Norwegian translation
.08527   Russian translation
.08528   Spanish translation
.08529   Swedish translation

This device would still leave room for critical works about *L'otage* which might be written by an author whose name alphabetically precedes that of Barna Avré.

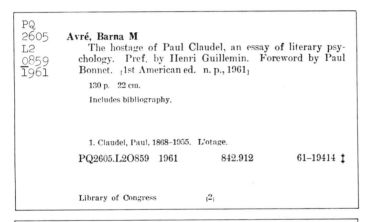

PQ
2605
L2
0859
1961

Avré, Barna M
  The hostage of Paul Claudel, an essay of literary psychology. Pref. by Henri Guillemin. Foreword by Paul Bonnet. ₁1st American ed. n. p., 1961₁

  130 p.   22 cm.

  Includes bibliography.

  1. Claudel, Paul, 1868–1955. L'otage.

  PQ2605.L2O859   1961   842.912   61–19414 ‡

  Library of Congress   ₁2₁

PQ
2605
L2
086

Avré, Barna M
  L'otage de Paul Claudel; essai de psychologie littéraire. Préf. de Henri Guillemin, avant-propos de Paul Bonnet. Québec, Soleil, 1961.

  122 p.   22 cm.

  1. Claudel, Paul, 1868–1955. L'otage.   I. Title.

  PQ2605.L2O86   61–30789 ‡

  Library of Congress   ₁3₁

While translations of a specific title are arranged to follow the original language editions, the two examples by Avré which appear to be the same work are arranged alphabetically by title because neither the English nor the French edition is identified as a translation of the other.

```
PQ
2605    Claudel, Paul, 1868–
L2          ... L'ours et la lune; farce pour un théâtre de marionnettes.
O9      Paris, Éditions de la Nouvelle revue française, 1919.
1919
                2 p. l., ₍7₎–67 p., 1 l.; ₍3₎ p. (music) 1 l.  26ᶜᵐ.




            I. Title.
                          ₍Full name: Paul Louis Charles Marie Claudel₎
                                                        19–16416 Revised

            Library of Congress             PQ2605.L2O9  1919
            Copyright  D 52618                  ₍r35c2₎
```

A play in the language of the original titled *L'ours et la lune.*

```
PQ
2605    Claudel, Paul, 1868–1955.
L2          ... Le pain dur: drame en trois actes.  Paris, Nouvelle
P3      revue française, 1918.
1918
                5 p. l., 13–158 p.  19 cm.




            I. Title.
            PQ2605.L2P3   1918                        19—2645



            Library of Congress        ₍a66r30g½₎
```

A play in the language of the original titled *Le pain dur.*

```
PQ
2605    Claudel, Paul, 1868–1955.
L2          Two dramas: Break of noon (Partage de midi)   The tid-
P353    ings brought to Mary (L'annonce faite à Marie)   Trans-
        lations and introductions ₍by₎ Wallace Fowlie.  Chicago,
        H. Regnery Co., 1960.
                295 p.  illus.  19 cm.




            I. Title: Break of noon.  II. Title: The tidings brought to Mary.

            PQ2605.L2P353            842.912            60—14057 ‡

            Library of Congress        ₍a68f½₎
```

An English translation of two plays, *Partage de midi* and *L'annonce faite à Marie.* Notice that the Cuttering for this edition is taken from *Partage de midi* and not from the title *Two Dramas*. This device places this English translation next to the French edition of *Partage de midi*.

```
PQ
2605      Czaschke, Annemarie.
L2             Der Cantique de Mesa in Paul Claudels Drama Partage
P373      de midi. Münster, Aschendorff ₁1964₎

               189 p.  25 cm.  (Forschungen zur romanischen Philologie, Heft
          13)

               Includes the text and variants of the poem.
               "Verzeichnis der Abkürzungen und Bibliographie": p. 171-179.



               1. Claudel, Paul, 1868-1955.  Partage de midi.    I. Title.
          (Series)

          PQ2605.L2P373                                     68-46917

          Library of Congress                 ₂₂₎
```

A critical work about Claudel's *Partage de midi*.

```
PQ
2605      Claudel, Paul, 1868-
L2             ... Le père humilié, drame en quatre actes.  2. éd.   Paris,
P4        Éditions de la Nouvelle revue française, 1920.
1920           4 p. l., 11-189 p., 1 l.  19½ cm.




               I. Title.
                         ₍Full name: Paul Louis Charles Marie Claudel₎
                                                        21—1597
               Library of Congress        PQ2605.L2P4  1920
                                          ₁49r37e½₎
```

A play in the language of the original titled *Le père humilié*.

```
PQ
2605      Claudel, Paul, 1868-
L2             ... Protée, illustré par Daragnès.   ₁Paris, ᶜ1920₎
P7
1920           ₍90₎ p., 1 l.  illus.  24 x 19½ᶜᵐ.

               Colophon: Achevé d'imprimer le quinze février, mil neuf cent vingt, sur
          les presses de Coulouma, imprimeur Argenteuil.
               Imprint on cover: Paris, Éditions de la Nouvelle revue française, 1919.
               "Cette édition sur papier pur fil Lafuma-Navarre a été tirée à dix exem-
          plaires hors commerce marqués ... A à J, et trois cent quatre-vingt-dix
          exemplaires numérotés ... 1 à 390 ... Copyright by Librairie Gallimard.
          1920.  Exemplaire n° 189."


               I. Title.

                                                        24-22839

               Library of Congress        PQ2605.L2P7  1920
```

A play in the language of the original titled *Protée*.

```
PQ
2605        Claudel, Paul, 1868–1955.
L2               ... Deux farces lyriques: Protée—L'ours et la lune.  8. éd.
P7          Paris, Gallimard, Éditions de la Nouvelle revue française
1927        [ᶜ1927]

                 5 p. l., [13]–222 p., 1 l.  19 cm.

                 Without music (music for "Protée" was composed by Darius Mil-
            haud)


                 I. Milhaud, Darius, 1892–      II. Title.  III. Title: Protée.
            IV. Title: L'ours et la lune.

                                   Full name: Paul Louis Charles Marie Claudel.


            PQ2605.L2P7   1927          842.91               37—7908

            Library of Congress         [a58d½]
```

An edition of two plays *Protée* and *L'ours et la lune* in the language of the
original. Notice that the title Cuttering is from the name of the first play
cited, *Protée,* and not from *Deux farces lyriques.*

```
PQ
2605        Claudel, Paul, 1868–1955.
L2               ... Le soulier de satin; ou, Le pire n'est pas toujours sûr
S6          ...  Paris, Gallimard, Éditions de la Nouvelle revue fran-
1929        çaise [ᶜ1929]

                 2 v.  19 cm.

                 "Action espagnole en quatre journées."

                 CONTENTS.—I. Première et deuxième journées.—II. Troisième et
            quatrième journées.



                 I. Title.


            PQ2605.L2S6   1929                          30—10002

            Library of Congress         [a70i1]
```

A play in the language of the original titled *Le soulier de satin.*

```
PQ
2605        Claudel, Paul, 1868–.
L2               The satin slipper; or, The worst is not the surest, by Paul
S62         Claudel.  Translated by the Rev. Fr. John O'Connor, with
1931        the collaboration of the author.  London, Sheed & Ward,
            1931.

                 xxvi, 310 p.  front.  22½ cm.

                 "Spanish play in four days."



                 I. O'Connor, John, 1870–    tr.  II. Title.

            PQ2605.L2S62   1931          842.91               32—4996



            Library of Congress         [a66i½]
```

An English translation of *Le soulier de satin.*

```
PQ
2605     Claudel, Paul, 1868-1955.
L2          Der seidene Schuh; oder, Das Schlim-
S624     mste trifft nicht immer ein. [Für die
         9.  Aufl. neu gestaltet und mit einem
         Nachwort und einer Schlussbemerkung
         versehen von Hans Urs von Balthasar]
         Salzburg, O. Müller [1959, c1939]

            415 p.

            "Schlussbemerkung" dated 1959.

               I. Title.


         [PQ2605.L2S624]
```

A German translation of *Le soulier de satin.* The call number was locally assigned to place the German translation alphabetically by language among other translations of this work.

```
PQ
2605     Brunel, Pierre.
L2          Le soulier de satin devant la critique; dilemme et contro-
S633     verses.  Paris, Lettres modernes, 1964.

            127 p.  19 cm.  (Situation, no 6)
            Bibliography · p. [120]-125.




              1. Claudel, Paul, 1868-1955.  Le soulier de satin.    I. Title.

            PQ2605.L2S633                                         67-2627

            Library of Congress              [3]
```

A critical work written by Brunel about *Le soulier de satin.*

```
PQ
2605     Lerch, Emil, literary critic.
L2          Versuchung und Gnade.  Betrachtungen über Paul
S634     Claudel und sein Schauspiel Der seidene Schuh.  Wien,
         Heiler [1956]

            140 p.  20 cm.
            Bibliography : p. [138]-140.




              1. Claudel, Paul, 1868-1955.  Le soulier de satin.    I. Title.

                                                       A 56-5408

            Illinois.  Univ.  Library
            for Library of Congress          [8]
```

A critical work written by Lerch in German about *Le soulier de satin.* The call number has been locally assigned. No attempt is made to group critical material about a particular work by the language in which it is written; it is grouped alphabetically by the author of the critical material through the use of successive Cutter numbers. This and the next three examples demonstrate this practice.

```
PQ
2605      Lindemann, Reinhold.
L2             Kreuz und Eros.  Paul Claudels Weltbild im "Seidenen
S6343      Schuh."  Frankfurt am Main, J. Knecht [1955]

               188 p.  port.  20 cm.

               "Die Zitate sind der deutschen Übersetzung des 'Seidenen Schuh'
               von Hans Urs v. Balthasar entnommen."

               CONTENTS.—Das Erosthema im Abendland.—Divina commedia.—
               Kraftfelder.—"Afrikas Ruf."—Fegefeuer Mogador.—Gegenstimmen.—
               Der gekreuzigte Eros.—Sternbild der Liebe.—Welteroberung und
               Restitution.

               1. Claudel, Paul, 1868–1955.  Le soulier de satin.    I. Title.

                                                              A 56–2585

               Illinois.  Univ.  Library
               for Library of Congress              [2]
```

A critical work written by Lindemann in German about *Le soulier de satin.* The call number has been locally assigned.

```
PQ
2605      Petit, Jacques.
L2             Pour une explication du Soulier de satin.  [Paris, Lettres
S637       modernes] 1965.

               59 p.  19 cm.  (Archives des lettres modernes : études de critique
               et d'histoire littéraire, no 58)

               Bibliography : p. [2]

               1. Claudel, Paul, 1868–1955.  Le soulier de satin.    I. Claudel,
               Paul, 1868–1955.  Le soulier de satin.  II. Title.

               PQ2605.L2S637                                    67–105025

               Library of Congress              [2]
```

A critical work written by Petit in French about *Le soulier de satin.*

```
PQ
2605      Willems, Walter, 1894–
L2             Ce cœur qui m'attendait.  Dona musique et l'amour.  De
S657       la note unique à l'accord final [par] D. W. Willems.  Bru-
               xelles, Paris, Amiens, Société générale d'éditions, Sodi,
               1967.

               135 p.  illus.  20 cm.  (Amour, couple et famille)  bfr 150.–

                                                              (Be 68–343)

               1. Claudel, Paul, 1868–1955.  Le Soulier de satin.    I. Title.

               PQ2605.L2S657                                    68–141748

               Library of Congress              [1?]
```

A critical work written by Willems in French about *Le soulier de satin.*

```
PQ
2605      Claudel, Paul, 1868–
L2              ... Tête d'Or, drame orné de compositions dessinées par
T4        Maxime Dethomas.  Paris, Société littéraire de France, 1920.
1920
                2 p. l., 265 p., 1 l.  fold. plates.  22½ cm.

                "Cette édition de Tête d'Or comprend ... douze cents exemplaires
            sur vélin de Lafuma marqués de 51 à 1250.  Exemplaire numéro 803."


                I. Title.
                            ₁Full name: Paul Louis Charles Marie Claudel₁

                PQ2605.L2T4 .1920                              24–24610

                Library of Congress            ₁a48c1₁
```

A play in the language of the original titled *Tête d'or*.

```
PQ
2605      Claudel, Paul, 1868–1955.
L2              Tête-d'Or; a play in three acts, by Paul Claudel, trans-
T5        lated from the French by John Strong Newberry.  New
          Haven, Yale university press; London, H. Milford, 1919.
                178 p.  21½ cm.




                I. Newberry, John Strong, 1883–     tr.  II. Title.

                PQ2605.L2T5                                    19—16750

                Library of Congress            ₁a68r36h½₁
```

English translation of *Tête d'or*. Notice that the Cuttering for an English
translation of *Tête d'or* in 1919 was quite different from the examples supplied for later shelflisting. Even though it is Cuttered .T5, the English translation will stand next to the French original.

```
PQ
2605      Claudel, Paul, 1868-1955.
L2              Testa d'oro, nella versione di G. F.
T525      Ponti.  [Milano] Schwarz [1959]

                155 p.  (Dialoghi col poeta, 52)




                I. Ponti, Gian Felice.



          [PQ2605.L2T525]
```

An Italian translation of *Tête d'or*. Notice that with this locally devised call
number for the Italian translation of *Tête d'or* space has been left for the
insertion of a German translation when and if necessary.

```
PQ
2605      Fragonard, Marie Madeleine.
L2            Tête d'or, ou l'imagination mythique chez Paul Claudel.
T534      ₁Paris₁ École normale supérieure de jeunes filles, ₁196-  ₁

              68 p.   27 cm.   (Collection de l'École normale supérieure de jeunes
          filles)   11 F
                                                                    (F•••)
              Bibliography :  p. 67.




              1. Claudel, Paul, 1868-1955.   Tête d'Or.   I. Title.

          PQ2605.L2T534                                       68-138499

          Library of Congress                ₁18₁
```

A critical work written by Fragonard about *Tête d'or.*

```
PQ
2605      Sarrasin, Chantal.
L2            La Signification spirituelle de "Tête d'or."   Aix-en-Pro-
T538      vence, la Pensée universitaire, 1966.

              188 p.   21 cm.   (Publications des Annales de la Faculté des lettres,
          Aix-en-Provence.   Série : Travaux et mémoires, no 39)   10 F
                                                                    (F 66-11893)
              Bibliography : p. 175-184.



              1. Claudel, Paul, 1868-1955. Tête d'Or.   I. Title.   (Series :
          Aix-Marseille, Université d'. Faculté des lettres et sciences hu-
          maines, Aix.   Travaux et mémoires, no 39)

          PQ2605.L2T538                                       68-137818

          Library of Congress                ₁18₁
```

A critical work written by Sarrasin about *Tête d'or.*

```
PQ
2605      Claudel, Paul, 1868-1955.
L2            ... Trois poèmes de guerre.   Paris, Éditions de la Nou-
T7        velle revue française ₁ᶜ1915₁
1915          3 p. l., 9-26, ₁1₁ p., 1 l.   25½ cm.

              CONTENTS.—Tant que vous voudrez, mon général!—Derrière eux.—
          Aux morts des armées de la République.



              1. European war, 1914-1918—Poetry.

          PQ2605.L2T7   1915                                 16—1950

          Library of Congress                ₁a65r37d½₁
```

A separate work in the language of the original titled *Trois poèmes de guerre.*

```
PQ
2605     Claudel, Paul, 1868–
L2           Three poems of the war, by Paul Claudel.  Tr. into English
T72      verse by Edward J. O'Brien.  With the French text.  Intro-
1919     duction by Pierre Chavannes.  New Haven, Yale university
         press; [etc., etc.] 1919.
             53, [1] p.  21ᶜᵐ.


             1. European war, 1914–1918—Poetry.     I. O'Brien, Edward Joseph
         Harrington, 1890–1941, tr.

                             [Full name: Paul Louis Charles Marie Claudel]

                                                       20—3006
         Library of Congress         PQ2605.L2T72  1919

                                      [a43r34h1]
```

An English translation of *Trois poèmes de guerre*. Notice that the numeral 2 has been added to the title Cutter of the French original.

```
PQ
2605     Claudel, Paul, 1868–1955.
L2           La Ville.  Édition critique avec étude, variantes et notes
V5       par Jacques Petit.  Paris, Mercure de France, 1967.
1967         447 p.  20 cm.  38 F.

                                                       (F 67–3380)

             Bibliography: p. [431]–432.




             I. Petit, Jacques, ed.  II. Title.

         PQ2605.L2V5  1967                             67–87360

         Library of Congress         [2]
```

A separate work in the language of the original titled *La ville*.

```
PQ
2605     Claudel, Paul, 1868–
L2           The city: a play, by Paul Claudel.  Translated from the
V53      French by John Strong Newberry.  New Haven, Yale uni-
         versity press; [etc., etc.] 1920.
             115, [1] p.  21 cm.



             I. Newberry, John Strong, 1883–    tr.  II. Title.
                             [Full name: Paul Louis Charles Marie Claudel]

         PQ2605.L2V53                            20—22679

         Library of Congress         [51r32h½]
```

An English translation of the play *La ville*.

```
PQ
2605    Claudel, Paul, 1868-1955.
L2          Mémoires improvisés.  [Entretiens avec Paul Claudel]
Z52       recueillis par Jean Amrouche.  Paris, Gallimard [1954]
           349 p.  21 cm.




           I. Amrouche, Jean, 1906–      II. Title.
                        Full name: Paul Louis Charles Marie Claudel.

           PQ2605.L2Z52                                  54—27010 ‡

           Library of Congress              [a55b1]
```

Inasmuch as published conversations of a given author with another person are regarded as autobiographical along with journals, diaries, and memoirs, the practice used by the Library of Congress is to reserve .xZ5–52 for this type of material. Since in Table IXa autobiographical material is on .xZ5–52, the first item received is assigned the Cutter .Z5 and the second item received is assigned Cutter .Z52. If both items are received on the same day, the successive Cutter number is further extended to effect an alphabetical sub-arrangement by title. By implication, the second item received by L.C. in the example was *Mémoires improvisés, entretiens avec Paul Claudel recueillis par Jean Amrouche* and was consequently Cuttered .Z52.

```
PQ
2605    Claudel, Paul, 1868-1955.
L2          Mémoires improvisés; quarante et un entretiens avec Jean
Z52       Amrouche.  Texte établi par Louis Fournier.  [Paris]
1969      Gallimard [1969]
           380 p.  17 cm.  (Collection Idées, 190.  Littérature)  unpriced
                                                                       F•••




           I. Amrouche, Jean, 1906–      II. Fournier, Louis, ed.  III. Title.

           PQ2605.L2Z52  1969                            74–436365

           Library of Congress              69 [1]
```

Since this is a later edition of the conversations of Claudel and Amrouche, the successive Cutter number stays the same, differentiated by imprint date.

```
PQ
2605    Claudel, Paul, 1868-1955.
L2          Journal ...  Introduction par François Varillon.  Texte
Z524      établi et annoté par François Varillon et Jacques Petit.
           [Paris,] Gallimard, 1968–69.
           2 v.  18 cm.  (Bibliothèque de la Pléiade, 205, 213)  60.00 (v. 1)
                                                                 F 69–2121 (v. 1)
           Includes bibliographical references.
           CONTENTS.—1. 1904–1932.—2. 1933–1955.



           I. Varillon, François, ed.  II. Petit, Jacques, ed.

           PQ2605.L2Z524                                  73–395567

           Library of Congress              69 [r70c2]  rev
```

A journal of Claudel's which was received by L.C. later than the 1954 edition of *Mémoires improvisés*.

```
PQ
2605      Claudel, Paul, 1868-1955.
L2            Paul Claudel par lui-même.  ₍Par₎ Paul-André Lesort.
Z525      ₍Paris₎ Editions du Seuil ₍1963₎
              191 p.  illus., ports., map  (on lining paper)  facsims.  18 cm.
          (Écrivains de toujours, 63)

              Includes bibliographical references.




              I. Lesort, Paul André, 1915-      ed.

          PQ2605.L2Z525                                      64—27780

          Library of Congress            ₍68b1₎
```

On the basis of the established L.C. practice of expanding successive Cutter numbers on .xZ52 for autobiographical material according to the order in which the item was received, the assumption would be that *Paul Claudel par lui-même* was received after the Claudel journal above.

NOTE: Remember that diaries, memoirs, and conversations are regarded as autobiographical and are arranged in the manner described and illustrated above. With regard to the published correspondence of a given author, the Library of Congress at present attempts to reserve .xZ53 for collected or selected letters with subsequent differentiation supplied by the addition of an imprint date. As far as the arrangement of letters to a particular person is concerned, the Cutter sequence .xZ54 plus is used. The .xZ54 plus successive Cutter is extended to maintain an alphabetical order by the name of the person to whom the letters were written. While the examples below do not respect the current practice of reserving the .xZ53 notation for collected or selected letters, they do demonstrate the method of arranging alphabetically an author's correspondence to a particular person by the name of the recipient.

```
PQ
2605      Claudel, Paul, 1868-1955.
L2            Correspondance, 1899-1926 ₍de₎ Paul Claudel et André
Z53       Gide.  Préf. et notes par Robert Mallet.  ₍Paris₎ Gallimard
          ₍1949₎
              399 p.  ports., facsims.  23 cm.



              I. Gide, André Paul Guillaume, 1869-1951.  II. Mallet, Robert,
          1915-     ed.
                          Full name: Paul Louis Charles Marie Claudel.

          PQ2605.L2Z53              928.4                  50—2368

          Library of Congress            ₍58e₁₎
```

An edition in the language of the original of the correspondence of Claudel and Gide. Since in this case .xZ53 was not reserved for an edition of selected or collected letters of Claudel, it would be necessary, if and when such an edition were published, to interpolate between the successive Cutter numbers .xZ528 and .xZ53 to place a general collection of letters before a collection of letters to a particular person.

```
PQ
2605        Claudel, Paul, 1868-1955.
L2              The correspondence, 1899-1926, between Paul Claudel and
Z532        André Gide.  Introd. and notes by Robert Mallet, prefaced
            and translated by John Russell.  ₍New York₎ Pantheon
            ₍1952₎

                299 p.  22 cm.




                    I. Gide, André Paul Guillaume, 1869-1951.

                PQ2605.L2Z532            928.3             A 53—9861

                Allegheny College.  Libr.
                for Library of Congress       ₍a68m½₎†
```

Translations of collections of letters to a particular person stand next to the original language edition and are arranged alphabetically by language; the bracketed call number is extended to effect this grouping. With the addition of a terminal 2 to the successive Cutter number of the original French edition, the English translation would stand next to the French original.

```
PQ
2605        Claudel, Paul, 1868-
L2              Correspondance, 1897-1938 ₍de₎ Paul Claudel, Francis
Z54         Jammes ₍et₎ Gabriel Frizeau; avec des lettres de Jacques
            Rivière.  Préf. et notes par André Blanchet.  ₍Paris₎ Galli-
            mard ₍1952₎

                465 p.  23 cm.



                    I. Jammes, Francis, 1868-1938.  II. Frizeau, Gabriel.  III. Rivière,
                Jacques, 1886-1925.
                            Full name: Paul Louis Charles Marie Claudel.

                PQ2605.L2Z54                          52-3789

                Library of Congress        ₍2₎
```

An edition in the language of the original of the correspondence of Claudel with Jammes, Frizeau, and Rivière. The alphabetical order is established on the basis of the first correspondent.

```
PQ
2605        Claudel, Paul, 1868-1955.
L2              Claudel et l'Amérique II; lettres de Paul Claudel à Agnès
Z543        Meyer, 1928-1929; Note-book d'Agnès Meyer, 1929.  Édition
            établie, avec introduction et notes, par Eugène Roberto.
            ₍Ottawa₎ Éditions de l'Université d'Ottawa, 1969.

                322 p.  plates.  20 cm.  (Cahier canadien Claudel 6)  unpriced
                                                                        C•••
                English or French.


                    I. Meyer, Agnes Elizabeth (Ernst) 1887-    Note-book.  II. Roberto,
                Eugène, ed.  III. Title.  (Series)

                PQ2605.L2Z543                          75-418268

                Library of Congress        69 ₍2₎
```

A collection of letters in the language of the original written to Agnès Meyer.

NOTE: The following group of examples demonstrates the manner in which biography and criticism about an author and his work are organized alphabetically by the author of the criticism using successive Cutter numbers within the number span .xZ5–Z99. Remember the grouping is a one alphabet arrangement devised on the basis of main entry without regard to the language in which the biography and/or criticism is written.

PQ
2605
L2
Z554

Alter, André.
  Paul Claudel. Textes de Claudel. Points de vue critiques, témoignages ... bibliographie ... Paris, Seghers, 1968.
    192 p. illus., plates. 16 cm. (Théâtre de tous les temps, 8)
    9.25 F
                                                              (F 68–10989)
    Illustrated cover.
    Bibliography : p. ₁185₁–189.

    1. Claudel, Paul, 1868–1955.   I. Claudel, Paul, 1868–1955.

  PQ2605.L2Z554   70–364367

    Library of Congress   69 ₁18₁

PQ
2605
L2
Z556
1965a

Andersen, Margret.
  Claudel et l'Allemagne. ₁Ottawa₁ Éditions de l'Université d'Ottawa, 1965.
    358 p. 20 cm. (Cahier canadien Claudel, 3) $5.50 Can.
                                                        (C 66–1611)
    Les Publications sériées de l'Université d'Ottawa, 80.
    First issued as the author's thesis, Montréal, 1965, under title : Le théâtre de Paul Claudel en Allemagne.
    Bibliography : p. ₁303₁–316.
    1. Claudel, Paul, 1868–1955. 2. Literature, Comparative—French and German. 3. Literature, Comparative—German and French. I. Title. (Series. Series: Ottawa. University. Publications sériées. 80)

  PQ2605.L2Z556 1965a   67–76318

    Library of Congress   ₁3₁

PQ
2605
L2
Z559

Barbier, Joseph.
  Claudel, poète de la prière. ₁Tours₁ Mame ₁1962₁
    329 p. 20 cm. (Sélection Mame)
    Bibliography : p. 325–326.

    1. Claudel, Paul, 1868–1955.

  PQ2605.L2Z559   68–48128

    Library of Congress   ₁13/8₁

```
PQ
2605    Beaumont, Ernest, 1915–
L2          The theme of Beatrice in the plays of Claudel.  London,
Z57     Rockliff [1954]
1954        102 p.  23 cm.




            1. Claudel, Paul, 1868–      2. Dante—Characters—Beatrice.
        I. Title.
            PQ2605.L2Z57   1954          842.91            55—632 ‡



        Library of Congress           [66e½]
```

```
PQ
2605    Cattaui, Georges.
L2          Claudel, le cycle des Coûfontaine et le mystère d'Israël.
Z597    Paris, Desclée, De Brouwer, 1968.
            254 p.  port.  21 cm.  (Temps et visages)  23.90 F
                                                              (F 68–8029)
            Bibliographical footnotes.




            1. Claudel, Paul, 1868–1955.

        PQ2605.L2Z597                                     68–137208

        Library of Congress           [18]
```

Notice that critical works about Claudel have been started on the notation
.xZ55 plus; other critical material will be interpolated into the sequence on
the basis of the entry for any other critical work about this author.

```
PQ
2605    Chaigne, Louis, 1899–
L2          Vie de Paul Claudel et genèse de son oeuvre.  [Tours]
Z612    Mame [1961]
            282 p.  illus., ports., facsims.  22 cm.
            Bibliographical footnotes.




            1. Claudel, Paul, 1868–1955.
        PQ2605.L2Z612                              A 61—4855
        Illinois.  Univ.  Library
        for Library of Congress        [a67c3]†
```

A locally assigned call number devised on the basis of L.C. cataloging for
an English translation for the same work (see following example). Naturally
it would be necessary to determine that this title is actually the French
original of the English translation. If the work is not the original language
edition, the arrangement would be alphabetical by title.

```
PQ
2605    Chaigne, Louis, 1899–
L2          Paul Claudel: the man and the mystic.  Translated from
Z6123    the French by Pierre de Fontnouvelle.  New York, Apple-
         ton-Century-Crofts [1961]

             280 p.  21 cm.

             Includes bibliography.




             1. Claudel, Paul, 1868–1955.

             PQ2605.L2Z6123              928.4              61—14364 ↕

             Library of Congress         [a66q1]
```

If L.C. assigns this call number to an English translation of this critical work
by Chaigne, it would be possible to assign the call number PQ2605.L2Z612
to the French original (see previous example).

```
PQ
2605    Claudel newsletter.
L2          [Kingston, R. I.]
Z622            v.  22 cm.







             1. Claudel, Paul, 1868–1955—Societies, periodicals, etc.

             PQ2605.L2Z622              841'.9'12              75–216086

             Library of Congress         69 [2]
```

A newsletter which deals with literary criticism of Claudel's work. The successive Cutter number is adjusted to allow for its filing as a title main entry
among other works about Claudel.

```
PQ
2605    Coenen-Mennemeier, Brigitta.
L2          Der aggressive Claudel; eine Studie zu Periphrasen und
Z623     Metaphern im Werke Paul Claudels [von] Brigitta Men-
1957     nemeier.  Münster Westfalen, Aschendorff [1957]
             xvi, 188 p.  24 cm.  (Forschungen zur romanischen Philologie,
             Heft 2)

             Issued also as thesis, Münster.
             Bibliography p. vii–x.

             1. Claudel, Paul, 1868–1955.    I. Title.    (Series)

             PQ2605.L2Z623   1957                          58–21749 rev


             Library of Congress         [r66b½]
```

This call number is the result of a revised main entry. See what the original
entry and call number were by referring to PQ2605.L2Z8155 1957. Remem-

ber that a revised surname in the main entry will affect the call number, for the object is to keep critical material about a particular author arranged alphabetically by the name of the author of the critical material.

PQ
2605
L2
Z635

Donnard, Jean Hervé.
　　　Trois écrivains devant Dieu : Claudel, Mauriac, Bernanos
　　　... Paris, Société d'édition d'enseignement supérieur, 1966.
　　　　99 p.　24 cm.　10 F.

　　　　　　　　　　　　　　　　　　　　　　　　　(F 67–407)

　　　　"Extrait des Annales de la Faculté de philosophie de l'Université
d'Athènes."—Bibl. de la Fr.

　　　　1. Claudel, Paul, 1868–1955.　2. Mauriac, François, 1885–
3. Bernanos, Georges, 1888–1948.　I. Title.

　　　PQ2605.L2Z635　　　　　　　　　　　　　67–81777

　　　Library of Congress　　　　　(2)

An English translation of the title would be *Three Writers Before God: Claudel, Mauriac, Bernanos.* Notice that the classification is for the first named writer, Claudel, and added entries are made for Mauriac and Bernanos.

PQ
2605
L2
Z645

Espiau de la Maëstre, André.
　　　Das göttliche Abenteuer.　Paul Claudel und sein Werk.
Salzburg, O. Müller (1968).
　　　　380 p.　21 cm.　S 180.–

　　　　　　　　　　　　　　　　　　　　　　　　　(Au 68–9–97)

　　　　1. Claudel, Paul, 1868–1955.　I. Title.

　　　PQ2605.L2Z645　　　　　　848'.9'1209　　　　68–105724

　　　Library of Congress　　　　(15)

PQ
2605
L2
Z647

Formes et figures.　[Ottawa] Éditions de l'Université
d'Ottawa, 1967.
　　　　204 p.　illus.　21 cm.　(Cahier canadien Claudel, 5)　$4.25 Can.

　　　　Bibliographical footnotes.　　　　　　　　　(C 68–1137)

　　　　1. Claudel, Paul, 1868–1955.　(Series)

　　　PQ2605.L2Z647　　　　　　848'.9'1209　　　　68–106716

　　　Library of Congress　　　　(18)

PQ
2605
L2
Z654

Franco López, Concepción.
Paul Claudel y el teatro histórico-mistico. México, 1953.

188 p. ports., facsim. 21 cm.

Tesis—Universidad Nacional Autónoma de México.
Bibliography: p. ₁184₁-188.

1. Claudel. Paul, 1868–1955.

PQ2605.L2Z654   57–15487

PQ
2605
L2
Z6725

Griffiths, Richard M
Claudel: a reappraisal edited by Richard Griffiths. London, Rapp & Whiting, 1968.

x, 197 p. 23 cm. 55/-   B 68–22660
Bibliography: p. 197.

1. Claudel, Paul, 1868–1955.   I. Title.
PQ2605.L2Z6725   1968   848'.9'1209   70–352767

PQ
2605
L2
Z673

Guillemin, Henri, 1903–
Claudel et son art d'écrire. Paris, Gallimard ₁1955₁

195 p. illus. 19 cm.
Includes bibliography.

1. Claudel, Paul, 1868–1955.   I. Title.

PQ2605.L2Z673   55—41491 ‡

PQ
2605
L2
Z674

Guillemin, Henri, 1903–
Le "Converti" Paul Claudel. ₁Paris,₁ Gallimard, 1968.

247 p. 21 cm. 16.00
Bibliographical footnotes.   (F•••)

1. Claudel, Paul, 1868–1955.   I. Title.

PQ2605.L2Z674   76–364371

PQ
2605
L2
Z68

Hubert, Marie Clotilde.

Paul Claudel, 1868–1955. Préface de Pierre-Henri Simon ... ₁Catalogue par Marie-Clotilde Hubert. Avant-propos par Étienne Dennery.₁ Paris, Bibliothèque nationale, 1968.

xxiv, 174 p. plates. 21 cm. 17 F

At head of title: Bibliothèque nationale.
Illustrated cover.

(F 68–5061)

1. Claudel, Paul, 1868–1955. ɪ. Paris. Bibliothèque nationale.

PQ2605.L2Z68   016.848′9′1209   68–111244

Library of Congress   ₁18₁

PQ
2605
L2
Z697

Kempf, Jean Pierre.

Études sur la "Trilogie" de Claudel ₁par₁ Jean-Pierre Kempf, Jacques Petit ... Paris, Éditions Lettres modernes, 1966–68.

3 v. 19 cm. (Archives des lettres modernes, 69, 77, 87. Archives claudéliennes, 5–7) 16.00   F 66–10561 (v. 1)

Includes bibliographical references.

CONTENTS.—1. L'otage.—2. Le pain dur.—3. Le père humilié.

1. Claudel, Paul, 1868–1955. ɪ. Petit, Jacques, joint author.
ɪɪ. Title.

PQ2605.L2Z697   68–73991

Library of Congress   ₁r69c2₁   rev

PQ
2605
L2
Z745

Lima, Alceu Amoroso, 1893–

O teatro claudeliano. Rio de Janeiro, AGIR, 1959.

69 p. 20 cm. (*His* Ensaios, 1)

1. Claudel, Paul, 1868–1955. ɪ. Title.

PQ2605.L2Z745   60–27886 rev ‡

Library of Congress   ₁r68b2₁

PQ
2605
L2
Z77

Madaule, Jacques, 1895–

Claudel et le langage. Paris, Desclée, De Brouwer, 1968.

320 p. 22 cm. (Temps et visages) 29.50   F•••

Illustrated cover.

1. Claudel, Paul, 1868–1955. ɪ. Title.

PQ2605.L2Z77   71–380169

Library of Congress   69 ₁18₁

PQ
2605
L2
Z813
Marcel, Gabriel, 1889–
    Regards sur le théâtre de Claudel.   Paris, Beauchesne
₍1964₎
        174 p. 18 cm. (Collection Beauchesne 7)
        "Gabriel Marcel: bibliographie": p. ₍173₎-174.

        1. Claudel, Paul, 1868–1955.   ɪ. Title.

    PQ2605.L2Z813   65—38328

    Library of Congress   ₍66b1₎

PQ
2605
L2
Z8155
1957
Mennemeier, Brigitta.
    Der aggressive Claudel; eine Studie
zu Periphrasen und Metaphern im Werke
Paul Claudels. Münster Westfalen,
Aschendorff [1957]

    188 p. (Forschungen zur romanischen
Philologie, Heft 2)
    Issued also as thesis, Münster.

    1. Claudel, Paul, 1868-1955.   I.
Title.   (Series)

    PQ2605.L2Z8155 1957

PQ
2605
L2
Z8157
Mercier-Campiche, Marianne.
    Le Théâtre de Claudel ou la Puissance du grief et de la
passion. Paris, J.-J. Pauvert, 1968.
        277 p. 22 cm. 28.50   F***
        Bibliographical footnotes.

        1. Claudel, Paul, 1868–1955.   ɪ. Title.

    PQ2605.L2Z8157   71–400528

    Library of Congress   69 ₍1⅜₎

PQ
2605
L2
Z823
Ormesson, Wladimir, *comte d'*, 1888–
    Discours prononcé le 31 mars 1966 à l'occasion de l'in-
auguration de la place Paul Claudel sur le 6ᵉ arrondisse-
ment de Paris ... Paris, impr. Firmin-Didot et Cⁱᵉ, 1966.
        6 p. 28 cm. 3 F
                                            (F 67–1505)
        At head of title: Institut de France. Académie française.

        1. Claudel, Paul, 1868–1955.   ɪ. Académie française, Paris.

    PQ2605.L2Z823   68–114777

    Library of Congress   ₍13₎

In the event that an author writes two separate critical works about the same author, the successive Cutter number is extended to effect an alphabetical subarrangement by title.

PQ
2605
L2
Z824

Ormesson, Wladimir, *comte* **d',** 1888–
    Paul Claudel et son fauteuil, par Wladimir d'Ormesson et Daniel-Rops. Paris, A. Fayard ₁1957₁

unpaged. 22 cm.

Ormesson's discourse on his reception into the Académie française and the reply of Daniel-Rops.

1. Claudel, Paul, 1868–1955. 2. Ormesson, Wladimir, Comte d', 1888–   I. Daniel-Rops, Henry, 1901–   II. Title.

PQ2605.L2Z824   57–35435 ‡

Library of Congress   ₁8₁

PQ
2605
L2
Z827

Paris. Bibliothèque Sainte-Geneviève. *Collection Doucet.*
    Paul Claudel, premières œuvres, 1886–1901, manuscrits, inédits, éditions originales, œuvres de Camille Claudel. ₁Catalogue par François Chapon.₁ Préface de François Mauriac ... 29 november–23 décembre 1965. Paris, Bibliothèque littéraire Jacques Doucet, 1965.

67 p. port., facsims. 27 cm. unpriced

(F 66–6608)

1. Claudel, Paul, 1868–1955—Exhibitions.   I. Chapon, François.

PQ2605.L2Z827   68–138612

Library of Congress   ₁13₁

PQ
2605
L2
Z853

Roberto, Eugène.
    Visions de Claudel. Marseille, Leconte, 1958.

viii, 282 p. 25 cm.

Bibliographical footnotes.

1. Claudel, Paul, 1868–1955.   I. Title.

PQ2605.L2Z853   59–23631

Library of Congress   ₁8₁

PQ
2605
L2
Z88

Société Paul Claudel du Canada.
Claudel et l'Amérique. ₍Ottawa₎ Université d'Ottawa, 1964.

265 p. 21 cm. (Cahier canadien Claudel, 2)

Publications sériées de l'Université d'Ottawa, 75.
Bibliographical footnotes.

1. Claudel, Paul, 1868–1955. ɪ. Title. (Series. Series: Ottawa. University. Publications sériées, 75)

PQ2605.L2Z88   68–53486

Library of Congress   ₍18₎

PQ
2605
L2
Z914

Tricaud, Marie Louise.
Le baroque dans le théâtre de Paul Claudel. Genève, Droz, 1967.

283 p. 23 cm. sfr 36.–

(Sw 67–A–4040)

Bibliography: p. ₍271₎–278.

1. Claudel, Paul, 1868–1955. ɪ. Title.

PQ2605.L2Z914   842'.9'12   67–107691

Library of Congress   ₍2₎

PQ
2605
L2
Z94

Vachon, André, 1926–
Le temps et l'espace dans l'œuvre de Paul Claudel; expérience chrétienne et imagination poétique. Paris, Éditions du Seuil ₍1965₎

455 p. 21 cm. (Collection "Pierres vives")

Bibliography: p. 441–448.

1. Claudel, Paul, 1868–1955. 2. Time and space. ɪ. Title.

PQ2605.L2Z94   65–53391

Library of Congress   ₍1₎

PQ
2605
L2
Z96

Varillon, François, 1905–
Claudel ... ₍Textes de Paul Claudel.₎ ₍Paris,₎ Desclée, De Brouwer, 1967.

144 p. plates. 16 cm. (Les Écrivains devant Dieu, 14) 5.75 F.

(F 67–13142)

Illustrated cover.
Bibliography: p. 141–143.

1. Claudel, Paul, 1868–1955.

PQ2605.L2Z96   848'.9'1209   68–76892

Library of Congress   ₍2₎

```
PQ
2605    Willems, Walter, 1894–
L2          Paul Claudel; rassembleur de la terre de Dieu ₁par
Z98      Walther Willems.  Bruxelles, Renaissance du livre ₁1964₁
            251 p.  illus.  20 cm.  (La Renaissance du livre)
            CONTENTS. — L'Homme et le poète.—Commentaire sur l'Annonce
         faite à Marie.—Partage de midi ou le lien entre l'homme et l'œuvre.—
         Introduction au Soulier de satin.—Quelques dates et souvenirs.



            1. Claudel, Paul, 1868–1955.    (Series)

         PQ2605.L2Z98                                    68–111647

         Library of Congress          ₁1⅜₁
```

3.2.8 EXAMPLE OF THE ARRANGEMENT OF TRANSLATIONS INTO LANGUAGES OTHER THAN ENGLISH, FRENCH, OR GERMAN

TRANSLATIONS. OTHER   By language   .x5–59

The following examples of the arrangement of translations of the selected works of Bertolt Brecht into Hebrew, Russian, and Spanish demonstrate the manner in which translations of collections of the works of a given author into languages other than English, French, and German are to be organized. Also, the example has been expanded to show the method used to arrange more than one edition of translations of the selected or collected works of a given author into a language other than English, French, or German. The point to remember is that after alphabetical subarrangement by language further differentiation is effected by arranging the works alphabetically by translator by expansion of the successive Cutter number. If there are two different editions by the same translator, the successive Cutter number is extended to supply an even further alphabetical subarrangement by title. If no translator is identified, the editor of the collection is used and if no editor then the publisher.

```
PT
2603    Brecht, Bertolt, 1898–1956.
R397       מבחר שירים ₁מאת₁ ברטולט ברכט.  עברית: מרדכי אבי-שאול.
A53        הציורים: דב בן-דוד.  ₁מהד׳ ב.₁ מרהביה, ספרית פועלים ₁1967₁
            140 p.  illus., port.  19 cm.  (ספרי מופת) IL 6.00
            Added t. p.: Gedichte; Auswahl und hebräische Übersetzung
         von Mordechay Avi-Shaul.



            I. Avi-Shaul, Mordechai, 1898–    tr.
                              Title romanized: Mivhar shirim.
         PT2603.R397A53                          HE 68–654
                                                 PL 480: Is–5728
         Library of Congress          ₁5₁
```

A Hebrew translation of a collection of Brecht's poetry.

```
PT
2603    Brecht, Bertolt, 1898–1956.
R397       Стихи. Роман. Новеллы. Публицистика. Предисл.
A57     И. Фрадкина. Редакторы: Р. Гальперина и И. Фрадкин.
        Москва, Изд-во иностранной лит-ры, 1956.
           658 p.  illus.  21 cm.




                                    Title transliterated: Stikhi.  Roman.

           PT2603.R397A57                      57–29142 ‡

           Library of Congress        ⟨8⟩
```

A Russian translation edited by Gal'perina of a collection of Brecht's poetry, novels, articles, etc. Ordinarily where there are two collections of an author's works translated into the same language, the successive Cutter number is expanded to keep an alphabetical order by translator (or by editor, if no translator is indicated, or by publisher, if no editor is cited).

```
PT
2603    Brecht, Bertolt, 1898–1956.
R397       Пьесы. ⟨Перевод А. Голембы и др. Составитель С. С.
A573    Мокульский⟩ Москва, Искусство, 1956.
           764 p.  illus.  23 cm.




                                    Title transliterated: P'esy.

           PT2603.R397A573                     57–37290 ‡

           Library of Congress        ⟨8⟩
```

A Russian translation of Brecht's plays. Notice that the successive Cutter number has been extended to place this edition of plays translated by Golemba after the edition cited above, which was edited by Gal'perina.

```
PT
2603    Brecht, Bertolt, 1898–1956.
R397       Bertolt Brecht.  Introducción y recopilación de Juan
A584    Larco. Habana, Ediciones del Teatro Nacional, 1961.
           unpaged.  illus.  21 cm.
           CONTENTS.—Introducción a la obra de Bertolt Brecht, por A. Gissel-
           brecht.—El actor de la era científica, por W. Weideli.—Textos de
           Brecht.


              I. Larco, Juan, comp.
                         Full name: Bertolt Eugen Friedrich Brecht.

           PT2603.R397A584                     62–67400 ‡

           Library of Congress        ⟨1⟩
```

A Spanish translation of a collection of Brecht's works edited by Larco.

```
PT
2603    Brecht, Bertolt, 1898-1956.
R397        Poemas y canciones.  Versíon de Jesus
A5844   Lopez Pacheco sobre la traduccíon di-
        recta del alemán de Vincente Romano.
        Prólogo de Jose Maria Carandell.
        [Madrid] Editorial Horizonte [1964,
        c1960]

            216 p.   21 cm.   (Biblioteca de
        literatura actual, 8)

            Translated from the German.

            I. Title.


        [PT2603.R397A5844]
```

A Spanish translation of a collection of poems and songs by Brecht translated by Jesus Lopez Pacheco. The call number was locally assigned to place this Spanish translation of collected works by Brecht with other Spanish translations of collected works by Brecht. Notice that the successive Cutter number has been extended to place this edition, translated by Lopez Pacheco, after the edition cited previously, which was edited by Larco. The subarrangement of collections in translation into a given language is alphabetical by (1) translator or (2) editor or (3) publisher.

3.2.9 EXAMPLE OF THE ARRANGEMENT OF DIFFERENT LANGUAGE TRANSLATIONS OF AND CRITICAL MATERIALS ABOUT A SEPARATE WORK

SEPARATE WORKS   .xA61–Z49

The following example of the arrangement of translations of James Joyce's *Ulysses* demonstrates the manner in which different language editions of a separate work are to be organized. The arrangement of editions in different language translations of a separate work is alphabetical by language by adding an extra number to the title Cutter of the original language edition. The example has been expanded beyond editions in translation to show how critical material about a separate work would be grouped alphabetically by author through the use of successive Cutter numbers following editions in translation. Notice that the arrangement of critical works about a specific title varies markedly from the arrangement of general biography and criticism about a given author which would be organized alphabetically by author writing the general biography using successive Cutter numbers within the number span .xZ5–99.

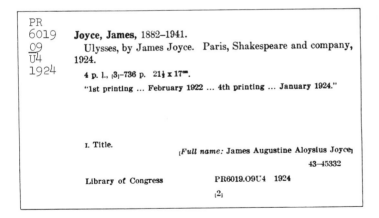

```
PR
6019    Joyce, James, 1882–
  09        Ulysses, by James Joyce.   London, Egoist press, 1922.
  U4
1922a    4 p. l., 732 p., 1 l.  23ᶜᵐ.

         First published by Shakespeare and company, Paris, February 1922.
         Printed at Dijon, France.
         "This edition is limited to 2000 copies on handmade paper ...  no. 417."
         Errata : 7 p. inserted.




         I. Title.
                          ₍Full name: James Augustine Aloysius Joyce₎
                                          23—4811

         Library of Congress          PR6019.09U4  1922 a

                          ₍a36c1₎
```

An edition of *Ulysses* in the original language. Inasmuch as this edition is a limited edition, L.C. has classified it into its appropriate literature class rather than into PZ3 where a novel in English would ordinarily be put. The lower case "a" following the imprint date in the call number is a device used by L.C. to differentiate this edition which was published in 1922 from other editions of the same title published in the same year. Each different edition of a title published in the same year would have a different terminal letter appended to the imprint date in the call number.

```
PR
6019    Joyce, James, 1882–1941.
  09        Ulysses, by James Joyce.  Paris, Shakespeare and company,
  U4    1924.
1924      4 p. l., ₍3₎–736 p.  21½ x 17ᶜᵐ.
          "1st printing ... February 1922 ... 4th printing ... January 1924."




         I. Title.
                          ₍Full name: James Augustine Aloysius Joyce₎
                                          43–45332

         Library of Congress          PR6019.09U4  1924

                          ₍2₎
```

An edition of *Ulysses* in the original language published in 1924. Again this is a special edition and has been classified into its appropriate literature class rather than into PZ3.

```
PR
6019    Joyce, James, 1882–1941.
09          Ulysses [by] James Joyce. [New York, Random house,
U4      c1934]
1934
            xvii, 767, [1] p.  illus. (music)  21½ cm.

            Title on two leaves.
            "Second printing, January 1934."




            I. Title.
                    Full name: James Augustine Aloysius Joyce.

        PZ3.J853U 5
                                                    34—2348

        Library of Congress          [57p1]
```

Conversely, this edition was not regarded as special in any way and was classed into PZ3, that is, fiction in English, including English translations of foreign authors. (See Section 3.2.5.)

```
PR
6019    Joyce, James, 1882–1941.
09          Ulysses, by James Joyce; with an introduction by Stuart
U4      Gilbert and illustrations by Henri Matisse.  New York, The
1935    Limited editions club, 1935.

            1 p. l., v–xv, [1] p., 1 l., 363 p., 1 l.  illus., plates.  30½ x 24 cm.

            "This edition ... consists of fifteen hundred copies ... This copy ...
        [is] copyright copy."  This copy not signed.
            Includes music.



            I. Gilbert, Stuart.  II. Matisse, Henri, 1869–      illus.  III. Limited
        editions club, inc., New York.  IV. Title.

        PR6019.O9U4  1935        823.91               36—943

        Library of Congress          [a68e½]
```

The call number as printed on the unit card is incorrect. Joyce's special Cutter is .09 and not .06.

```
PR
6019    Joyce, James, 1882-1941.
09          Ulysses.  Paa dansk ved Mogens Boisen.
U415    København, Martins Forlag, 1961.

            765 p.   20 cm.




            I. Title.



        [PR6019.09U415]
```

A Danish translation of *Ulysses*. This is a locally devised call number. Remember than translations of a separate work are arranged alphabetically by the language of the translation. The addition of the numerals 15 to the title

Cutter of the original language edition still allows for the interpolation of Dutch, Esperanto, Estonian, and Finnish translations of this title before the French translation which L.C. title Cuttered .U44.

```
PR
6019    Joyce, James, 1882–
09          ... Ulysse ; traduit de l'anglais par M. Auguste Morel, assisté
U44      par M. Stuart Gilbert, traduction entièrement revue par M.
1929     Valery Larbaud avec la collaboration de l'auteur.  Paris, A.
         Monnier, 1929.
            4 p. l., 870 p., 1 l.  23½ᶜᵐ.


         I. Morel, Auguste, tr.  II. Gilbert, Stuart, joint tr.  III. Title.
                         ₍Full name: James Augustine Aloysius Joyce₎
                                                          29–20042
         Library of Congress          PR6019.O9U44  1929
         Copyright  A—Foreign          3259
                                        ₍2₎
```

A French translation of *Ulysses*.

```
PR
6019    Joyce. James, 1882–1941.
09          Ulysses.  (Vom Verfasser autorisierte Übersetzung von
U45      Georg Goyert.)   Einführung von C. Giedion-Welcker.
1967     (Frankfurt a. M.) Suhrkamp (1967).
            835 p.  19 cm.  19.80              GDNB 68–A11–229




         I. Title.
         PR6019.O9U45  1967                     76–411487



         Library of Congress      69 ₍18₎
```

A German translation of *Ulysses*. Notice that the numeral 5 has been added to the original English language title Cutter.

```
PR
6019    Joyce, James, 1882-1941.
09          Ulisse, romanzo.  Unica traduzione
U46      integrale autorizzata di Giulio de
         Angelis.  Consulenti: Glauco Cambon,
         Carlo Izzo, Giorgio Melchiori.  [4. ed.
         Milano] A. Mondadori [1961, c1960]

            1025 p.  20 cm.  (Medusa, v.441)

         I grandi narratori d'ogni paese.


            I. Title.  (Series: La Medusa degli
         Italiani, v.      441)

         [PR6019.O9U46]
```

An Italian translation of *Ulysses*. A locally devised call number to keep translations of *Ulysses* organized alphabetically by the language of the translation.

```
PR
6019    Joyce, James, 1882-1941.
09          Ulisses.  Trad. [por] Antônio Houaiss.
U465    Rio de Janeiro, Editôra Civilização
        Brasileira [1966]

            846 p.  21 cm.  (Biblioteca do leitor
        moderno, v.72)



        I. Title.


        [PR6019.09U465]
```

A Portuguese translation of *Ulysses*. A locally devised call number to keep translations of *Ulysses* organized alphabetically by the language of the translation.

```
PR
6019    Joyce, James, 1882–1941.
09          ... Ulises, traducido por J. Salas Subirat.  Buenos Aires, S.
U47     Rueda [1945]

        3 p. l., ix–xv, 833 p., 2 l.  23ᶜᵐ.

        "Esta primera edición en castellano ... se publica bajo la dirección de
        Max Dickmann."



            I. Salas Subirat, J., tr.  II. Title.

                        [Full name: James Augustine Aloysius Joyce]

        PR6019.09U47              823.91              46–23091

        Library of Congress          [2]
```

A Spanish translation of *Ulysses*.

```
PR
6019    Hanley, Miles Lawrence, comp.
09          Word index to James Joyce's Ulysses, by Miles L. Hanley,
U488    assisted by Martin Joos and others.  Madison, University of
        Wisconsin Press, 1951.

        xxiii, 392 p.  28 cm.




        1. Joyce, James, 1882–1941.  Ulysses.

                                            A 52—5368

        Brown Univ.  Library
        for Library of Congress       [64k½]
```

The assigned subject heading does not indicate that this title is a concordance to *Ulysses*, which it is. Conforming to the pattern implied by the classification of the Thornton concordance below, the call number was locally assigned to place this concordance to *Ulysses* with other concordances to *Ulysses* arranged alphabetically by compiler or author.

```
PR
6019      Thornton, Weldon.
09            Allusions in Ulysses; an annotated list.   Chapel Hill,
U49       University of North Carolina Press [1968]
1968         viii, 554 p.  24 cm.

                 Bibliography: p. 507–522.




                 1. Joyce, James, 1882–1941.  Ulysses—Concordances.     I. Title.
                 PR6019.O9U49   1968           813′.5′4                68–14359



             Library of Congress                    [3]
```

A concordance to *Ulysses* which L.C. has Cuttered .U49. This places concordances after translations of the specific title and before critical works about this title.

```
PR
6019      Adams, Robert Martin, 1915–
09            Surface and symbol; the consistency of James Joyce's
U515      Ulysses.  New York, Oxford University Press, 1962.
1962         290 p.  21 cm.




                 1. Joyce, James, 1882–1941.  Ulysses.    I. Title.
                 PR6019.O9U515   1962           823.912          62—16573 ↕



             Library of Congress                    [a68f½]
```

A critical work about *Ulysses* by Adams. Notice that in this instance L.C. has started works about *Ulysses* on .U5.

```
PR
6019      Schutte, William M
09            Joyce and Shakespeare; a study in the meaning of
U56       Ulysses.  New Haven, Yale University Press, 1957.
             xiv, 197 p.  25 cm.  (Yale studies in English, v. 134)

                 "This study, in an earlier version, was presented to ... Yale Uni-
             versity as a dissertation for the doctorate."
             Includes bibliographical references.



                 1. Joyce, James, 1882–1941.  Ulysses.  2. Shakespeare, William—
             Influence—Joyce.     (Series)
                 PR6013.O9U56                823.91                    57–6345
                 ———  ——— Copy 2.           PR13.Y3  vol. 134
             Library of Congress                    [15]
```

Notice that there are two call numbers supplied for this title on the unit card. The call number PR13.Y3 vol. 134 is a series classification for the *Yale Studies in English*. It is not recommended that series classification be used in open-stack libraries. (See Section 3.2.1 on the nonuse of series call numbers.) With respect to the other call number, it is absolutely wrong. Joyce's literature number is PR6019.09 and not PR6013.09. The Cutter .U56 does not place this title by Schutte in its proper alphabetical relationship among other works about *Ulysses*. The call number should be PR6019.09U72. See discussion under the revised call number PR6019.09U72.

```
PR
6019
09
U625
```

Beach, Sylvia.
　　Ulysses in Paris.　[1st ed.]　New York [Priv. print.] Harcourt, Brace [1956]
　　24 p.　20 cm.

　　1. Joyce, James, 1882–1941.　Ulysses.　I. Title.

　　PR6019.09U625　　　　823.91　　　　57–13531 ‡

Library of Congress　　　　[2]

```
PR
6019
09
U627
```

Boldereff, Frances Motz.
　　A Blakean translation of Joyce's Circe [by] Frances M. Boldereff.　Woodward, Pa., Classic Non-fiction Library [1965]
　　xii, 178 p.　21 cm.

　　1. Joyce, James, 1882–1941.　Ulysses.　2. Blake, William, 1757–1827.　I. Title.　II. Title: Circe.

　　PR6019.09U627　　　　823.912　　　　65–4645

Library of Congress　　　　[3]

```
PR
6019
09
U63
1960
```

Budgen, Frank Spencer Curtis, 1882–
　　James Joyce and the making of Ulysses. With a portrait of James Joyce and four drawings to Ulysses by the author. Bloomington, Indiana University Press [1960]
　　339 p.　illus.　20 cm.　(A Midland book, MB26)

　　1. Joyce, James, 1882–1941.　Ulysses.　I. Title.

　　PR6019.09U63　1960　　　823.912　　　　60—50081 ‡

Library of Congress　　　　[70x¼]

```
PR
6019     Budgen, Frank Spencer Curtis, 1882-
09           James Joyce and the making of Ulysses. With a portrait
U63       of James Joyce and four drawings to Ulysses by the author.
1960a     Bloomington, Indiana University Press [1960]

             339 p. illus. 21 cm.




             1. Joyce, James, 1882-1941. Ulysses.    I. Title.
             PR6019.O9U63   1960a          823.912          61—3004 ‡


         Library of Congress          [66c2]
```

A different edition of *James Joyce and the Making of Ulysses* published in
1960. Notice that L.C. has added a lower case "a" to the imprint date in the
call number.

```
PR
6019     The Celtic bull; essays on James Joyce's Ulysses, by students
09           of the honors seminar in Ulysses, Hunter College, Dept. of
U633      English. Edited by Judy-Lynn Benjamin. Tulsa, Okla.,
          University of Tulsa [°1966]
             xi, 100 p. 23 cm. (University of Tulsa. Dept. of English. Mono-
          graph series, no. 1)
          Includes bibliographical references.


             1. Joyce, James, 1882-1941. Ulysses.    I. Benjamin, Judy-Lynn,
          ed.  II. Hunter College, New York. Dept. of English.    (Series:
          Tulsa, Okla. University. Dept. of English. Monograph series, no. 1)

          PR1.T8   no. 1                              68-3136

          Library of Congress          [3]
```

Since this group of essays about *Ulysses* was classified as part of a series
(Tulsa, Okla. University. Dept. of English. Monograph series no. 1) and no
alternative national literature number was supplied by L.C., the item has
been reclassified locally to place it alphabetically among other works about
Ulysses. (See Section 3.2.1 on the nonuse of series call numbers.)

```
PR
6019     Gilbert, Stuart.
09           James Joyce's Ulysses; a study. [2d ed., rev.]  New York,
U65       Knopf, 1952.
1952         407 p. 22 cm.
             Bibliographical footnotes.




             1. Joyce, James, 1882-1941. Ulysses.
             PR6019.O9U65   1952          823.91           51—11996


         Library of Congress          [61h1]
```

```
PR
6019      Gilbert, Stuart.
09             James Joyce's Ulysses, a study.   [New rev. and slightly
U65        enl. ed.]  London, Faber & Faber [1952]
1952a          407 p.  23 cm.




               1. Joyce, James, 1882–1941.  Ulysses.
               PR6019.O9U65   1952a          823.91          52–3498


           Library of Congress          [2]
```

A different edition also published in 1952 of *James Joyce's Ulysses, A Study.*
Notice that a terminal lower case "a" has been added to the imprint date in
the call number.

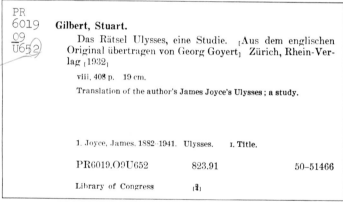

```
PR
6019      Gilbert, Stuart.
09             Das Rätsel Ulysses, eine Studie.   [Aus dem englischen
U652       Original übertragen von Georg Goyert]  Zürich, Rhein-Ver-
           lag [1932]
               viii, 408 p.  19 cm.
               Translation of the author's James Joyce's Ulysses ; a study.




               1. Joyce, James, 1882–1941.  Ulysses.   I. Title.

               PR6019.O9U652          823.91          50–51466

           Library of Congress          [3]
```

A German translation of Gilbert's *James Joyce's Ulysses, A Study.* Notice
that in this instance the numeral 2 has been added to the call number of the
English original. The arrangement of translations of critical works is alphabetical by language through the use of successive Cutter numbers following
the original language edition.

```
PR
6019      Goldberg, Samuel Louis.
09             The classical temper; a study of James Joyce's Ulysses.
U653       New York, Barnes & Noble [1961]
1961           346 p.  22 cm.




               1. Joyce, James, 1882–1941.  Ulysses.   I. Title.
               PR6019.O9U653   1961          823.912          61–66090 ‡




           Library of Congress          [5]
```

PR
6019
09
U658

Jackson, Holbrook, 1874–1948.
    Ulysses à la Joyce.   Berkeley Heights, N. J., Oriole Press
[1961]
        [13] p.   20 cm.
        "Ed. lim. to 150 copies for private distribution."

        1. Joyce, James, 1882–1941.   Ulysses.   I. Title.

        PR6019.O9U658   63–46295

        Library of Congress   [1]

PR
6019
09
U67
1959

Kain, Richard Morgan, 1908–
        Fabulous voyager; James Joyce's Ulysses.   [3d impression,
    with corrections and additions]   Chicago, University of Chi-
    cago Press [1959]
        299 p.   21 cm.

        1. Joyce, James, 1882–1941.   Ulysses.   I. Title.

        PR6019.O9U67   1959   823.912   59—2709 ‡

        Library of Congress   [64c½]

PR
6019
09
U675
1961

Litz, A   Walton.
        The art of James Joyce: method and design in Ulysses and
    Finnegans wake.   London, New York, Oxford University
    Press, 1961.
        152 p.   illus.   23 cm.
        Includes bibliography.

        1. Joyce, James, 1882–1941.   Ulysses.   2. Joyce, James, 1882–1941.
    Finnegans wake.
        PR6019.O9U675   1961   823.912   61–2855 ‡

        Library of Congress   [10]

PR
6019
09
U675
1964

Litz, A   Walton.
        The art of James Joyce, method and design in Ulysses and
    Finnegans wake [by] A. Walton Litz.   New York, Oxford
    University Press, 1964.
        x, 150 p.   facsim.   21 cm.   (A Galaxy book)
        "GB121."
        Includes bibliographies.

        1. Joyce, James, 1882–1941.   Ulysses.   2. Joyce, James, 1882–1941.
    Finnegans wake.   I. Title.
        PR6019.O9U675   1964   823.912   64–7100

        Library of Congress   [5]

PR
6019
09
U68

Loehrich, Rolf Rudolf, 1913–
      The secret of Ulysses; an analysis of James Joyce's Ulys-
ses.   McHenry, Ill., Compass Press [1953]
      viii, 200 p.   24 cm.

      1. Joyce, James, 1882–1941.   Ulysses.   I. Title

      PR6019.O9U68   823.91   53—13389

      Library of Congress   [66h½]

PR
6019
09
U685

Parr, Mary.
      James Joyce: the poetry of conscience; a study of Ulysses.
With figures by Karl Priebe.   Milwaukee, Inland Press,
1961.
      205 p.   illus.   25 cm.

      1. Joyce, James, 1882–1941.   Ulysses.

      PR6019.O9U685   823.912   61–18825 ‡

      Library of Congress   [10]

PR
6019
09
U72

Schutte, William M
      Joyce and Shakespeare; a study in the meaning of
Ulysses.   New Haven, Yale University Press, 1957.
      xiv, 197 p.   25 cm.   (Yale studies in English, v. 134)
      "This study, in an earlier version, was presented to ... Yale Uni-
versity as a dissertation for the doctorate."
      Includes bibliographical references.

      1. Joyce, James, 1882–1941.   Ulysses.   2. Shakespeare, William—
Influence—Joyce.   (Series)

      PR6013.O9U56   823.91   57–6345
      ———— ———— Copy 2.   PR13.Y3   vol. 134

      Library of Congress   [15]

This call number has been corrected in order to place the item in its proper
alphabetical relationship to other books about *Ulysses*. In those cases where
a call number is corrected or changed, the fact that the call number has been
altered should be recorded on the main entry so that any future conflict with
a correct L.C. number may be resolved. A useful method is to type the revised class number in the bottom left corner of the main entry and enclose
the entire number in brackets, [PR6019.09U72].

```
PR
6019    Sultan, Stanley.
09          The argument of Ulysses.  ₁Columbus₁ Ohio State Uni-
U73      versity Press ₁1965, *1964₁
            485 p.  24 cm.
            Includes bibliographical references.




         1. Joyce, James. 1882–1941.  Ulysses.    I. Title.

         PR6019.O9U73              823.912            64–22634

         Library of Congress          ₍3₎
```

3.3 THE L.C. SYSTEM FOR AUTHOR NUMBERS

Library of Congress call numbers consist in general of two principal elements: class number and author number, to which are added, as required, symbols designating a particular work and a particular book. This statement offers a brief explanation of the Library's system of author numbers, or, more properly, of assigning the symbols by which names are designated and differentiated in call numbers.

Library of Congress author symbols are composed of initial letters followed by Arabic numbers. The numbers are used decimally and are assigned on the basis of the tables given below in a manner that preserves the alphabetical order of names within a class.

1. After the initial letter S

for the second letter:	a	ch	e	hi	m	o p	t	u
use number:	2	3	4	5	6	7–8	9	

2. After other initial consonants

for second letter:	a	e	i	o	r	u
use number:	3	4	5	6	7	8

3. After initial vowels

for second letter:	b	d	l m	n	p	r	s t
use number:	2	3	4	5	6	7	8

Letters not included in the foregoing tables are assigned the next higher or lower number as required by previous assignments in the particular class.

The following examples illustrate the application of these tables.

1. Names beginning with consonants:

Carter	.C3	Cox	.C65
Cecil	.C4	Crocket	.C7
Cinelli	.C5	Croft	.C73
Corbett	.C6	Cullen	.C8

2. Names beginning with vowels:

Abernathy	.A2	Appleby	.A6
Adams	.A3	Archer	.A7
Aldrich	.A4	Arundel	.A78
Allen	.A45	Atwater	.A87
Ames	.A5	Austin	.A9

3. Names beginning with the letter S:

Sabine	.S15	Shank	.S45
Saint	.S2	Shipley	.S5
Schaefer	.S3	Smith	.S6
Schwedel	.S35	Steel	.S7
Scott	.S37	Storch	.S75
Seaton	.S4	Sturges	.S8
Sewell	.S43	Sullivan	.S9

Since the tables provide only a general framework for the assignment of author numbers, it should be noted that the symbol for a particular name is constant only within a single class.

NOTE: The material on Author Numbers is from the Library of Congress Processing Department, Subject Cataloging Division. This chart is dated March 30, 1962 and is available free from the Subject Cataloging Division, Library of Congress.

$$\boxed{4}$$

Mechanical Decisions
Prior to Reclassification

While many political, financial, and classificatory decisions concerning reclassi-fication will naturally precede any consideration of the mechanics of physical reprocessing, there is no question that a smoothly organized project will only result from a carefully developed plan for conversion from one class scheme to the other. Among such considerations will be (1) an evaluation of equipment needs based on the anticipated number of catalogers and clericals assigned to the project, (2) the development of a catalog card duplication procedure which will supply a steady flow of new card sets, (3) the establishment of catalog card pulling and replacement routines which will maintain collection accessibility, (4) the design of marking routines which will assure easy collection maintenance and finally a plan for the termination of the project.

4.1 EQUIPMENT NEEDS

The following equipment is recommended on the basis of full-time personnel. If some part of the work is to be carried on by part-time employees, the equipment requirements should be adjusted accordingly.

1 Electric typewriter, IBM	for each clerk responsible for cata-log card typing (pica type is rec-ommended as more readable than elite).	$395.00
1 Electric typewriter, IBM	for each clerk responsible for typ-ing cards and pockets.	$395.00
1 Bulletin 8-pitch typewriter, R. C. Allen	for use with the Se-lin labeler. (This is available only as a manual typewriter. Other manufacturers can supply electric typewriters which will work as well.)	$270.00 (manual only)

1 Se-lin labeler, Gaylord	for use in book marking (a special platen is required for whatever typewriter is to be used).	$197.00
1 Electric eraser, Bruning	for every clerk responsible for cleaning Dewey cards to be used as masters for duplication.	
1 Book truck, Remington Rand	for every 200 volumes processed per week (this figure assumes that the book truck will be completely loaded on both sides).	$120.00
1 Worktable (3' x 8')	for every three clerks assigned to marking.	
1 Glue machine, Pot-Devin	for pasting pockets in books (this machine is only useful where the gluing is an internal technical services operation).	$120.00 (manual) $190.00 (electric)
1 Xerox machine	for catalog card reproduction as well as reproduction of temporary slips for the public catalog (the rental cost of the Xerox machine may be shared with other institutional copying requirements—see Table 2.1).	
1 Heavy duty paper cutter, Homs M15 (with extra blade)	for cutting catalog cards after they are duplicated.	$194.00 (manual)

An added factor in determining equipment needs will be the smoothness and continuity of reclassification procedures; for example, if 1000 volumes are processed by the classifiers, but there are only enough clerks to physically handle 500 volumes, the requirements for book trucks, etc., will be altered.

4.2 CATALOG CARD DECISIONS

In a reclassification project the achievement of a fast, effective technique for card duplication is one of the initial problems to be solved. At the beginning of the reclassification project at the University of Puget Sound, all possibilities were explored until a method was found which would generate card sets rapidly enough to answer the requirements of the project.

1. Pulling complete card sets from the catalog, erasing Dewey numbers, and retyping L.C. numbers was found to be the most inefficient approach.
   (a) Subject approach was lost in the public catalog for as long as it took to redo the cards.
   (b) Erasing an entire set of cards proved too time-consuming.
   (c) Pulling and refiling entire card sets wasted too much time.
   (d) Quality control of erasing and retyping was difficult to maintain.
   (e) Many of the cards in the public catalog had become so marked, worn, and dirty that to return them to the catalog seemed ridiculous.

(f) Much of the descriptive cataloging done in the early years of the library's history was so inaccurate and incomplete that it was impossible to use the information.

2. Typing complete new card sets proved time-consuming and expensive for obvious reasons.

3. Ordering new card sets proved very expensive in terms of card costs and clerical time and in time lost waiting for card sets to arrive, but this method was used notwithstanding until a method of card duplication was decided upon and perfected.

4. Copying masters on the Xerox 914 and later on the Xerox 720 proved ultimately to be the most efficient method of supplying new card sets for the reclassification project.

The initial frustrations of using the Xerox process of card duplication are outweighed by its ability to produce quickly a clean, sharp catalog card in whatever quantity needed. Admittedly there will be a time of trial when the mechanics of card duplication are being learned, but beyond this modest inconvenience few problems will be encountered. Ordinarily the greatest problem associated with duplicating catalog cards is the need to share one machine with other institutional copying requirements. Few libraries can justify the expense of a Xerox 914, 720, 2400, or 3600 for the exclusive use of the technical services division; therefore, it will be necessary to achieve a *modus vivendi* with other claimants upon the machine.

The following decisions, steps, and procedures are recommended when setting up a Xerox card duplication program.

1. Enlist the interest and sympathy of the Xerox maintenance representative. He will undoubtedly be the one to make the necessary initial adjustments in the machine before card duplication can begin.

2. Carefully consider the choice of card stock. While numerous brands are available (some prepunched and perforated, some prepunched and nonperforated), it is wise to consider exactly what kind of a physical card catalog will be built—for in a very real sense you are rebuilding the entire catalog. Are catalog cards to have the rough edges a perforated card stock will produce? Are the cards to be cleaned if in duplicating they are shadowed or soiled? Are the cards going into the public catalog to be covered with plastic overlays to protect them?[1]

3. Make one clerk responsible for card duplication, thereby eliminating the need to constantly retrain and supervise rotating personnel. Naturally while some other clerks will have to be trained for emergency purposes, there is a real advantage in having the accumulated experience of one clerk trained for

---

[1] *Plastic covers should be given some thought, since most cards remain in the public catalog for decades. With the repeated thumbing a group of cards receives through the years, no one really knows how long a duplicated catalog card will last.*

card duplication. The analysis and adjustment of small problems by this clerk can save a lot of time and maintain the flow of high quality cards.

4. The Xerox 914 was the machine recommended by the company for catalog card duplication at the time the 720 became available; however, it was felt that hours spent by a clerk in card reproduction had to be considered in determining card costs. After a careful time and motion study, it was decided that to bring the per card cost down it was necessary to move to the Xerox 720, which copies almost two times faster than the Xerox 914 with comparable quality. The incidence of the card stock jamming in the machine is no greater than it is with the 914.

5. An extra drum, which is used only for card reproduction, is recommended for the machine, and it is wise always to wax this drum prior to card duplication. This waxing tends to reduce background haze and sharpen the print on the finished cards. (The recommended wax is Vista car wax or the wax available from the Xerox Corporation.)

4.3 CATALOG CARD DUPLICATION

4.3.1 THE XEROX 914 OR 720 COPIER

The method of producing catalog cards from typed masters, galley slips, or L.C. printed cards is essentially the same when using either the Xerox 914 or the Xerox 720 because there is outwardly little variation between the two machines. The significant difference between the models is that the Xerox 720 will copy nearly twice as fast as the older 914. In terms of the unit cost of a single catalog card, this capability of the 720 will be important in deciding which machine will be leased for the purposes of card duplication. While the impression was mostly subjective, it was our feeling that the Xerox 720 did produce a sharper image and a cleaner product than did the 914; in the sequence of photographs below, the Xerox 720 was in use. Inasmuch as no interior adjustments need to be made in either the 914 or the 720 when it is used for catalog card duplication, either machine can be used for general purpose copying which might arise from other library or institutional requirements. This fact tends to bring the cost of the machine into perspective as the rental and copying charges are then spread over a wider use base than would be otherwise possible.

Setting of Controls for Catalog Card Duplication

While no interior adjustments are necessary on the Xerox 914 or 720 for catalog card duplication, there are external controls which must be changed when card stock is used in either machine. The photograph in Figure 4.1 illustrates the various control settings which have proven most effective over a period of a year. It must be understood, of course, that these settings were the best only when the machine was working at its best. The phrase "working at its best" implies proper maintenance on the part of the personnel responsible for the machine, proper storage of card stock, careful operation of the machine during the actual catalog card duplication phase of the procedure, and certain atmospheric conditions.

FIGURE 4.1

1. The print lever setting determines the amount of toner used during any given printing sequence. The normal setting for all manner of copying is between the 2 and 3 on the scale. If the master is clear and sharp, there should be no reason why the print lever should have to be set beyond 3 on the scale. In the event that the copy is too light, the print lever may be advanced on the scale until the desired contrast is achieved. Even though the print lever may be advanced, it is recommended that careful controls be established with regard to the print lever setting to prevent haphazard overtoning of the machines. Aside from the position of the print lever, another reason for light copy may be that the toner in the toner well has become "caked" due to excessive humidity. If this is the case, *gently* move the dipstick two or three times around the edges of the toner well while the scan lamps are lit. If copy is still not darkened by the above maneuvers, move the print lever back and forth rapidly between the 0 and 6 while the scan lamps are lit. Then return the print lever to the normal setting between 2 and 3 on the scale.

2. The paper feed lever controls the pressure of the feed rollers which draw the card stock from the paper tray into the machine. When printing is being done on card stock, the setting which has proved most generally useful is D. This recommendation is advanced on the assumption that the card stock has been properly stored, adequately fanned, and correctly loaded into the machine prior to the copying run.

3. The paper registration buttons determine the location of the copied master's impression on the card stock. The "14" button should be completely depressed for all lengths of copy paper.

NOTE: The 720 will scan continuously without copying unless the "14" button is depressed completely. (The "M" and "11" buttons should not be used.)

4. The fuser controls, that is, the fuser and fuser range, must work in conjunction with each other. These two controls regulate the amount of heat needed to fuse or "bake" the toner into the card stock for a finished copy. These buttons permit the fusing temperature to be regulated for various types of paper. Remember that one fuser button (yellow) and one fuser range button (red) must always work as a pair. In order to achieve a well-fused image on card stock it is necessary to use the highest possible fusing temperature; that is, the fuser button must be set on "hi," and the fuser range button set on "3." This setting, of course, is definitely not the setting when 20 lb. copy paper is being used for general purpose copying—the setting in this instance would be fuser "lo" and fuser range "2."

Preparation of Card Stock

The recommended kind of card stock to be used with either the Xerox 914 or 720 is the multistrip 6-up, cut, perforated, and punched style. There should be no compromise as to the quality of the card stock—use the best 100% rag available. It is definitely not recommended that the style of card stock that is only punched and perforated be used because of numerous mechanical feeding problems which result in fires in the machine. In Figures 4.2 and 4.3, the manner in which the recommended style of card stock is to be broken and fanned is illustrated. Notice that in Figure 4.2 the slits in the multistrip 6-up card stock are examined to make sure that they have been completely and uniformly cut. If the cuts are not complete and uniform, the card stock should be twisted gently back and forth until cuts are opened. After examining the cuts, the card stock should be held first on one side of the long dimension and fanned and then held on the other side of the long dimension and fanned again as illustrated in Figure 4.3. This maneuver assures that the punches in the card stock are completely separated.

Loading the Paper Tray with Card Stock

Since the dimensions of the recommended card stock are 8⅜ by 11 in., it is necessary to adjust the guide arms which center the card stock left to right in the paper tray. Be sure that each of the guide arms is set the same distance from the center of the paper tray, for this location determines whether or not there will be a dark shadow on the right or left side of the card stock when it

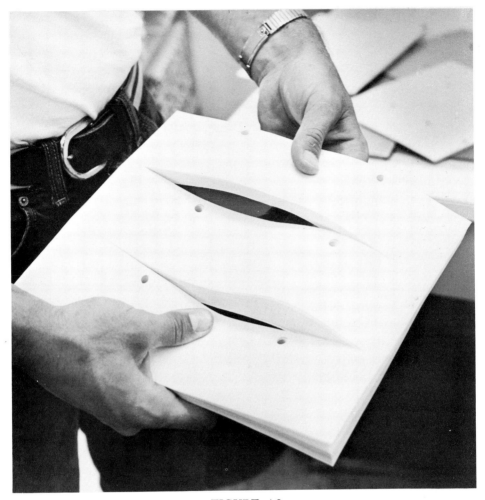

FIGURE 4.2

is fed through the machine. Be sure that the slide assembly, which adjusts to the length of the card stock, is firmly set in the 11 in. setting. By holding a quantity of card stock flat on one's hand, it is possible to see that there is a curl side. The card stock should be squared and loaded into the paper tray with the curl side down. Notice in Figure 4.4 that the punches have been loaded to the left-hand side of the paper tray. Do not fill the paper tray higher than the top red line on the paper guide. Be sure that the leading edge of the stack of card stock is even with the leading edge of the paper tray. The machine is now loaded with card stock, and the paper tray should be pushed gently back into the machine as far as it will go.

Placement of Masters on the Document Glass

If careful examination is made of Figure 4.5, it will be possible to see that a plastic template has been used to position the masters in an ordered and controlled manner on the document glass. (The dimensions and characteristics of the plastic template will be supplied below for the purpose of special ordering on a local level.) This plastic template is absolutely necessary, and any attempt to place and hold six masters on the document glass without one is the ultimate study in futility. Notice that the template has a long end and a short end. It is the short end that is placed against the top guide scale. The masters are inserted under the plastic holders in an range of three at the top and three at the bottom. Notice that the punches on all the masters are to the right-hand side of the document glass. This positioning of the punches is important because according to Figure 4.4 the card stock has been loaded into the paper tray with the punches favoring the left-hand side of the paper tray. Inasmuch as the image is reversed in the copying, it is necessary that the punches on the card stock and the punches on the masters point in opposite directions. When placing the masters in the template, take care to fit them very closely together, for any gap which exists between any side of any two cards will be copied as a dark shadow line. The

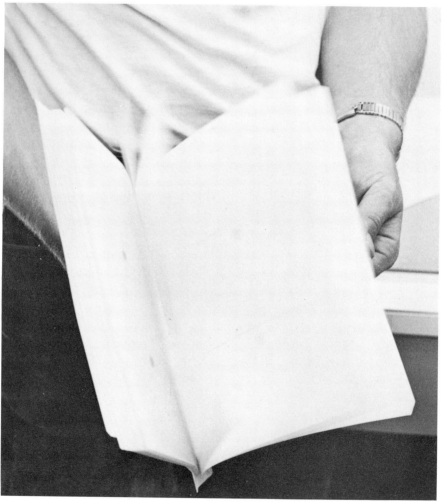

FIGURE 4.3

FIGURE 4.4

closer the masters are together, the smaller the shadow line. Ordinarily, the 0 on the top guide scale should be used to center the masters after they have been placed in the template on the document glass; however, some experimentation will be necessary to obtain a finished copy which will appear on the printed card stock in proper relationship to card edges and punches. (It should be remarked that there is a magnification ratio of 1 percent in the copying of the Xerox 914 and 720 and that *exact* relationships will not be possible.) If the register on the printed copy is too far to the left or right, then the template should be moved slightly to the right or to the left until the error has been corrected. The vertical scale on the right side of the document glass is used to determine where the image will appear on the long dimension of the finished copy. Sometimes it may be necessary to lap the lead edge of the template over the top guide scale to get a printed image falling on the card stock in proper relationship to edges and punches. Once it has been established where the template should be placed in relation to the two scales for acceptable copying, mark the location with a soft pencil and be sure that it stays in the same position for each copying run. After template positioning has been determined, set the print quantity selector to the number of copies needed for the masters being copied and print.

The location of the duplicated image on the punched, cut, and perforated card stock after it has been fed through the machine is illustrated in Figure 4.6. Notice that the shadow lines, caused by fitting the masters together on the template, are located on the bottom edge of each of the cuts in this style of card stock. Though some may not regard it as important to produce a catalog card which is thoroughly clean and legible, the suggestion seems not inappropriate that if it can be done with not too much effort then why not do it? In the three manual cuts necessary to separate the six cards, it is possible with a heavy-duty paper cutter to shear off the end perforations and/or shadows. As for the cut needed in the center, it is possible to double cut and remove both shadow and perforation. In those cases where class numbers have been typed on the masters prior to the copying run, it is important to check before making a cut through a large stack of duplicated 6-up cards to see that no part of the call number will be removed when the cut is made. Remember that the Xerox machine is not a printing press and that the register on any two sheets of 6-up card stock will not necessarily be exactly the same. Additional suggestions when using the multi-strip, cut, punched, and perforated style of card stock with the Xerox 914 or 720 follow:

1. When beginning a copying run for any group of six masters, it is best to run off only one copy at first to see that the image location is correct on the 6-up sheet of card stock. After it is determined that the image location is correct, dial the print quantity selector to the required number of additional cards and print.

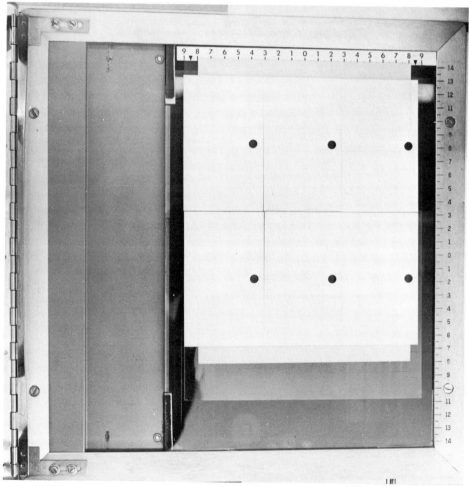

FIGURE 4.5

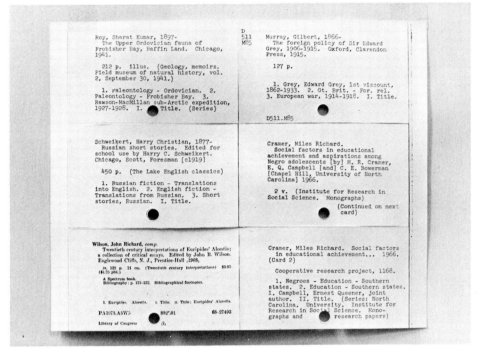

FIGURE 4.6

2. Keep the level of card stock in the paper tray as full as possible. Do not allow the level of card stock to become so low that the machine needs to indicate that more stock is necessary.

3. Be sure to watch the card stock as the machine pulls it from the paper tray. Sometimes, particularly if the card stock has not been fanned and the cuts broken prior to loading the paper tray, the machine will pull more than one sheet of card stock into the machine at one time. This will invariably result in these sheets catching fire or possibly jamming. Neither the fires nor the jammings harm the machine, but the time lost waiting for a service representative to come and clean up or unjam the machine can be an annoyance and disrupt an otherwise smooth copying run.

4.3.2 THE XEROX 2400 OR 3600 COPIER

In duplicating catalog cards with either the Xerox 2400 or 3600, the recommended style of card stock is punched only. Since these two machines are more complicated than either the Xerox 914 or the 720, the company sends an instructor to orient the library staff in their operation. Because of this company-supplied instruction, it will not be necessary to go through a step-by-step outline of the procedures necessary for catalog card duplication. The advantage of these two machines is, of course, their speed and the almost totally foolproof paper feed. When it is planned to use either the Xerox 2400 or 3600 for catalog card duplication, it will be necessary to have a variable weight paper tray installed on the machine. (See Table 2.1 for the cost of this adaptation.) For purposes of illus-

FIGURE 4.7

tration of 6-up card stock loading of either the 2400 or the 3600, Figure 4.7 shows that the card stock is loaded to the extreme left of the paper tray with the punches in the card stock facing out.[2]

Like the placement of masters in the plastic template described for catalog

[2] *The Xerox 3600 with variable weight paper tray is pictured in Figure 4.7. The variable weight paper tray is identical for both the 2400 and 3600.*

card duplication on the Xerox 914 or 720, the masters on the Xerox 2400 or 3600 should be positioned with the punches facing to the right. With the two faster machines the punches on the card stock and the punches on the masters are always to the right-hand side as you face the machine. (With the Xerox 914 and 720, the punches in the masters faced to the right and the punches in the paper stock in the paper tray faced to the left.) The positioning of the plastic template is accomplished by inserting its right-hand edge under the rubber frame which surrounds the document glass and by fixing its left-hand edge under the flange which frames the left side of the document glass. The location of the template front to back is determined by lining up the upper left-hand corner of the upper left-hand master with the 10.5 marking on the scale. For an illustration of this positioning see Figure 4.8.

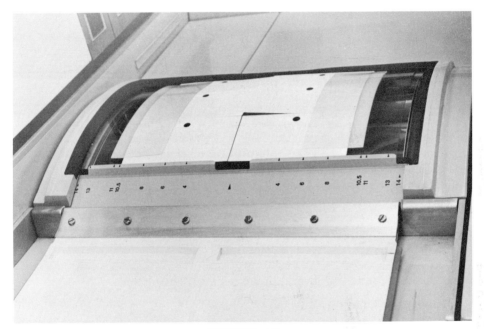

FIGURE 4.8

The template as pictured in Figure 4.9 was designed and manufactured locally. The design has proven versatile and has actually been used on the Xerox 720, 2400, and 3600 with equal success—there is no reason to assume that it will not work on the Xerox 914. The materials in the template are neither exotic nor expensive, and every effort should be made to have at least two templates on hand at all times because with use the plastic surface which is against the document glass can become scratched or marred. These scratches or mars will copy as lines or smudges on the card stock when it is fed through the machine.

The dimensions of the template and the materials used in its construction are listed in Table 4.1.

Figure 4.10 shows the relationship of one of the holding flaps to the top of the template. Notice that the top of the base sheet, the adhesive strip, and

FIGURE 4.9

the leading edge of the holding flap are all on the same line. The holding flap and the adhesive strip have been centered left to right on the base sheet.

Figure 4.11 shows the relationship of the other holding flap to the bottom of the template. The adhesive strip is positioned parallel with and exactly 9⅞ in. from the adhesive strip at the top of the template. The holding flap and the adhesive strip have been centered left to right.

While undoubtedly other types of templates may be designed and found useful, the one described and illustrated has provided trouble-free duplication of catalog cards.[3]

Organization of Masters for Duplication Prior to a Copying Run

While each library will undoubtedly develop those procedures which will mesh most readily with its own work flow, it might be helpful to offer the follow-

TABLE 4.1

	Base sheet	Holding flaps*	Adhesive strips
Dimensions	12 by 19 in.	2½ by 8 in. each	8 in. each
Materials	Clear acetate† (gauge .020)	Clear acetate† (gauge .010)	3M double-sided tape (½ in., white, cushioned)

* *The opening between the two holding flaps is 9⅞ in.*
† *The manufacturer of the acetate is Universal Plastics.*

[3] *It has been suggested that a sheet of 6-up card stock be used as a template. One can prepare this by using a piece of double-sided adhesive tape which is centered down the short dimension of the sheet of card stock. One would then stick the back side of the masters to the tape, turn it over, and copy. Turning it over, positioning it, and covering it with the document cover, however, can introduce a number of uncontrollable variables.*

FIGURE 4.10

FIGURE 4.11

ing suggestions on the method which has been used locally to organize masters for a copying run on Xerox machines. The procedure for organizing masters can be adapted regardless of whether the masters to be duplicated are for new books or reclassified books or whether they are typed masters, galley slips, or L.C. printed cards.

1. If the master to be copied is a typed master, the original can be used as the main entry with additional cards made for each subject entry and for each added entry plus one card for the shelflist record. (It is advisable to use a copy of the main entry for the shelflist record so that if it becomes neces- sary to update subject headings the subject heading which has been used will be on the shelflist card. After the subject heading has been altered, the shelflist card can then be used to generate a new main entry for the making of a new card set.) In the event that a given library is a member of a re- gional bibliographic center which maintains a union list of participating libraries' holdings, an extra card can be made for this purpose.

Formula: 1 card for each subject entry.
          1 card for each added entry.
          1 card for each title.
          1 card for each series (when appropriate).
          1 card for the bibliographic center (if needed).
          1 card for the shelflist record.

NOTE: If the typed masters are done on a pica or an elite typewriter, the call num- ber can be typed onto the master prior to duplication.

2. If the master to be copied is a galley slip supplied from the Library of Congress, the galley slip itself will not be usable as a main entry. The main entry will have to have a card made for it, along with a card for each sub- ject entry and for each added entry, plus one card for the shelflist record, plus one card for the regional bibliographic center.

Formula: 1 card for the main entry.
          1 card for each subject entry.
          1 card for each added entry.
          1 card for each title.
          1 card for each series (when appropriate).
          1 card for the bibliographic center (if needed).
          1 card for the shelflist record.

NOTE: Because galley slips are only work slips as far as the Library of Congress is concerned, they sometimes will not have enough margin for the call number if a pica typewriter is used for catalog cards. The reason for this is that there is 1 per- cent image magnification which results when a master is duplicated. If the card stock following duplication is cut with a heavy-duty paper cutter, some portion of the left margin of the call number occasionally will be sheared off. On the other hand, if the typewriter used to type catalog cards has elite type, it is possible to space in far enough on the galley slip to allow for the magnification ratio and not lose some part of the call number in cutting.

3. If the master to be copied is an L.C. printed card which has been erased and cleaned for a reclassification project, the original may or may not be usable as a new main entry. The decision to use the old printed L.C. card

will be determined by what card quality is acceptable for the new public catalog which will be built as the result of the reclassification project. (See Section 4.4 for the kinds of coding that will be necessary when copying L.C. printed cards for this purpose.)

Formula: 1 card for the main entry (when appropriate).
1 card for each subject entry.
1 card for each added entry.
1 card for each title.
1 card for each series (when appropriate).
1 card for the bibliographic center (if needed).
1 card for the shelflist record.

NOTE: Since L.C. printed cards have been a standard size for many years, it is recommended that the new call numbers be typed on the masters prior to duplication regardless of whether pica or elite typewriters are used for catalog cards.

These three formulas will vary only when there are special departmental card catalogs to be maintained or when the decision has been made to build a special subject/title catalog for the reference department. For arguments in favor of a special subject/title catalog for the reference department, see Section 3.1.1.

The method of organizing masters for duplication is to group, behind a series of numbered guide cards, all masters, regardless of kind, which require the same number of copies. This grouping, of course, will be determined by which of the three formulas is used. It should be mentioned that it is a good idea to duplicate the same kinds of masters together; that is, copy six typed masters at once or six galleys at once. Naturally as you get to the end of a group of masters for which you are, for instance, making seven copies, it will not always be possible to keep like master with like master, and greater care in positioning the masters on the template will be necessary.

4.4 CARD PULLING AND REPLACEMENT

4.4.1 WHEN MAIN ENTRY IS AN L.C. PRINTED CARD

Assume the shelflist following is the first card with a 1950 or later copyright date in a Dewey shelflist drawer which holds the 831's. (Notice that unfortunately the Dewey shelflist card is not an L.C. printed card. If an L.C. printed card had been used, the shelflist card could be used to generate a new card set without having to pull any main entries from the public catalog.)

Pull the corresponding main entry, which is a unit card, from the public catalog. (Drop a colored filing flag into this position which will facilitate filing the temporary slip after it is made.) After this main entry is pulled, proceed to the next Dewey shelflist card with a copyright or imprint date of 1950 or later. No more than 50 main entries per clerk should be pulled from the public catalog at any given time. It takes approximately 40 or 50 minutes to pull a group of 50 main entries, although this estimate, of course, depends upon the size of the catalog and the speed of the clerks assigned to this work.

DEWEY SHELFLIST CARD

```
831       Goethe, Johann Wolfgang von, 1749-1832.
G554go    Goethe, the lyrist  [1955]


9my63
EBS
1.54
```

The Dewey main entry is duplicated for use as a temporary main entry which is refiled in the public catalog. By using standard 8½ by 14 in. paper, one can duplicate five main entries at a time to make temporary cards for the public catalog. These temporary cards should be refiled in the public catalog as soon as the group of 50 has been cut. Duplicating, cutting, and refiling take approximately 1 hour.

The Dewey class number is penciled in the lower right-hand corner of the main entry before it is removed by one of three methods.

1. By erasing. (An electric eraser does a good job and is the recommended method, although a combined use of a single-edge razor blade and typewriter eraser also works well.)

2. By placing a gummed label over the Dewey number. (A shadow will be produced by the edges of the label when the card is duplicated.)

3. By covering the Dewey number with an opaque correction fluid such as Sno-pake. (Due to the quick-drying nature of this product, it is difficult to produce a smooth surface on which to type the L.C. class number.)

L.C. PRINTED DEWEY MAIN ENTRY DRAWN FROM PUBLIC CATALOG

```
831       Goethe, Johann Wolfgang von, 1749-1832.
G554go      Goethe, the lyrist; 100 poems in new translations facing
            the originals, with a biographical introduction by Edwin H.
            Zeydel. With an appendix on musical settings to the poems.
            Chapel Hill, University of North Carolina Press [1955]

              xvii, 182 p.  23 cm.  (North Carolina. University. Studies in the
            Germanic languages and literatures, no. 16)




            I. Zeydel, Edwin Hermann, 1893-    ed. and tr.   (Series)

          PD25.N6  no. 16           831.69              55—63007
          —————— Copy 2.           PT2026.A3Z4

          Library of Congress          [62k1]
```

DEWEY MAIN ENTRY ERASED

Goethe, Johann Wolfgang von, 1749–1832.
    Goethe, the lyrist; 100 poems in new translations facing
the originals, with a biographical introduction by Edwin H.
Zeydel. With an appendix on musical settings to the poems.
Chapel Hill, University of North Carolina Press ₍1955₎

      xvii, 182 p. 23 cm. (North Carolina. University. Studies in the
Germanic languages and literatures, no. 16)

     I. Zeydel, Edwin Hermann, 1893–   ed. and tr.   (Series)

PD25.N6 no. 16   831.69   55—63007
———— Copy 2.   PT2026.A3Z4
                                         831
Library of Congress   ₍62k1₎   *G55430*

It is recommended that experimentation with the three methods be tried because the method chosen will determine the quality of the cards which will
ultimately be filed in the public catalog.

The L.C. class number is typed onto the erased main entry. The card is now
ready to be used as a master for duplicating a complete card set. (Notice that
the unit card following supplies two L.C. class numbers. The PD class number is
a series classification for studies in Germanic philology and languages by various
authors; the PT class number is a national literature classification for English
translations of Goethe's poetry arranged by translator. For the relative merits of
the use of the series classification, see Section 3.2.1.)

After the set has been duplicated (see Section 4.3), cut, and any shadowed
card edges cleaned, it will be filed along with other completed card sets behind
the Dewey shelflist card in the Dewey shelflist file. When enough new card sets
have been made for the 831's to warrant pulling books from the Dewey collection, a clerk goes to the stacks with a book truck, a workbox, and the Dewey
shelflist drawer for the 831's. On the basis of the information on the Dewey
shelflist card for each title for which there is a new card set, the clerk will draw
the book from the shelf, put it on the truck, and place the Dewey shelflist card

MAIN ENTRY PREPARED FOR DUPLICATION

PT
2026   **Goethe, Johann Wolfgang von, 1749–1832.**
A3   Goethe, the lyrist; 100 poems in new translations facing
Z4   the originals, with a biographical introduction by Edwin H.
       Zeydel. With an appendix on musical settings to the poems.
       Chapel Hill, University of North Carolina Press ₍1955₎

         xvii, 182 p. 23 cm. (North Carolina. University. Studies in the
       Germanic languages and literatures, no. 16)

         I. Zeydel, Edwin Hermann, 1893–   ed. and tr.   (Series)

       PD25.N6 no. 16   831.69   55—63007
       ———— Copy 2.   PT2026.A3Z4
                                      831
       Library of Congress   ₍62k1₎   *G554.90*

---

and the new card set in the workbox. The sequence of books on the truck and cards in the workbox should be kept in Dewey order so that the book can be retrieved at any point in the recataloging process. If all copies or volumes listed on a shelflist for which there is a new card set are not on the shelf, the clerk should bypass the title and go on to the next shelflist where all copies and volumes are present.

4.4.2 WHEN MAIN ENTRY IS A TYPED CARD

Assume that the shelflist card following is the first card with a 1950 or later copyright date in the Dewey shelflist drawer which holds the 831's.

DEWEY SHELFLIST

```
831      Goethe, Johann Wolfgang von, 1749-1832.
G554go   Goethe, the lyrist  [1955]


9my63
EBS
1.54
```

Pull the corresponding main entry, which is a typed card, from the public catalog. After this main entry is pulled, proceed to the next Dewey shelflist card with a copyright date of 1950 or later. No more than 50 main entries per clerk should be pulled from the public catalog at any given time.

The typed Dewey main entry is duplicated to be used as a temporary main entry which is refiled in the public catalog as described previously. Since a typed main entry does not carry the L.C. call number, it will be necessary to search the

TYPED DEWEY MAIN ENTRY DRAWN FROM THE PUBLIC CATALOG

```
831      Goethe, Johann Wolfgang von, 1749-1832.
G554go   Goethe, the lyrist; 100 poems in new
         translations facing the originals, with
         a biographical introduction by Edwin H.
         Zeydel.  With an appendix on musical
         settings to the poems.  Chapel Hill,
         University of North Carolina Press
         [1955]

         xvii, 182 p. 23 cm. (North Carolina.
         University.  Studies in the Germanic
         languages and literatures, no.16)
             I. Zeydel,     Edwin Herman, 1893-.
         ed. and tr.     (Series)
```

ERASED TYPED DEWEY MAIN ENTRY WITH L.C. CALL NUMBER

```
Goethe, Johann Wolfgang von, 1749-1832.
   Goethe, the lyrist; 100 poems in new
translations facing the originals, with
a biographical introduction by Edwin H.
Zeydel.  With an appendix on musical
settings to the poems.  Chapel Hill,
University of North Carolina Press
[1955]

   xvii, 182 p. 23 cm. (North Carolina.
University.  Studies in the Germanic
languages and literatures, no.16)
   I. Zeydel,      Edwin Herman, 1893-
ed. and tr.      (Series)          831
PT2026.A324                        G554 90
```

National Union Catalog for the call number, which is typed onto the bottom of the card in the lower left-hand corner. In the event that an original call number must be assigned by the local cataloger, it is recommended that the book number be enclosed in brackets in case a conflict later occurs with a number assigned by the Library of Congress. If the quality of the typed card is good, it will be possible to use it as a master for duplicating as soon as the L.C. call number is found and typed onto the card. If the quality is poor, a new master must be typed. From this point on, the procedure with the typed main entry is the same as that described for L.C. printed cards.

4.4.3 FILING NEW CARD SETS AFTER BOOKS HAVE BEEN RECLASSIFIED

Since the decision was made to use an altered master for the generation of new catalog card sets, the problem of removing from the public catalog corresponding cards which still carried Dewey call numbers was resolved in the following manner. If only the Dewey main entry had been pulled and a temporary slip refiled in the public catalog, there still remained all other tracings associated with the pulled main entry. It was determined that leaving in the public catalog the other cards for the pulled main entry was, in fact, the best way to retain a subject approach to the materials which were in the process of reclassification. With a well-designed reprocessing procedure it was possible to retrieve any title which might be requested at any time. The method used was to alert the circulation department staff to the fact that if there was a temporary main entry in the public catalog the initial step would be to check with the technical services department to see whether the Dewey shelflist was still in the file. If the shelflist card was still in the Dewey shelflist, then the requested title would be somewhere in the library but not in some step in the reclassification process. If the Dewey shelflist card was not in the Dewey shelflist, the assumption would be that the item was in process of reclassification. In setting up a book truck for reclassification, the basic rule was that books and catalog cards be kept in a Dewey shelf order through these steps: by removing internal Dewey markings, verifying title page against catalog card information, removing external Dewey markings, remarking with L.C. call numbers, pasting new book pockets, and retyping the headings on the new card sets. If this rule was strictly followed, there would be no point in the process when a title could not be found, if needed. Even if the book was to be mended, the rule still held—keep the item filed by Dewey call number.

In all probability by the time the card sets for reclassified titles were in the final typing phase, the books themselves would already have been returned to the shelves under their new L.C. call numbers. Remember that in the coding of the Dewey main entry the Dewey call number had been penciled in the lower right-hand corner of the card prior to its being erased, cleaned, and prepared for use as a master in the reclassification process. The presence of that Dewey coding still allowed the arrangement of the new card sets by Dewey number and could be used as a means of finding the new L.C. call number when needed. (If L.C. printed cards have been used in a given library for a number of years, it is possible to alert the user to the fact that the L.C. call number printed at the bottom left or bottom center of the card, depending upon the vintage of the card, is probably where the book will be found in the new scheme.)

It was only after the card sets for the reclassified titles had been completely typed that the group was then arranged alphabetically for filing in the public catalog. If there had been no changes or additions effected in the form of the various added entries which pertained to any given title in the process of reclassification, the method of refiling the new cards and pulling the old was a simple one of replacement. The new main entry replaced the temporary slip, and all subsequent entries—subject headings and added entries—"bumped" the corresponding Dewey cards in the catalog. In the event that some subject heading or added entry had been altered or canceled in the recataloging phase, the appropriate Dewey card or cards would naturally have been removed from the public catalog at that time. No procedure was ever made in heaven; if a procedure works, use it.

4.5 PHYSICAL PROCESSING OF BOOKS

While the following remarks about the physical processing of books tend to be more descriptive than prescriptive, the conviction remains that no library procedure should be allowed just to develop. A procedure must have specifically designed rules which effect a smooth operation from the initial bibliographic search for a title to the ultimate cancellation of records after a book has been lost or discarded. The way in which a book is processed prior to its going onto the open stacks will determine how easily it is shelved by the circulation department, how quickly it is found on the shelf by the user, how effortlessly it is returned to the collection after circulation, and ultimately how smoothly it may be inventoried and possibly even discarded. If this sounds modestly authoritarian, it is. Beyond this, one might suggest that it simply assures uniformity in the kinds of signals we supply to ourselves and to library users—a uniformity which promises better control and consequently more effective use.

4.5.1. MARKING

If a poll were taken among library users, spine marking with its unintelligible characteristics would stand high on a graded scale of irritants. There is absolutely no reason why order cannot be imposed upon the nature of spine marking. In the first place, marking should be done with a typewriter and not by hand lettering; in the second place, it should be done on a typewriter with an eight pitch letter size, and, if possible, the letter style should be sans serif. With this size and style of type, a user with 20/20 vision can read a call number from six feet away —a fact which implies that it is a respectable size for people with less than 20/20 vision. This size character allows the use of a standard 1 by 1½ in. gummed label or a standard 1⅛ in. Se-lin tape. Because Se-lin tape is much more expensive than gummed labels, it has been our practice to use gummed labels on books which have dust jackets and can be covered with plastic book covers and to use the Se-lin tape on books without dust jackets. If the call number is broken down according to the method recommended in Section 3.1.4, the label or Se-lin tape of this width can accommodate a linear sequence of eight characters, which is the extreme limit required by any part of the L.C. Classification system. It should be remarked that in extremely large subject areas the Cutter numbers can exceed this length; however, that is a problem of the exception and not the rule and can be resolved when necessary. At the outset of our reclassification project, it was decided that no spine marking would ever be placed on the face of a book but rather always on the spine regardless of the width of the book or the length of the elements of the call number. This was accomplished by always using a plastic book jacket on all items which were too narrow to accommodate their call numbers. The label was always placed on the spine favoring the left-hand margin of the call number so that the class or subclass was always visible along with some elements of the subsequent numerical breakdown as well as the Cutter designation. This decision has proven a useful and worthwhile one, for, consequently, shelving is easier, locating a specific book on the shelf is easier, and shelf reading has become less tedious.

In selecting the 1 by 1½ in. gummed label, the 1½ in. dimension was established as a standard length for all spine marking, whether Se-lin tape or gummed labels were used. With this decision it was possible to determine exactly the location of the call number on any given label. The rule was established that the first line of the call number, that is, the class or subclass, would be typed on the first full space down from the top of the gummed label with all subsequent elements typed in descending order on the basis of an established left-hand margin. The left-hand margin was determined by centering left to right on the label the longest single element in the call number. After this pattern of typing the call number on a gummed label was set and after the length of the label was determined, the same pattern and length were to be used whenever Se-lin tape was used. This length of 1½ in. will accommodate, with few exceptions, all call numbers, volumes, and parts plus whatever special location designation might be necessary (e.g., Reference, Rare Book Room, Music Dept., Chem. Dept., Special, etc.).

F	M	QD
899	3	1
T2	B44	C57
T45	v.3	v.65
Rare	pt.1	pt.2
Book		
Room	Music	Chem.
(Cases)	Dept.	Dept.

The configuration of spine markings resulting from a mixing of gummed labels and Se-lin tape is illustrated in Figure 4.12. Notice that examples 1, 3, 4, 7, 14, 15, and 16 have been marked with Se-lin tape which has been cut to the same length as the gummed labels marking the remaining examples. Since Se-lin tape cannot be ironed beyond and around the extreme edges of a book spine, it is necessary to cut the edge of the tape to fit the spine as in examples 3, 14, and 15. Inasmuch as all efforts failed to make people—clerks and students in particular—understand or appreciate what ¼ in. was, it was decided that the best compromise with reality was to have the label or the cut Se-lin tape, both·of which were the same length, positioned at the extreme bottom of the spine thereby assuring a uniform spine marking pattern as demonstrated in Figure 4.12. By virtue of this early concern with how a shelf of books would look and how easily a book might be removed or returned to the shelf, there is now a collection of 125,000 cataloged volumes marked uniformly and legibly.

FIGURE 4.12

4.5.2 INFORMATION ON AND PLACEMENT OF BOOK CARD AND POCKET

The information required on the book card and pocket was cut to its barest essentials. The book card shows call number, author's surname and first given name, and an abbreviated title; in those cases where the entry is a corporate author the whole corporate entry plus an abbreviated title is shown. The book pocket information is restricted to only the call number.

As far as the location of the pocket in the book is concerned, it was felt that only one location would be acceptable for the obvious purpose of simplifying the slipping (carding) of books returned from circulation. The location chosen was the flyleaf inside the back of a book, since it is obviously easier for staff working in circulation to open the back cover of a book and know that the pocket will always be found there. The location of the pocket on the flyleaf is at the very bottom of the page and centered left to right. The point of selecting this location was that if in the future the library were to move to a computerized circulation system most books with the pockets glued in this place would accommodate whatever IBM card would be used for circulation charges. See Figure 4.13 for an example of book card and pocket information as well as for the

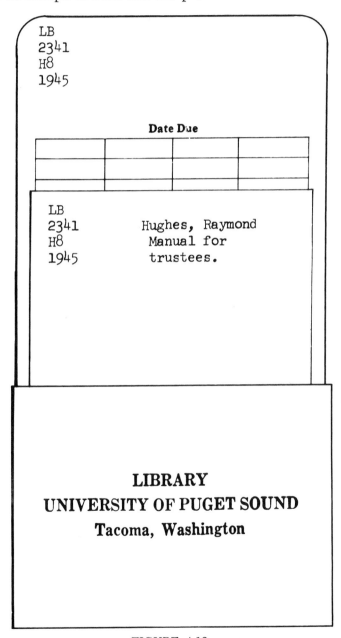

FIGURE 4.13

location of the pocket on the flyleaf inside the back cover. In those cases where there is information pertinent to the text printed on endpapers, the practice has been to tip-in a blank piece of 20 lb. paper cut to the appropriate page size for the purpose of maintaining uniformity in the location of the book pocket. In those cases where the information is reproduced elsewhere in the book or is strictly of a decorative nature, the book pocket is glued over the information or decoration (see Figure 4.13).

4.6 TERMINATION OF THE PROJECT

With the last book truck of Dewey titles drawn from the stacks and processed, with the last tray of reprocessed cards typed and filed, the final step of the reclassification project has been reached. Without question there will remain a number of Dewey shelflist cards for which no books are found. These, in effect, represent an inventory count of missing and lost books which have been unreported for whatever reasons. The Dewey shelflist cards can now be used in the last step of reclassification as a means for clearing the public catalog of all remaining Dewey cards, except for a few which will have been inadvertently overlooked and can be discovered and discarded as the catalog is used.

The procedure is the simple one of organizing the Dewey shelflist alphabetically by author (this rearrangement of the Dewey shelflist means nothing because there is no longer a shelf order in Dewey on which to maintain a file) and having the corresponding cards pulled from the catalog. If at all possible, it is well to save the main entry and selflist for each title for assorted reasons. For instance, the possibility does exist that some of the books not now available will be returned and that the old main entry can be used as a master for a new card set. In addition, these cards can form the basis for a reordering record with the possibility of editing the descriptive cataloging to match a replacement copy of any given title in this group. The shelflist record can also supply copy information on a specific title which might be important in the reordering process. If all copies of a title have disappeared over the years, it might indicate that some kind of special handling is required.

$\boxed{5}$

Reclassification Considered: A Bibliography

This bibliography is selective. It is not intended to be inclusive of any and all references to reclassification or even to the Library of Congress Classification. It is our purpose to include only those citations that offer some useful suggestions, practices, or critical comments on the implementation and use of LC and, of course, reclassification to LC. Representative historical and descriptive sources have been included as well. On the other hand, all of the literature cited is not necessarily complimentary or even favorable to LC and/or reclassification. Some especially pertinent references to just the Dewey Decimal Classification have been included because of a particular emphasis, for example, an article or two by the prestigious and idiosyncratic classification war-horse, Thelma Eaton.

The intent of this bibliography is to include primarily the materials that will provide helpful as well as critical comment by those who were or still are involved in the matter of reclassification and classification with LC. It has been a frustrating experience to read much of the literature from which this list has been prepared. Not only are the same problems repeatedly dealt with, but, in addition, many of those libraries using LC are still muddling through by employing practices and procedures that often seem calculated to counteract many of the intrinsic advantages of using the LC scheme.

All citations have been personally examined unless otherwise indicated. Moreover, the annotations are often critical and evaluative, not just descriptive. This list is offered not only as evidence of our tedious and frustrating journey into the past, but also as a handy reference guide for the zealous librarian or library school student who must see for himself.

The library literature has been covered to August 1969. Later references are included whenever we have had the opportunity to examine them.

1. Anderson, LeMoyne W. "The Classification Game as Played at Colorado State University." Unpublished. Fort Collins: Colorado State University. 1964?

A somewhat facetious article revealing the reasons for the change from DC to LC, as well as a superficial view of the preparations for reclassification. Strong emphasis on the need for and development of a procedure manual. Some of the reasons for the change to LC are presented with positive and emphatic conviction.

2. Angell, Richard S. "Development of Class K at the Library of Congress." *Law Library Journal* 57 (1964):353–360.

The article briefly covers the history and character of the LC Classification in general, as well as the progress of Class K. Angell emphasizes the pragmatic advantages of the LC system, including the up-to-date additions and changes. He acknowledges the serious absence of a complete law schedule and a general index. Chiefly of interest for historical information.

3. ———. "On the Future of the LC Classification." In *Classification Research: Proceedings of the 2d International Study Conference, 14–18 September 1964,* edited by Pauline Atherton, pp. 101–112. Copenhagen: Munksgaard, 1965.

"The Library of Congress Classification is characterized by its scope, notation, principle of class construction and provisions for revision. The areas most in need of completion and correction . . . are reviewed. Problems of accommodating classification systems to major changes in the content and relationship of fields of knowledge are illustrated and generalized solutions are suggested." Angell comments on the implication of two statements in the 1964 report, *Automation and the Library of Congress,* that indicate a strongly reduced need for subject-related classification. He feels strongly that the LC scheme will be continually developed and expanded as circumstances demand. He briefly reviews the areas of the schedules that should be given revision and reconstruction in the future, that is, subject bibliography, fiction in English and juvenile literature, language and literature separations, social sciences, law, etc. A valuable viewpoint from the subject Cataloging Division Chief of the Library of Congress.

4. Anstaett, Herbert B. "Franklin and Marshall's Reclassification Project: The Initial Phase." *P.L.A. Bulletin* 21 (1966): 177–181.

A discussion of the conception and development of the reclassification project. LC cards are duplicated by means of the Xerox 914. Cost of card duplication is about $.03 per card. Sketchy information is provided on their reclassification procedures—of some value for any library considering a change to LC. Mainly, this is a brief résumé of how the project was started, with some indications of the preparations required.

5. Baer, Karl A. "Reclassifying and Recataloging the Chemical Club Library." *Special Libraries* 36 (1945):150–153.

Describes the reclassification of a 60,000-volume library. In 1918 the library was reclassed to LC, but the classification was tied to a system of fixed locations which later proved unsatisfactory. The present reclassification project is a revision of the old LC collection. Cutter book numbers were originally omitted, with their place taken by the date of publication. Some special modifications were used, such as devising their own call numbers when dissatisfied with the LC assigned number. LC subject headings were modified whenever it was found necessary. The local modifications and practices of this reclassification would hardly recommend this project. Mainly of interest as to how *not* to proceed.

6. Batts, Nathalie C. "LC in NY." *Library Journal* 91 (1966):3649–3650.

This is chiefly a news article on the activities of the Institute on the Use of the Library of Congress Classification. However, Batts reports that Tauber feels that the decimal point before the author Cutter in the LC call number serves no useful purpose. We agree wholeheartedly with this view. (See Reference 76.)

7. Batty, C. D. "Which Classification?" *Assistant Librarian* 57 (1964):178–180.

An analysis of six of the general classifications of medium book capacity or greater: Bliss, Brown, LC, DC, Colon, and UDC. The analyses determined how many volumes the various schemes could handle, their performance, and their quality of construction. The DC 16th edition was considered incapable of satisfactorily handling much over 250,000 volumes, whereas LC, UDC, and Colon were considered to be extremely expandable. Batty concludes that LC suffers serious defects because of the lack of an index, and is somewhat suspect because of its notation. The only drawback to the DC 16 was its lack of accurate detail. He concludes that the UDC and the DC 16 are the "best buys!" The article is a somewhat facetious analysis that completely overlooks really crucial elements in the evaluation of a classification system, such as up-to-dateness, economy, and ease of application, adaptability, etc. Mainly a curiosity with only minimal usefulness.

8. Bentz, Dale M. and Thera P. Cavender. "Reclassification and Cataloging." *Library Trends* 2 (1953):249–263.

"In the past thirty years many institutions have made conversions, and for the most part this has meant a shift from the Dewey Decimal or Cutter to the Library of Congress Classification." This article analyzes the reasons for reclassification in libraries. It recommends that a critical examination of circulation procedures and the routines of technical services be made prior to reclassifying. Careful organization and strict economy are imperative. This is a general review of current practices. The conclusion: with proper planning, reclassification can be done smoothly and effectively.

9. Bliss, Henry E. *The Organization of Knowledge in Libraries.* 2d ed. rev. New York: Wilson, 1939. (Chaper XII, pp. 242–278.)

Bliss briefly describes, reviews, and analyzes the LC Classification along both theoretical and practical lines. As an example of Bliss's animus, he remarks in reference to the claim of centralized processing for LC that

"Unless the libraries take the notations from the cards without adapting them to their individual classification, the schedule would have to be handled and studied and altered; and the time and trouble would greatly reduce the savings of centralized service [!]." In summary, Bliss concludes that the LC classification "is very commendable in much of its detail . . . and good use can be made of this detail; but the system is too cumbersome and complicated; has too many faults, and it is on the whole inadaptable. The advantages and economies . . . are overborne by the disadvantages . . . and wastes of the system . . . it is unscientific and inadaptive . . . uneconomical; as a standard it is disqualified." Bliss also offers his critical analyses of both the LC and DC systems. Mainly of historical interest.

10. Boisen, Harold L. "A Venture in Reclassification." *College & Research Libraries* 6 (1944):67–72.

A report of a reclassification project that changed to LC but compressed or severely abridged the Library of Congress Classification for use in a small academic library. Definitely *not* a recommended policy.

11. Bond, Ethel. "Economies in Cataloging As Reported at the Cataloging Section of the American Library Association." *Illinois Libraries* 16 (1934):99–101.

A brief report on the ALA program. The consensus was that "The most tactful inquiries have failed to produce any epoch-making suggestions." And "while economies are necessary, many of the economies which we are using at present are not true economies." An excellent example of the usual malarkey so characteristic of most pronouncements on cataloging economies.

12. Bull, Helen S. "A Year's Experience with the Library of Congress Classification." *Wisconsin Library Bulletin* 63 (1967):47–48.

This is a very short report on a conversion project to LC by the Technical Services Unit for Library Services of the Department of Public Instruction of Wisconsin. Bull seems very pleased with the results. The article is really too brief to be of very much practical assistance. A detailed report of the procedures used in conversion is available on loan from the library. Unfortunately, we have been unable to borrow a copy. Bull's report seems useful only for matter-of-fact enthusiasm.

13. Bushnell, George H. "Notes by a British Librarian on the Library of Congress Classification Scheme." *Special Libraries* 24 (1933):41–43.

Enthusiastically in favor of the LC scheme, Bushnell embarked on a reclassification project to LC at Scotland's oldest university library, St. Andrews. Useful only for enthusiasm.

14. Casellas, Elizabeth R. "Relative Effectiveness of the Harvard Business, Library of Congress, and the Dewey Decimal Classifications for a Marketing Collection." *Library Resources & Technical Services* 9 (1965):417–437.

A detailed analysis of all three systems, covering such areas as basic characteristics, appropriateness for marketing, business classification, form divisions, geographic subdivisions, etc. The author concludes DC is the least desirable because of its lack of detail and cumbersome notation. The Harvard class system is the second choice because of its limited subject scope and inadequate treatment of industries. LC is the first choice as it "affords a detailed analysis of industries that is absolutely unavailable in the DC or the Harvard." Also, LC cards give the LC classification number which is generally unchanged in current LC additions and changes. By contrast the DC number on printed cards is sometimes completely out-of-date because of revisions in later editions. LC numbers are usually stable. "The Library of Congress Classification remain the best choice. . . ."

15. Clapp, Verner W. "DC Numbers on LC Cards." *Library Resources & Technical Services* 9 (1965):393–403.

An analysis of the history of the movement to include DC numbers on the LC printed cards. Clapp indicates that 99 percent of LC cards in regular series had DC numbers assigned in 1964. Clapp feels definitely that there has been a trend to de-emphasize the inclusion of DC numbers on printed cards. He indicates probable reasons and recommends a return to the Putnam recommendations of 1933 which called for giving DC "equal time," that is, DC numbers listed on *all* LC cards. Clapp considers the Library of Congress has a conflict of interest in classification which has de-emphasized the application of DC. (See Mumford's reply, Reference 98.)

16. Classification Committee, RTSD Cataloging & Classification Section, 15 May 1964. "Statement on Types of Classification Available to New Academic Libraries" (Report). *Library Resources & Technical Services* 9 (1965):104–112.

17. ———. Correction by B. A. Custer (letter). *Library Resources & Technical Services* 9 (1965):212.

The committee report emphasizes that the "LC system becomes the chosen one where centralized cataloging is done." It also emphasizes that nearly 85 percent of LC cards give the LC class number as well as the LC style Cutter number, whereas it seems only about 35 percent give the suggested DC number (without any Cutter number). "It is obvious that the LC system is less expensive even though some LC numbers are lacking and the problems of law, fiction, and series remain." The report, however, considers the DC notation easier to handle for a mechanized/computer system. Custer alleges that the above report is misleading. He claims DC numbers appear on 80 percent of the LC cards that are sold, and that discussions are being held as to how to increase the DC class numbers on L.C. cards. Custer may be correct, but his comments do not substantially change the fact that using LC is practicing centralized cataloging (providing the class numbers are accepted), whereas the DC, by no stretch of the imagination, comes even close to the efficiencies of the LC system in this regard.

18. Clemons, Harry. "D.C. versus L.C." *Libraries* 35 (1930):1–4.

A somewhat dated discussion of the pros and cons of both classifications. The LC scheme seems to be slightly favored.

19. Collins, Walter S. "A Change of Horses: Some Aspects of Reclassification." *Library Journal* 86 (1961):757–759.

A report on the reclassification (DC to LC) of 8000 volumes in the library of the Southern Research Institute. A questionnaire survey of 40 libraries was conducted before the decision to reclassify. Some cost figures are supplied. This is a report of a very small project, with no real consideration or discussion of the primary issues involved in evaluating the LC scheme as compared to the DC. The general reasons for reclassifying were "lack of expansive qualities for technical material and the length of the class numbers." No consideration was given to centralized cataloging, use of LC cards, subject headings, costs, etc.

20. Colmer, Mary W. "LC: Problems Inherited." *Louisiana Library Association Bulletin* 31 (1968):15–18.

Although Colmer is involved in a project of reclassification to LC, she raises several critical points concerning the practices of LC. Her first comment deals with the complete acceptability of LC call numbers (for our answer to this criticism see text) and echoes Richmond's "Ha, Ha" statement in *Library Journal.* Another criticism deals with LC's confused handling of monographic series and on this point there is no quarrel (see Section 3.2.1). Useful comments are included on the LC shelflisting procedures at the Library of Congress. She obviously has been there! Colmer tends to think of reclassification in a strict sense, discouraging the use of the project as an occasion for taking inventory, serial revision, correcting descriptive cataloging, etc. This, of course, may be a tenable position, but it is quite self-limiting and even arbitrary. Nevertheless, the point is important. The scope of the reclassification project must be carefully thought out in terms of the total benefits and costs.

21. Comins, Dorothy. "The Library Case for Conversion." In *Problems in Library Classification—Dewey 17 and Conversion,* edited by Theodore Samore, pp. 83–92. Milwaukee: University of Wisconsin, School of Library and Information Science; published in cooperation with R. R. Bowker, 1968.

Comins lists a few arguments for and against conversion to LC. There are mostly general comments on advantages of using LC when involved in the PL 480 and Shared Cataloging Programs, etc. Comins is on solid ground concerning a policy of general acceptance of LC cataloging information. She effectively meets Talmadge's argument on the high cost of reclassification by indicating that little-used materials need not be reprocessed, but can be retired to a storage area under the old classification number without any problems resulting.

22. Conference on Reclassification, University of Maryland. *Reclassification: Rationale and Problems; Proceedings.* Edited by Jean Perreault. College Park, Md.: University of Maryland, School of Library & Information Services, 1968.

> The papers of Elton Shell, Harry Dewey, Desmond Taylor, and James Gaines make this the best collection on reclassification yet to be published. For a fuller description and evaluation of each paper, refer to the author entries in this bibliography. The other papers may be of academic interest but contribute little, if anything, to the success of the collection. Batty's paper is especially irrelevant. Perreault, of course, is riding his UDC hobby-horse for all it is worth.

23. Connors, William E. "Reclassification at the University of Maryland." *Library Resources & Technical Services* 11 (1967):233–242.

> The Maryland reclassification project was started in July of 1963 with a collection of nearly 350,000 volumes. Connors offers a brief résumé of reasons for changing from DC to LC. A special reclassification unit was created to handle the project. Some general problems and procedures are discussed. A detailed reclassification procedure, which may be very useful as a guide, is outlined. The Library of Congress is accepted as the ultimate authority for entry and classification with practically no exception. Cost figures are supplied for card duplication as well as for various other reclassification procedures. What seems so utterly fantastic, however, is that new copies of books were added to the DC collection despite the reclassification in progress. This is hardly a recommended policy—in fact, it is wasteful, ill-conceived, and should be severely condemned. One wonders at these confessional revelations and begins to consider seriously the charges of Gore in his notorious article "Mismanagement of College Libraries."

24. Cox, Carl R. "Costs of Reclassification." In *Problems in Library Classification —Dewey 17 and Conversion,* edited by Theodore Samore, pp. 101–111. Milwaukee: University of Wisconsin, School of Library and Information Science; published in cooperation with R. R. Bowker, 1968.

> This is a very basic and general discussion of reclassification costs. No specifics are presented since "even more important to remember, is the fact that costs are valid only in context—they do not translate from one system to another without mutation." Cox does present a useful step process for reaching a "workable cost of conversion" for a specific library operation. A highly useful article. Essential reading.

25. ————. "Reclassification Planning at the University of Maryland." Mimeographed. University of Maryland, 22 April 1963.

> A statement of preparations to reclassify over 300,000 volumes from DC to LC. The LC classification will be accepted without alteration. A valuable outline of preparations, procedures, and problems of reclassification planning. Some of this material is included in the article by Connors (see Reference 23).

26. Datta, D. G. "The Classification of Maps and Geographical Publications." *IASLIC Bulletin* 8 (1963):78–86.

Datta comments on the merits and demerits of the Dewey, LC, Williams, American Geographical Society, and the Boogs and Lewis schemes for the classification of maps. He concludes that the Boogs and Lewis and the LC schemes offer the best solution for map classification. However, Datta cautions that it is only logical to use the same scheme for maps that is already in use for the book collection in order to (as he so nicely puts it) avoid the use of two classifications.

27. Dawson, John M. "The Library of Congress: Its Role in Cooperative and Centralized Cataloging." *Library Trends* 16 (1967):85–96.

A review of the work of the Library of Congress in cooperative and centralized cataloging. A detailed analysis of the L.C. printed card situation with a basis for estimating costs. This is primarily an historical review of L.C. activities emphasizing the recent acceleration of centralized cataloging activities.

28. Dewey, Harry. "The Relationships between the Headings in the Subject Catalog and the Classification Numbers of the Books." In *Reclassification: Rationale and Problems; Proceedings,* edited by Jean M. Perreault, pp. 57–75. College Park, Md.: University of Maryland, School of Library & Information Services, 1968.

Dewey's thesis is that LC subject headings are not an acceptable substitute for subject classification. (See the article by Sidney Jackson, Reference 77.) However, subject catalogs do effectively supplement a shelf classification. Dewey attempts to contrast and compare the LC subject headings with the classified arrangement provided by subject classification. He presents an argument against assuming that all LC subject headings are automatically correct and beyond improvement. The principle of specific entry at the Library of Congress is most severely criticized. Dewey offers a special plea for the necessity of cross-references in any dictionary catalog. The paper concludes with a critical blast at the "stampede" from DC to LC by citing a number of what Dewey considers to be devastating weaknesses of LC, and especially of "economy," as the sole rationale for all classification and cataloging application. A firm statement against any thoughtless and uncritical acceptance of LC. A useful point of view.

29. Dougherty, Richard M. "The Realities of Reclassification." *College & Research Libraries* 28 (1967):258–262.

The author reviews the pros and cons of reclassification and examines three common assumptions concerning reclassification. The merits of partial reclassification are presented as an alternative to total reclassification. Serials reclassification is a complex problem. The economies of classifying with LC are "erroneously claimed for reclassification to retrospective collections." Caution is counseled, for no matter how it is viewed, reclassification is expensive. This article is an important prerequisite for any consideration of reclassification.

30. Downey, Howard R. "Dewey or LC?" *Library Journal* 89 (1964):2292–2293.

A short article limited to a selected group of institutions with an enrollment of between 5000 and 6000 students. A brief survey of opinion. Downey concludes with: "Don't believe that by changing to another system all your problems will be solved." Hardly a profound conclusion.

31. Downs, Robert B. "The Administrator Looks at Classification." In *Role of Classification in the Modern American Library*, University of Illinois, Graduate School of Library Science, pp. 1–7. Champaign, Ill.: Illini Union Bookstore, 1960.

This is one of the notable articles against reclassification, be it to LC or DC. While Downs makes a thoughtful presentation, the years since 1959 have brought enough changes to alter radically the premises that he accepts in order to support his arguments.

32. Doyle, Irene M. "Library of Congress Classification for the Academic Library." In *Role of Classification in the Modern American Library*, University of Illinois, Graduate School of Library Science, pp. 76–92. Champaign, Ill.: Illini Union Bookstore, 1960.

Doyle recounts the use of the Cutter classification at the University of Wisconsin, the crisis with Cutter in 1953, and the introduction of the LC classification in 1954. She cites the familiar arguments for and against the use of LC and discusses opinions on the effectiveness of LC from the point of view of catalogers, reference librarians, faculty, and herself. She reviews the general climate of opinion concerning the use of LC by large and small libraries. Doyle strongly supports the use of the LC classification.

33. Eaton, Thelma. "Classification in College and University Libraries." *College & Research Libraries* 16 (1955):168–176.

Eaton reports the results of a library survey based upon Kephart's library survey of 1893. Her survey indicates that the use of varied classifications is almost past. Now the LC or DC systems are predominately in use. DC is still used in 84.6 percent of all libraries. However, Eaton indicates that there is a growing dissatisfaction with DC. She gives no consideration to classification costs, but does point out some of the inadequacies of DC. The survey and Eaton are mainly of historical interest.

34. ———. *Classification in Theory and Practice, a Collection of Papers*. Champaign, Ill.: Illini Union Bookstore, 1957.

This collection includes her articles "Dewey Re-examined," "Classification in College and University Libraries," and "Epitaph to a Dead Classification," which are discussed elsewhere in this bibliography. Only one of the remaining four papers has any particular value for the purpose of this study. "The

Classification of Books in Public Libraries" illustrates exceedingly well the disastrous consequences of the use of the DC editions, especially those after the 14th edition. Once again, the use of DC has resulted in the ever-present special modifications of its schedules to suit local practices or the individual temperament and judgment of the cataloger. This particular article points out only too well the handicaps of DC use. Eaton's data are based on a survey she conducted in early 1955 of 863 public libraries.

35. ———. "Dewey Re-examined." *Library Journal* 77 (1952):745–751.

A very critical review of the 15th edition of DC. Eaton strongly favors the DC 14 over the DC 15. She characterizes the DC 15 as "this skimpy classification," totally unsuitable for teaching purposes in graduate library schools, and concludes that it "obviously does not satisfy many libraries." She makes a number of specific critical points.

36. ———. "Epitaph to a Dead Classification." *Library Association Record* 57 (1955):428–430.

Eaton maintains that with the DC 15 the familiar skeleton of the Dewey scheme, as displayed in the 3rd summary table, was scrapped along with the principle of logical classification. The DC arrangement "is best described as a tabulation." Since it appears that the DC 16 will be much farther from the DC 14 and quite different from the DC 15, it only remains for classifiers to accept the fact that the decimal classification of Melvil Dewey ended with the 14th edition, and to plan their work with that fact always in mind. In general, the college libraries have repudiated the new classification on two counts: "(1) it is too broad for most collections, and (2) changes in the scheme involve expensive reclassification." Eaton also criticizes public librarians' acceptance of the 15th edition because they tend to view the notation as useful for shelving. There is a great concern by Eaton for patrons who expect to find all books on a subject in one place! "After 14 editions, the classification as prepared by Dewey has reached the end of its life . . . *We must accept the fact that with the 14th edition Melvil Dewey's classification died.*" (Italics ours!) Of course, we heartily agree.

37. "Editorial Comment: Classification." *Library Resources & Technical Services* 9 (1965):413.

This article makes further comments on the emotional reception of the RTSD Classification Committee's Report (see Reference 16). "We would never recommend wholesale or impetuous revision or 'adaptation' of existing classification schemes. Too many libraries have faced or are facing expensive reclassification because of past improvisation. Once tampering of numbers is begun . . . the innovator finds himself committed to moving farther and farther out of cooperative and centralized movements as well as contributing to confusion of library users . . . 'custom' cataloging and classification are luxuries of the past . . . it is debatable if the scheme promising ideal break-down is possible in today's world of interlocking subject disciplines

. . . it would seem more prudent to organize . . . around a chosen classification than to distort the classification to meet pre-determined ideas of department content."

38. Ellinger, Werner B. "Classification of Law at the Library of Congress, 1949–1968." *Law Library Journal* 61 (1968):224–236.

This paper contains a short history of the development of the K schedule. Ellinger also carefully describes the characteristics of the present KF schedule, as well as the implications of its formation and divisions to the future development of the K schedules which still remain to be finished. This article confirms the accuracy of the KF numbers and attempts to develop a sense of confidence in the present schedule construction and its subsequent developments.

39. Ellsworth, Ralph E. "Another Chance for Centralized Cataloging." *Library Journal* 89 (1964):3104–3107.

Ellsworth believes that the library profession is now approaching the time for action on the question of centralized cataloging. In spite of all that has been done (especially by the Library of Congress), we still have precious little centralized cataloging practice. A general survey of current practices and opportunities by one of the profession's long-term exponents of centralized cataloging. Essential reading.

40. Evans, G. Edward. "Dewey: Necessity or Luxury? A Study of the Practical Economies Involved in Continuing with Dewey vs. Converting to LC." *Library Journal* 91 (1966):4038–4046.

Evans offers some general comments on the classification changes in the various editions of Dewey and provides a critical examination of DC 17. He emphasizes the extra expense and time needed to conform to the numerous relocations, etc. Evans also reflects on the cost of transition from edition to edition of the DC as compared with the cost of reclassification to LC. He comments on the cost studies by Gore, Taylor, and the University of Oregon Library, as well as other statistics. Evans concludes that it "would appear to be . . . less expensive and less troublesome for major libraries to convert to LC than to continue with Dewey." This is a brief survey of twenty academic libraries on the LC vs. DC issue. A useful article.

41. Fellows, Dorcas. "Library of Congress Classification vs. Decimal Classification." *Library Journal* 50 (1925):291–295.

Fellows provides a very strong defense of DC. However, the changes during the forty-five years since 1925 have generally made irrelevant many of his objections to and criticisms of LC. For example, he feels a very serious objection to the LC scheme of notation which requires that a library use the full notation. With DC, it is possible to use whatever length number best fits the collection size. Also, Fellows never discusses the problems of volume cost, centralized cataloging and processing, etc.

42. "Forward or Backward?" (Symposium) *Library Journal* 91 (1966):4047–4051.

This is a collection of six statements by classifiers and teachers of classification dealing with the DC 17 and reclassification to LC. One is in favor of LC. Four raise numerous objections about DC 17, and one lauds Dewey while castigating projects of reclassification to LC.

43. Foskett, Douglas J. *Classification and Indexing in the Social Sciences.* London: Butterworths, 1963. (pp. 66–88.)

Foskett explains how LC was originally based on the now defunct Expansive Classification made in the late 19th century by C. A. Cutter. He presents a brief history of its development. The following comments are a general summary of his position. "For all its detail the Library of Congress scheme cannot claim to offer an adequate system for information retrieval. It can show in places an approach to division into categories that appear in the modern literature but this division does not give the impression of being systematic and is by no means consistent. When one finds categories used, but in a confused way, one cannot but believe that the use is unconscious. LC fails to give the individual librarian a method for coping with new subjects or new complexes; all it does is to lay down a list of subjects that, however extensive, cannot hope to enumerate all those that will ever be written about, and the extreme lack of flexibility that comes from absence of synthesis makes it unsuitable for a documentation center in which specific classification is required." Of historical interest only.

44. Fraser, Lorna D. "Cataloging and Reclassification in the University of Toronto Library, 1959/60." *Library Resources & Technical Services* 5 (1961):270–280.

Fraser gives an account of the decision and subsequent process of reclassification from a local scheme to the LC scheme. In this ten-year plan for reclassification, only about 300,000 of the most-used volumes of over a million-volume collection were to be reclassified. The plan would entertain a permanent two-collection library. This is an interesting account of a hurry-up decision characterized by confusion and pressure. Some procedures mentioned seem useless. Dual divided catalogs were used to better accommodate the two collections. From all indications, a rather cumbersome procedural situation.

45. Gaines, James E. "The Financial Aspects of Reclassification." In *Reclassification: Rationale and Problems; Proceedings,* edited by Jean Perreault, pp. 116–133. College Park, Md.: University of Maryland, School of Library & Information Services, 1968.

Gaines honestly and candidly admits that there is no magic formula for precisely determining what reclassification costs will be, but he does report on his findings in a survey of the reclassification projects of nine college libraries and, more importantly, on the experience gained in directing the

Antioch College Library reclassification project. Gaines is an advocate of LC, but he advises caution and careful evaluation of a library's existing circumstances before attempting a hasty and ill-advised reclassification project (something which he feels has occurred far too often). A careful analysis of reclassification fund distribution, expenses, and equipment is presented with appropriate cautions on the magnitude of the project. Reclassification procedural problems are presented with stress on what degree of quality should be considered during a project, along with some useful cost data. This is a carefully reasoned presentation. Gaines is one of the few who emphasize the need for maintaining standards of quality during a reclassification project as well as the need for economy and speed.

46. ———. "Reclassification in the Libraries of the Great Lakes Colleges Association." *College & Research Libraries* 29 (1968):292–296.

Gaines reports on a survey of 12 liberal arts colleges. Ten are on LC and two are continuing with DC. Gaines briefly lists the reasons for the change plus some separate institutional programs for funding the reclassification. Most libraries, however, did not make any large demands for reclassification funds. Thus, in most instances, the costs of the change are borne mostly by the regular operating budget. Unit cost figures are given wherever available. Gaines reports a wide variety of practices. Specific difficulties experienced in LC use are (1) lack of a guide; (2) use of schedules and special tables; (3) LC's Cuttering; (4) PZ3 and PZ4; (5) older and newer material separation by schedule revision; (6) original classification when a title is a part of a series classification; (7) lack of the K schedule. Advice is offered for libraries considering the change to LC. Gaines, who directed a model reclassification program at Antioch College, strongly emphasizes the need to standardize the best and most economical procedures. A valuable survey.

47. Gattinger, F. Eugene. "Reclassification—Are You Converted Yet?" *APLA Bulletin* 29 (1965):16–19.

This survey reveals that the subject of reclassification is far from dead, especially in the junior colleges and smaller universities of Canada. The thesis of the author is that all academic libraries not now using LC should begin a conversion as soon as possible. He discusses six major points in favor of the LC system and the concept of centralized cataloging. Another useful article.

48. ———. "Reclassification in Canadian Academic Libraries." *APLA Bulletin* 29 (1965):62–68.

This survey of Canadian academic libraries is similar to Eaton's (in the U.S.), done ten years earlier. A response of 97 percent was received. Only 31 percent are using DC, with 62 percent using LC, and about 7 percent using other systems. "Most librarians who have not converted to LC stress . . . that they would undertake the programme immediately if they could find professional staff."

49. Gjelsness, Rudolph H. "Reclassification: Its Problems and Technique." *Library Journal* 53 (1928):597–600.

> Great stress is placed on the fact that reclassification means reorganization. "It affects all the basic records and is felt in all departments of the organization." The writer considers specific methods and problems of reclassification. No choice of any specific classification system is considered, although LC is mentioned in passing. While this article is quite dated, some of the information is still relevant.

50. Gopinath, M. A. "Reclassification of a Library Collection: A Case Study in Cost-accounting." *Annals of Library Science* 9 (1962):108–114.

> Gopinath describes a project to change a library of nearly 30,000 books and about an equal number of unclassified, bound volumes of periodicals over from DC to Colon Classification. He indicates the six stages in the routine and the multiple purpose of the project, outlined by Ranganathan. He analyzes the manpower needed and estimates the cost of reclassification to be 1 rupee per book. On this basis, and on the method of osmosis of Ranganathan, the cost of classifying any library of whatever size is found to be 10,000 rupees, and the additional staff needed would be two professionals and four semiprofessionals for a period of eight months. The final cost estimate is .35 rupee per volume. A number of peculiar suggestions and routines, which are only useful in an academic discussion, are presented. A curious and interesting study with extremely limited application (if any) for American libraries considering a change to LC.

51. Gore, Daniel. "The 50 Cent Change—to the Library of Congress." *Colleges & University Business* 44 (1968):109–111.

> Gore examines the cost-of-reclassification issue. For a collection of 60,000 volumes, of which about 18,000 were reclassed in two months, he estimates the final per volume cost to be about $.50, or $30,000 for the entire collection. The key to this low cost is the utilization of a sizable staff of student workers, à la federal work-study program. Some details on Gore's procedures are presented, as well as some cost data. Gore indicates that a full report will be issued when the project is completed. Quite obviously no attempt is made to correct previous cataloging or typing errors, etc. This is a bare bones physical change of the books and the cards.

52. ——. "Further Observations on the Use of LC Classification." *Library Research & Technical Services* 10 (1966): 519–524.

> This is a continued development of Gore's thesis of the superiority of the LC system over the DC scheme. He states that any library will eventually recover the cost of any reclassification undertaken by virtue of the substantially lower cost of using LC. This article specifically answers the objections raised by O'Bryant in her article in *LRTS* regarding the use of LC. (See Reference 101.) An absolutely essential article.

53. ———. "In Praise of Error; with some Animadversions on the Cost of Descriptive Cataloging." *Library Journal* 90 (1965):582–585.

This is the third and final article in Gore's *LJ* series, dealing generally with the costs of cataloging. In this article he discusses descriptive cataloging verification procedures and their alternatives with the practice of centralized cataloging. Included is an exposé of what Gore refers to as "the absurd habits of descriptive catalogers." Essential reading.

54. ———. "The Mismanagement of College Libraries: A View from the Inside." *AAUP Bulletin* 52 (1966):46–51.

In general, Gore covers very much the same ground as described in his previous articles in *LJ* and elsewhere. This article is pitched to appeal to the academic profession as an indictment of academic librarianship for its inability to devote more monies to books instead of staff. Lack of centralized cataloging (and the resultant higher costs) and the old-fashioned technical processing constraints serve as the basis of Gore's repeated thrusts. He strikes at a basic weakness of librarianship.

55. ———. "A Neglected Topic: The Cost of Classification." *Library Journal* 89 (1964):2287–2291.

This is the first of Gore's several articles in favor of the LC system. Gore is, perhaps, the first writer to incisively raise the issue of the cost of classification. This issue of classification cost has burst upon a slumbering profession. The painful awakening is still going on, and much of the credit must go to Daniel Gore for this welcome turn of events. Gore provides cost data (comparative with DC) and a rationale for the use of LC. This is a most important article. In a sense, it inaugurated the public debate which is still in progress.

56. ———. "A Reply to Mr. Ramer." *The Southeastern Librarian* 15 (1965): 57–59.

Gore further amplifies his general thesis regarding the wasteful and costly practices of the library profession. The article is of value for its iconoclastic jabs at the traditional salary–book expenditure ratios and further reemphasis on the centralized cataloging feature of the Library of Congress system. Useful for general background information.

57. ———. "Subject Cataloging: Some Considerations of Cost." *Library Journal* 89 (1964):3699–3703.

Gore analyzes the practical alternatives that exist in the subject-cataloging phase of the total process. He indicates that substantial cost reduction is possible if his suggested procedures are used with the LC Classification. The second of Gore's articles on the use of LC and essential reading.

58. ———. "The Wasteful Profession." *The Southeastern Librarian* 15 (1965): 21–25.

This article on the lack of economy in academic library operations deals in a more general manner with some of the material covered in Gore's three-part series in *LJ*. More comment is made on the applicability of LC for a library operation. Of some usefulness as a complement to his other articles.

59. Grout, Catherine W. "An Explanation of the Tables Used in the Schedules of the Library of Congress Classification." Unpublished dissertation. New York: Columbia University, School of Library Service, 1940.

This is the first and only attempt to devise a manual for the LC schedules. Grout can serve as a general introduction and explanation of the schedules, but is not sufficiently detailed (in explanations, or examples) to answer many of the questions involved in the use of LC. Still, this is an admirable and praiseworthy effort to provide a manual for the LC schedules. A useful, if not a basic source of information.

60. Gulledge, J. R. "L.C. vs. D.C. for College Library." *Library Journal* 49 (1924):1026–1027.

The author recommends the adoption of LC for college libraries, large and small, as against any other system available. He feels that (1) LC is up-to-date, (2) the classification fits the subject (not as in DC, where the subject fits the classification), (3) the scheme is practical, not theoretical, and (4) LC has a shorter notation than does DC. Supporting the superiority of LC are eight points which are far more obvious today than they were in 1924. Gulledge attempts to deflate some of the traditional arguments used in support of Dewey, and offers a number of good comparative statements. This is still a useful article and an excellent indication that even then, some librarians were aware of the real issues. Far ahead of his time.

61. Hagedorn, Ralph. "Random Thoughts on LC Classification." *Special Libraries* 52 (1961):256–257.

Hagedorn engages in very brief speculative musing on the vagaries of Dewey (six-place decimals, etc.) and the centralized cataloging benefits and economies of LC. He concludes that although LC will save a considerable amount of cataloging time, the many topics LC scatters throughout the scheme raise questions about its applicability for a small, open-shelf collection.

62. Ham, Jessie Gilchrist. "Reclassification of the University of South Carolina Library Collection." *Journal of Cataloging & Classification* 11 (1955):221–232.

Ham gives a report on the reclassification from Cutter to the DC. Some procedures are listed, but their value is quite limited because of the local operating conditions and the classification involved. Some cost data is supplied, but it is rather out-of-date and only very generally comparable to routine-

time costs involved in the application of LC. Some of the problems encountered during the project may have value for present reclassification
activities in other libraries, but, on the whole, this report offers little that is
constructive.

63. Hanson, J. C. M. "Library of Congress Classification for College Libraries."
Library Journal 46 (1921):151–154.

Hanson generally favors the LC Classification for both large and small academic libraries. The article contains an informative but brief discussion of
the early development and origin of the LC Classification. Because of Hanson's personal involvement, this is of special interest. He comments on some
representative defects as well as the advantages of the LC system. He indicates that an overwhelming majority of university librarians favored the LC
schedules. Although the article is of interest primarily for historical purposes, most of the advantages listed for LC are still valid.

64. Haykin, David J. "Way to the Future: Cooperative and Centralized Cataloging." *College & Research Libraries* 3 (1942):156–162.

Haykin makes a general statement on the desirability of cooperative and
centralized cataloging. He stresses the need to reexamine the economics of
technical processing and discusses the problems involved in cooperative and
centralized cataloging. There is some speculation on how such activities
might be handled in the future. He suggests that the Library of Congress
will continue to play the prime role in any such projects. General and wide
cooperation is naturally the key for any substantial future development in
solving cataloging problems.

65. Henshaw, Marie. "Conversion Sampler." *Library Journal* 92 (1967):3964–
3966.

Henshaw presents charts covering the classificatory relationships between
DC and LC on one-to-one situations, span of notations situations, and combined conversion tables.

66. Herrick, Mary Darrah. "The Classified Catalog at Boston University, 1948–
1964." *Library Resources & Technical Services* 8 (1964):289–299.

Herrick claims that this is the only university library using a classified catalog as its only subject approach and basing this approach on LC. She reviews
the history, problems, and practices of their classified catalog development.
LC subject headings were used as the primary index of terms for the catalog.
Since this catalog has now been published in book form, it has been claimed
that it can function as a relative index to the LC schedules.

67. Hiatt, Peter. "Cooperative Processing Centers for Public Libraries." *Library
Trends* 16 (1967):67–84.

Hiatt comments on the interest of many libraries in the use of LC as opposed
to DC. Most school and public libraries have remained with Dewey, whereas

many university and college libraries have been using LC or have converted to LC. Hiatt raises the basic issue of lower costs as the use of LC becomes more general and more and more libraries begin to think in terms of centralized processing activities.

68. Hoage, Annette L. "Librarians Rate LC Classification." *Special Libraries* 53 (1962):484–485.

Hoage reports on a survey of the use of LC in U.S. libraries, as of May 1961. She considers the good and bad features of LC and also lists the operative LC practices used in libraries. Her study indicates that the advantages far outweigh the disadvantages.

69. ———. "The Library of Congress Classification in the United States: A Survey of Opinions and Practices, with Attention to Problems of Structure and Application." Unpublished dissertation. New York: Columbia University, School of Library Science, 1961.

This is one of the major studies on the LC Classification. Hoage's two articles are based on this dissertation, which is a valuable analysis from the user's standpoint. Hoage critically analyzes all the major subject divisions of LC on the basis of her surveys of the published literature and of librarians. This study was devised to "(1) survey the development and structure of [LC] in relation to use; (2) survey librarians' views and determine the extent of their direct and/or modified use of it as a classification aid; and (3) analyze and make suggestions for use of the classification by patrons."

70. ———. "Patron Use of the L.C. Classification." *Library Resources & Technical Services* 6 (1962):247–249.

This report is based on Hoage's study of patrons as discussed in her unpublished dissertation. (See Reference 69.) As might be expected, graduate students, as well as users of academic and special libraries, used the classification only as a shelf location. The libraries surveyed felt that "the average patron is not aware of the subject approach provided by the classification and is ignorant of the full meaning of the call numbers." This study effectively lays to rest the arguments of Eaton and others based on "patron" use to determine a choice of classification.

71. Holley, Edward G. "Reclassification in Texas Academic Libraries." *Texas Library Journal* 42 (1966):85–89.

Holley briefly reviews significant national developments in the movement to the LC Classification. He compares Texas activities and cites the standard reasons for a switch to LC, as well as the counterarguments. He concludes that the basic question to be asked is how to secure "the best reading for the largest number at the least expense." Holley unquestionably implies that LC is the best and most economical system. He indicates that half of the Texas libraries which have reclassified to LC did so with little or no extra funds for this purpose.

72. ———. "The Trend to LC: Thoughts on Changing Library Classification Schemes." In *Library Lectures,* University of Louisiana, Baton Rouge Libraries, pp. 29–46. Baton Rouge: The Library, 1967.

This is one of the best articles on changing to LC. Holley offers a brief survey and history of some of the reclassification projects of the last 25 to 30 years. He provides only very general cost information. What is more important, he offers a solid rationale for the application of LC. Great emphasis is placed on using the LC number as it appears on the LC card, although (happily) he has placed all fiction in the national literature numbers. What is more, he seems to be one of the few that have devised appropriate procedures to reclassify a fairly large number of volumes with a modest number of staff—for the most part clerical. Although some of his LC conversion guidelines may not be suitable or even desirable for general application, they are still useful criteria for establishing procedures. At the University of Houston, three full-time clerks do most of the reclassification, with the supervision and assistance of a professional cataloger about half the time. The monthly rate of reclassification has been about 1200 volumes and now is in excess of 2000 volumes. A very useful article.

73. Hughes, Margaret H. "DC to LC: Conversion at Shepherd College Library." *West Virginia Libraries* 22 (1969):5–11.

This is a report on a conversion project to LC that reclassified 8000 volumes (of a total 45,000 volume collection) in about two years. Hughes offers some reclassification procedures based on their local experience. Extensive recataloging was required due to the lack of properly trained personnel in the past. The Xerox 914 was used for catalog card duplication. Their procedures in some respects seem cumbersome (e.g., the substitute main entry practice), and their application for widespread library use seems ill-advised. The reclassification rate is extremely slow. Notwithstanding, some of the suggestions may be useful. No cost data is provided.

74. Immroth, John Phillip. *A Guide to Library of Congress Classification.* Rochester, N.Y.: Libraries Unlimited, 1968.

This book appears to have been designed primarily as a textbook for library science students, rather than as a manual to the LC schedules. The descriptions and explanations of the schedules are only partial and extremely brief. Although Immroth attempts to use examples of general application, too often the information supplied is so sparse and incomplete as to leave the cataloger unsure and even perplexed. Since the author has never visited the Technical Processing Department of the Library of Congress (according to the staff), and does not discuss the crucial LC shelflisting procedures, this book will be of little practical use in determining the how and why of LC schedule use. For the practicing cataloger, there are far too many questions raised and left unanswered for this book to serve as anything more than a convenient compilation of brief historical information and sample schedule and table snippets.

75. ———. "To PZ or Not to PZ" *Colorado Academic Library* 3 (1966):17–19.

The PZ 1, 3, and 4 classification numbers are one of the major disadvantages in adopting LC. Immroth cites the well-known problems associated with the PZ sections of LC. He concludes, as we do, that fiction is far better placed with the national literature materials.

76. Institute on the Use of the Library of Congress Classification, New York, 1966. *The Use of the Library of Congress Classification: Proceedings.* Edited by Richard H. Schimmelpfeng and C. Donald Cook. Chicago: ALA, 1968.

This is not "the long awaited definitive manual on the use of the Library of Congress Classification." However, it is probably the best all-around handbook on LC available, and an essential purchase for any library using or considering LC. A number of the papers were provided by the L.C. staff and represent authoritative and official information and views. The papers range over a number of special problem areas of LC and deal with organizational and procedural suggestions for LC Classification and reclassification. Special problem areas of the LC Classification are covered in literature, science, social science, etc., and the use of LC by public as well as academic libraries is discussed. This may not be a manual to the LC schedules, but it is far better than anything previously available. The Immroth book does not even begin to touch this publication for usefulness. It is unfortunate that it took so long (over two years) to publish this material. Inasmuch as all the papers are *essential* reading, they are not individually analyzed.

77. Jackson, Sidney L. "Long Files under LC Subject Headings, and the LC Classification." *Library Resources & Technical Services* 11 (1967):243–245.

He provides examples supporting his thesis that since many libraries make use of the LC subject heading service (and as more do so) "the adequacy of this service depends, to a degree not generally appreciated, upon using also the LC Classification. He feels the Library of Congress "Classification frequently affords more specific approaches to the material than its subject headings are capable of" and is "a resource not matched, by and large, by Dewey numbers." Something to think about!

78. Jacobs, Elizabeth P., and Spencer, Robinson. "What Price Reclassification?" *Catalogers' and Classifiers' Yearbook* no. 3 (1932), pp. 64–78.

Although this article is dated, it is still useful, though partly for showing what not to do. In this report of an LC reclassification project started in July 1927 at the University of Rochester Library, some curious reclassification procedures are outlined. Modifications of the LC schedules were made when required. Jacobs reports on faculty cooperation, accounting methods, statistical summaries, etc. This is a fairly detailed account of the change to LC, and one of the few efforts in the literature to provide careful cost and procedural information.

79. Jacobsen, Karl T. "The Re-organization of the Library of a Small College." *Library Quarterly* 4 (1934):234–243.

Jacobsen reports on a small library's general reorganization from classification to acquisition activities. The library changed from a modified Dewey to the LC system. "The library is best served by following the printed [LC] schedules quite closely."

80. Jefferd, Dorothy. "The Library of Congress Classification in a University Library." *PNLA Proceedings* 20 (1929):25–26.

Jefferd gives a statement in favor of the LC system, with some discussion of pros and cons. One of the objections is, that of the 21 divisions, 19 are subject oriented, while two (E and F) are geographical. LC is not a "perfect" classification of knowledge, but rather a special scheme devised solely for a particular library. As a result, this limitation must always be kept in mind. By implication, Jefferd stresses the great benefits of the centralized classification work of the Library of Congress.

81. Kilpatrick, Norman L. and O'Donnel, Anna M. "Reclassification at the State University of Iowa." *Journal of Cataloging & Classification* 8 (1952):12–17.

This is a review of the decision to reclassify from a modified Dewey scheme to the LC scheme, emphasizing the following reasons: "(1) To cut the cost of cataloging; (2) To get new acquisitions on the shelf more promptly; (3) To expand the usefulness of the bibliographic tools published by the Library of Congress." A collection of 66,200 volumes was reclassified in nine months, at a cost of 45 cents per volume. Kilpatrick places emphasis on the need for standardized policies. "As libraries increase in size and use of their book collection, the importance of classification diminishes . . . when 20,000 books are out on loan at any given time, the catalog, rather than the shelves, is where the researcher can gain a comprehensive picture of the library's book holdings on a given subject." Several very useful reclassification procedures are presented. A valuable report.

82. Lorenson, Robert. "Adapting LC Schedules to DC Notation." *Library Resources & Technical Services* 9 (1965):210–212.

Lorenson reports on the partial reclassification project at Indiana State College, where the LC national literature schedules were adapted to DC notation. "However, it is anticipated that conversions similar to the one we are doing in 810–899 are possible in other limited areas." LC/DC conversion tables are provided. This is a far-out solution to the literature problems of LC, and definitely not a recommended move. Another example of costly special practices and aborted professionalism.

83. LaMontagne, Leo B. *American Library Classification with Special Reference to the Library of Congress.* Hamden, Conn.: Shoe String Press, 1961.

This book contains a brief history of classification in western thought, although the emphasis is mainly on American library classification schemes. It provides an expanded history of classification in the Library of Congress, and a general review of the present LC Classification. A fairly detailed analysis of the subject construction and notation of LC is presented. Although valuable, the material is not presented in a form or in sufficient detail to answer anything more than general questions about LC use. This is basically an historical and descriptive work. A list of the advantages and disadvantages of DC is on pp. 223–225 and 232–233.

84. Lynn, Jeannette M. "Don't Reclassify . . . ." *Catholic Library World* 10 (1938):93–96.

Lynn considers the problems involved in reclassification and concludes that "reclassification is a costly, tedious, and lengthy process, but if a library needs such a major operation, the results in increased efficiency . . . make it well worth the labor involved." She considers DC and LC only briefly, and barely touches on the problems of classificatory superiority and cataloging efficiencies.

85. McGaw, Howard F. "Academic Libraries Using the LC Classification System." *College & Research Libraries* 27 (1966):31–36.

This is a list of those libraries listed in Table 3 in the Office of Education's *Library Statistics of Colleges and Universities, 1963–64; Institutional data* (1965) that use the LC Classification. The arrangement is by state. Outdated now, of course.

86. ———. "Reclassification: A Bibliography." *Library Resources & Technical Services* 9 (1965):483–488.

As a result of a reclassification project from DC to LC, the author made "a rather systematic study of the transitions experienced by other libraries, the strong and weak features of LC and DC. . . ." Some of the entries have annotations which are slanted toward an abandonment of DC. Upon publication it was a useful listing, but now is entirely superseded.

87. MacPherson, Harriet D. "Reclassification of College and University Libraries." *College & Research Libraries* 1 (1940):159–164.

MacPherson reports on a survey of 20 libraries involved in reclassification from one system to another. MacPherson observes that whenever "the bulk of a collection has been reclassified because of general inadequacy of an old classification system, the results have usually justified the means." Extensive modification of an old system is not recommended. Mainly an opinion poll on four rather general questions, this article provides no cost data and no evaluative comparisons of classification schemes.

88. Mann, Margaret. "Classification Chart." *Library Journal* 60 (1935):162.

Mann shows how the major divisions, as well as a few of the subdivisions, of the DC and the LC interrelate. The charts by Marie Henshaw (see Reference 65) are far more useful than Mann's.

89. Martel, Charles. "The Library of Congress Classification." In *Essays Offered to Herbert Putnam,* edited by W. William Bishop and Andrew Keogh, pp. 327–332. New Haven: Yale, 1929.

Martel quotes with approval the remark that "our conclusion is that the Congress schedules as such as will admit of the exact classification of the bulk of the world's literature to date at the lowest possible cost; and that in this respect the class headings of the Congress scheme have reached the theoretical high-water mark of efficiency. . . ." The essay by Martel has, admittedly, no practical value for today, but his comments, by one who played such an important part in the development of LC, do have interesting historical value.

90. Mason, Clyde W. "The Classification of a Chemistry Library, According to the Library of Congress System." *Journal of Chemical Education* 7 (1930):1887–1894.

This is a report of a project to reclassify to LC a collection of some 7500 volumes. While some costs are given, they are only of historical interest and deal primarily with the cost of the LC cards. Some discussion is given on the advantages of the LC Classification for a chemistry collection. Some modifications of the LC scheme were made. Mainly of historical interest.

91. Metcalfe, John Wallace. *Subject Classifying and Indexing.* Metuchen, N. J.: Scarecrow Press, 1959.

Metcalfe deals with LC on pp. 19, 20, and 113–117. LC "was devised to meet a practical purpose, as briefly stated as Cutter's, and has not been wrapped up in pseudoscience and muddled metaphysic, as three of the dead or dying classifications, SC, BC and CC have been. DC and UDC still hold the field, partly because each of these has an organization to maintain it, the only other classification having this being LC. This is another practical consideration of great importance often overlooked by theorists; the day of classification without a large, non-profit making, wealthy society or institution behind it is over, just because there is this business of keeping up-to-date, of issuing amendments, extensions and new editions. . . ."

92. Miller, H. G. "Why Library of Congress?" *New Zealand Libraries* 3 (1940): 137–138.

This brief report of visits to U.S. and English libraries indicates that the general opinion among university librarians is that if a library is likely to reach 100,000 volumes the LC system is the best. The author deals only very generally with the capabilities of the LC system. Cost factors are not mentioned.

93. Mills, Jack. *A Modern Outline of Library Classification.* London: Chapman & Hall, 1960. (Chapter 9, The LC Classification: pp. 89–102.)

Mills discusses the principles underlying the LC Classification system. This discussion is followed by a critical analysis of the main classes as well as of the notation. He concludes that (1) as a classification LC is very efficient; (2) the subject breakdown is generally helpful; (3) the detail provided by the classes allows for very close classification, if necessary (although in one area the detail would be inadequate for a special library); but (4) the "scheme can make no claim to 'universality' in the UDC sense." This discussion is primarily limited to the theoretical and scarcely touches the practical applications of LC and its centralized cataloging and processing implications.

94. Moon, Eric. "Rugged Stupidity." (Editorial) *Library Journal* 90 (1965):3406.

Moon suggests that vis-à-vis cataloging ". . . the most basic step . . . is . . . a profession-wide realization that 'rugged individualism' in cataloging practice is now only rugged stupidity." An incisive statement on the large cost of processing library materials. A reading must.

95. Morris, Leslie R. "The Argument for Dewey." *North Carolina Librarian* 26 (1968):58–62.

This article presents a number of arguments against reclassification to LC. Although Morris would use LC if he were starting a new academic library, the costs of reclassification, no matter how small (even 50 cents per volume), as well as the imperfections of the LC Classification, form the basis of his argument for Dewey. He brings no logic to the debate and tends to stop short of the implications of his discussion of various L.C. services.

96. Morrison, Perry D. "Use of Library of Congress Classification Decisions in Academic Libraries—an Empirical Study." *Library Resources & Technical Services* 9 (1965):235–242.

The "purpose of this study [is] to estimate amount of use made by academic libraries of classification information furnished on [LC] cards and extent to which it is modified to fit local needs." The "data [were] gathered by sampling at random the cards in the catalogs of three state college libraries and in [the] printed book catalog of . . . a state university. The total sample consisted of 588 cards. For comparison, a further sample of 135 cards was drawn from a state college library using the Dewey system of classification." This study indicates that, although minimal at some libraries, a degree of adaption seems to be required with LC, e.g., PZ, Z, and K. In comparison with the DC, 87 percent of cards with LC Classification were used without change, whereas only 26 percent of cards with DC Classification were used without change. The statistical data and also the opinions of the libraries using the LC Classification indicate that newer libraries tend to accept a large proportion of the classification information suggested by LC, with a subsequent increase in the efficiency of the classification project.

97. Mueller, Theodore A. "Workshop on the Library of Congress Classification and Its New BL–BX Schedules." In *Summary of Proceedings,* American Theological Library Association Conference, pp. 68–81. Washington, D.C.: The Association, 1961.

> Mueller briefly describes the schedules. Many of the major criticisms are discussed with genuine attempts to emphasize good points while recognizing the difficulties in devising schedules that will meet every special subject need. The notes on the subclasses should prove helpful in understanding the schedule decisions of L.C. as well as promoting the acceptance of the new BL–BX schedules.

98. Mumford, L. Quincy. "DC Numbers on LC Cards: A Supplement." *Library Resources & Technical Services* 9 (1965):405–413.

> Mumford addresses himself to the specific points of dispute in Clapp's article and attempts to counter every one with either documentary or personal testimonials by the participants. At least 80 percent of all cards *sold* carry the DC number. "The committee has erred in stating that 65 percent of all cards purchased from LC have no DC number!" In not recommending the addition of DC numbers to all titles cataloged by LC, the Library of Congress Librarians' Committee (1940) observed "that it should be recalled that this is primarily a service for popular libraries." The implications of this discussion are covered in the text of this manual.

99. Naeseth, Gerhard. "Problems of Reclassification: Academic Libraries." In *Problems in Library Classification—Dewey 17 and Conversion,* edited by Theodore Samore, pp. 140–150. Milwaukee: University of Wisconsin, School of Library and Information Science, published in cooperation with R. R. Bowker, 1968.

> Naeseth discusses some of the problems and the rationale of reclassification from Cutter to LC at the Madison campus library of the University of Wisconsin. A separate reclassification unit was established in 1954 with the aim of doing only a partial reclassification of the collection. This is primarily a "how-we-did-it" account with some telling examples of intraorganizational gaps in communication.

100. Nitecki, Joseph Z. "Speed Cataloging: Prudence and Pitfalls." *Library Journal* 94 (1969):1417–1421.

> The author reports on a two-year LC project at the Milwaukee campus library of the University of Wisconsin. Procedures are outlined and statistics given on production and error frequency. In this valuable progress report, some rather surprising statements about main entries occur: "The extent of adaptation of LC entries to local needs determines the percentage of errors made" and "a well written and up-to-date manual of operation allows for a high degree of flexibility in modifying LC entries!" Speed cataloging, as discussed in this article, would seem to be the natural outgrowth of using LC, rather than the convoluted process as described.

101. O'Bryant, Mathilda B. "Some Random Thoughts on the Cost of Classification." *Library Resources & Technical Services* 9 (1965):367–370.

O'Bryant critically evaluates Daniel Gore's article "The Cost of Classification: A Neglected Topic." She challenges Gore's claim that $300,000 could be saved by a one million-volume library using the LC scheme rather than DC. She feels that since a large research library only receives LC cards for about 50 percent of its acquisitions, the actual savings would not be as great as Gore claims. Further, she challenges Gore on the issue of the complete acceptance of the LC call number, in full or in part, by citing special needs of departmental libraries (i.e., engineering, chemistry, etc.), and cites the duplication of LC call numbers as a result of original cataloging performed by a local library before LC cards were available. O'Bryant dwells on the hoary argument that a library may have special local traditions and needs that absolutely prevent a down-the-line use of all LC call numbers. The desires of professors and other library users must be considered, she maintains, before complete adherence to LC call numbers can be accepted. In other words, each LC call number cannot be followed blindly, but must be evaluated in terms of the local library's needs and practices. In principle, the author favors centralized cataloging, but shows traditional rigidity and parochial resistance. A poor defense.

102. University of Oregon Library. "A Proposal to Adopt the L.C. Classification (A Summary Statement) and Report of the Ad Hoc Committee to Study the Advisability and Feasibility of Adopting Additional Cooperative Cataloging and Reclassification." Mimeographed. Eugene: University of Oregon Library, August 1964.

The data presented reveal that within the next ten years the library will spend more on continuing its use of DC than on an immediate change to the Library of Congress scheme. The basic argument is that of economy, although other advantages of LC are examined. A detailed cost analysis is presented to justify the change to LC. A careful study.

103. University of Oregon Library, Ad Hoc Committee. "L.C. Classification at the University of Oregon Library." *PNLA Quarterly* 29 (1965):249–250.

A partial summary of their 13-page unpublished report, emphasizing that "the most obvious present advantage is the economic one." (See Reference 102.)

104. Orne, Jerrold. "We Have Cut our Cataloging Costs!" *Library Journal* 73 (1948):1475–1478.

Orne feels that technical services librarians should deal only with that work which requires professional attention. Clericals can and should perform the rest. Information on LC cards is to be accepted in toto so that no work will be repeated. LC subject headings, as well, should be accepted. In other words, we should accept the work of LC and "we should not waste our time trying to improve on all of the work of LC. We accept this work as sound until it proves otherwise, and only then do we change it." He provides significant cost reduction figures. A useful attempt to change traditional library cataloging attitudes.

105. Ortopan, Leroy. "Support for Conversion to LC." In *Problems in Library Classification—Dewey 17 and Conversion,* edited by Theodore Samore, pp. 93–97. Milwaukee: University of Wisconsin, School of Library Information Science; published in cooperation with R. R. Bowker, 1968.

This paper argues, quite rightly, that classification numbers inevitably become a device for shelving books—even in small libraries. He presents general comments on the economics of LC application as well as the conversion experience at the Milwaukee campus library of the University of Wisconsin.

106. Osborn, Andrew D. "Cataloging Costs and a Changing Conception of Cataloging." *Catalogers' and Classifiers' Yearbook* no. 5 (1936), pp. 45–54.

The thesis which Osborn advances is that "the basic shortcoming has been and remains the lack of an adequate theory of cataloging" which has resulted in very high cataloging costs. The article contains a brief review of the literature on the cost of cataloging, with such incisive observations as ". . . many catalogers have set up a higher standard than that of the Library of Congress. They cannot even accept uncritically the cards they get from that source; they must criticize, add and subtract until they have spent possibly as much time and money in patching the entry as it would have taken to catalog the book afresh. Real economy can only come through big changes in cataloging methods . . . and through a willingness to cooperate and to accept the results of cooperation to the full." In some ways a landmark analysis of the cataloging "hangup" of the library profession.

107. ———. "The Crisis in Cataloging." *Library Quarterly* 11 (1941):393–411.

Osborn believes that cataloging is the major problem field. It has become elaborate and highly technical, too often existing in and for itself. Four principal theories of cataloging are presented: (1) legalistic—rules and definitions exist for all things, as ends in themselves; (2) perfectionistic—every possible aspect or detail is covered; (3) bibliographic—cataloging is a branch of descriptive bibliography, e.g., illustrated lining papers, etc.; (4) pragmatic—circumstances may modify cataloging application, e.g., school, college, public, etc., and because libraries all have different requirements, to standardize would result in much harm [!]. Osborn favors the pragmatic approach and feels that no ordinary library needs more detailed cataloging than the Library of Congress. Classification schemes, he points out, age rapidly. No one classification scheme is a panacea for classification problems regardless of the type of library. Pointing out that dictionary catalogs are becoming too complex and that the divided catalog offers no real solution, Osborn feels that the LC system shows ominous signs of breaking down (as of 1940) because of a several million-volume backlog of uncataloged items.

(Needless to say that as of 1970 it has not broken down.) He feels that the foremost problem confronting library administration is the cost of cataloging.

108. Perreault, Jean M. "Comparative Classification for Administrators: A Short Sermon." *College & Research Libraries* 29 (1968):46–50.

Perreault raises two issues. The first asks why library administrators are not familiar with comparative classification studies. The second asks why administrators refuse to view classification as a search strategy. Perreault indicates that the LC system is undoubtedly less desirable and effective, all aspects considered, than UDC, BC, or even DC. He again calls on librarians to resist the switch to LC and maintain their professional integrity by using one of the above-mentioned classification systems, even if this will mean original cataloging for all acquisitions. He follows up this heartwarming contribution by calling for some organization, preferably international in scope (but H. W. Wilson might be a good start), to form a centralized classification/information distribution base for one of the three systems mentioned previously (although he favors UDC). Each would provide for wide-ranging versatility, especially in view of the potential searching of electronically stored catalogs by automated search equipment. Cost isn't everything and, what is more, service should be uppermost—an interesting echo of Thelma Eaton. Finally, the only salvation for the library profession from the devilish fantasies of LC are the library schools! It is interesting to compare Perreault's article with the 1963 article of Ralph Shaw entitled "Classification Systems" (see Reference 134).

109. ———. "In the Mail: Classification." *Library Research & Technical Services* 11 (1967):245–246.

Perreault labels largely incorrect the claim that the use of the LC Classification system will result in greater economy! The article attempts to deal with the more theoretical aspects of the classification of books as a caution against changing to LC for reasons primarily of economy. This is an argument characteristic of schools of library science which, in the pragmatics of library classification, seem, by and large, to be clearly out of touch with the realities of the contemporary library scene. It is quite obvious that we need to look beyond LC, DC, or even subject headings, but to use this argument to bolster present complacency and the status quo is indeed specious!

110. ———. *Re-classification: Some Warnings and a Proposal.* Occasional Papers, no. 87. Urbana: University of Illinois, Graduate School of Library Science, September 1967.

Couched in "quasi-philosophicalese," this is a dire, finger-shaking warning about the illogical pitfalls of LC by the "enfant terrible" exponent of UDC. The author is staunchly in favor of UDC as a universal classification system, in spite of the fact (which he admits) that the FID has no prospect in sight for the massive financial support necessary to even begin to develop an LC-type operation. Nor are all the English schedules yet completed for UDC.

Mr. Perreault is to be admired for his messianic fervor, but until UDC has the financial support for centralized processing and cataloging similar to LC, he can at best be considered only a small noise in the ether. The real question to address to those who take Mr. Perreault's view is this: How much longer can libraries wait for the "ideal" machine-compatible classification to be developed and adequately funded? Still, a rather provocative point of view which all of those planning reclassification should be aware of when considering LC.

111. Phillips, W. Howard. *A Primer of Book Classification.* 5th ed. London: Association of Assistant Librarians, 1961.

Phillips lists the merits and defects of LC. He concludes that LC "seems to have in its schedules the essentials of an ideal bibliographical classification, suitable for all public libraries." But, he goes on to state, it is too "detailed and complex for widespread adoption." It needs to be modified and amended for application in almost every type of library! This, of course, has been proven to be complete hogwash.

112. Piercy, Esther J., and Talmadge, Robert L., eds. "Cooperative and Centralized Cataloging." *Library Trends* 16 (1967). (Special issue.)

The editors of this special issue cover the major categories of "(1) evaluation of processing centers, (2) types of centers, (3) processing centers for specific types of libraries, (4) developments abroad, and (5) the resurrection of the book catalog." Two of the 12 articles are helpful on the LC Classification issue. They are the Hiatt and Dawson articles, which are dealt with individually in this bibliography.

113. Pullen, William R. "We'd Rather Switch than Fight." *North Carolina Libraries* 26 (1968):62–66.

Pullen describes the rationale and arguments for the change to LC at Georgia State College Library. Over 93,000 volumes were to be reclassified. He comments on the eight-year experience with LC and, of course, is convinced that LC is the best for the library operation. No new data is presented. Usual arguments in favor of LC are presented. Mainly of testimonial value.

114. "Pure Science: L.C. vs D.C." *Library Journal* 58 (1933):124–127.

This article briefly outlines "some of the more salient weaknesses in these widely used . . . classifications." There is a comparison and examination of the Q schedule, published in 1921, and the 500's section of the twelfth edition of Dewey. This is of interest for historical development and comparison.

115. Ramer, James D. "Concerning the Wasteful Profession." *Eastern Librarian* 15 (1965): 26–28.

Ramer argues, inconclusively it seems (see Reference 56), that the basic weaknesses of Gore's thesis stem from the limited context of Gore's library operation (small college, Asheville–Biltmore, with a 20,000-volume collection). Further, Ramer quarrels with some of the cost figures of Gore. A thoughtful evaluation of some of the ideas promoted by Daniel Gore.

116. Rawson, Joan W. "Why Dewey?" *New Zealand Libraries* 4 (1940):4–5.

A very brief discussion of the advantages and disadvantages of the Dewey Decimal Classification. The advantages outweigh the disadvantages, according to Rawson. No discussion of costs or of centralized cataloging. A quite dated presentation.

117. Reichmann, Felix. "Cornell's Reclassification Program." *College & Research Libraries* 23 (1962):369–374.

Reichmann gives an account of the history and travail of changing from the Harris Classification to LC. He expresses regret at the modifications performed on LC in the early years of the program. Some arguments are presented for reclassifying the entire collection, rather than reclassifying only new acquisitions.

118. ———. "Costs of Cataloging." *Library Trends* 2 (1953):290–317.

Here is a brief historical review (allegedly the definitive study) of published reports on cataloging cost analysis. Reichmann concludes that the degree to which libraries exhibit a rugged individualism in cataloging practice has prevented a standard scale of measurement to be applied in determining costs. The general attitude of the article is traditional in viewing cataloging as an intellectual activity or game. He considers that real savings cannot be obtained at the expense of the reference need for subject approaches (although W. H. Brett suggests that this may not be the case). Reichmann concludes by indicating that the cost problem can only be solved by the library profession. The entire discussion seems to miss any really serious engagement with the factors that have, for so long, been ignored or only partially addressed concerning costs and library operation.

119. "Revolution at Enoch Pratt: Change to LC Classification." *Wilson Library Bulletin* 40 (1966):494.

This news item states that in 1920, Enoch Pratt adopted a modified LC system which gradually became confused by changes and substitutions, creating many problems. In 1964, Tauber advised a complete change to LC, with the project starting on May 1, 1965. The fact that not too many public libraries are on LC makes this change significant. It also should be noted that the Wisconsin State Library has (just recently) changed to the LC Classification.

120. Richmond, Phyllis A. "Switch without Deliberation" (Letter to editor). *Library Journal* 91 (1966): 4870.

Richmond advances four points of special consideration when considering a change to the the LC Classification. Her statement, most frequently quoted (especially by the anti-LC folk), is this: "Think you can take the LC call number right off the card and use it without checking it? Ha, ha." These four points are dealt with in detail in the text of this manual. Her remarks are not anti-LC (note the last paragraph), but rather a caution against ill-considered and ill-prepared switches to LC.

121. Roberts, Betty. "Reclassification from Dewey Decimal to LC in Subject Blocks." *Special Libraries* 60 (1969):297–298.

Roberts briefly reports on reclassification at Washington State University in Pullman, Washington. The policy was to minimize recataloging. Avery pressure-sensitive labels were used to cover the Dewey call numbers on catalog cards (which were never removed from the card catalog), as well as on the book cards and pockets. The procedure emphasizes speed as well as economy by using student help to the maximum with minimal professional activity. Data on the ratio of hours to the number of books reclassified are provided. A how-to-do-it procedure that may be potentially useful if speed is the *only* criteria.

122. Roberts, Martin A. *The Library of Congress in Relation to Research.* Washington, D.C.: GPO, 1939.

Roberts provides a clear examination of the LC system and enumerates the basic values of the scheme. This is still useful for a view of the merits that Roberts sees in the Library of Congress scheme.

123. Rogers, A. Robert. "LC and BG: Friendship without Marriage." *Library Resources & Technical Services* 13 (1969):47–61.

After some preliminary preparations for switching to LC, Bowling Green decided not to change because (a) output per cataloger and FTE cataloging staff clerk using DC did not seem to differ from some libraries using LC, (b) cost of reclassing would more than offset the savings, (c) computer costs would be doubled, and (d) public service departments would be inconvenienced. On the basis of the data in Table I, however, these conclusions are not very surprising. The question not discussed is why there are such low production figures of volumes processed for the number of technical services persons involved (even in the libraries already on LC!)—e.g., at BG: 4 catalogers, 6 semiprofessionals and clerks, and 7 to 8 students = 19,730 volumes; at UPS: 1 cataloger, 6¾ clericals, and about 179 hours per *week average* for student help = 33,742 volumes. *Very interesting.*

124. Rowell, Lois. "Additions and Changes: a Study of Selected LC Classification Schedules." *Library Journal* 94 (1969):3975–3977.

Although it seems well known that drastic relocations may be expected with each subsequent edition of Dewey, little has been reported about the practice of LC. As a result, the author has analyzed the *Additions and Changes* in the classes D (history), H (social sciences), and Q (sciences) for the periods August 1958 to July 1965, October 1949 to January 1964, and October 1949 to July 1966. All revisions were carefully counted, tabulated, etc., and the results presented in chart form. Rowell concludes that college and university libraries "need not consider relocations in LC as a deterrent to adopting a . . . classification that will . . . continue to provide success-fully for the needs of such collections in the future." An important up-to-date analysis and confirmation of the advantage of LC.

125. Sahaya, Shyamndan. "The Library of Congress and Its Classification." *Modern Librarian* 15 (1945):82–86.

Sahaya gives a brief survey of the Library of Congress and its classification, history, theory (outline, features, notation), defects, and merits. Compared with its rivals, LC is considered the most unsatisfactory scheme because its main classes do not modulate into one another; it shows an absence of his-torical or evolutionary order. It is a series of large special classes rather than a complete subjective compendium of knowledge. LC is considered to have too great a bulk, and the notation is inferior in every way. However, its merit consists in the minuteness of the scheme. Its indexing is exceptionally full and relative. He concludes that the scheme is a great achievement. An interesting viewpoint from the Alice-in-Wonderland of the Colon Classifica-tion.

126. Samore, Theodore. "Form Division in L.C. and D.C. Classification Schemes." *Library Resources & Technical Services* 6 (1962):243–246.

Samore compares form division in LC and DC, for example: "form divisions usually follow the general divisions in D.C., in L.C. form divisions precede the general." As a result of his study, he concludes that "L.C.'s theory behind the use of form divisions is both more logical and more practical than in D.C. In short, its rationale is functional, while in D.C. it is mnemonical . . . since the form divisions in D.C. are relatively inflexible, the subject is squeezed to fit the form divisions unless utterly inapplicable." Conclusion: LC uses its form divisions to maximum advantage because it is much more comprehensive, expansive, and flexible than DC. "D.C. is unable to match L.C.'s use for form divisions, because the scheme is limited by notational and mnemonic considerations."

127. Samore, Theodore, ed. *Problems in Library Classification—Dewey 17 and Conversion.* Library & Information Science Studies, no. 1. Milwaukee: University of Wisconsin, School of Library and Information Science; published in coopera-tion with R. R. Bowker, 1968.

This is a collection of papers originally presented at a two-phase conference held at the Milwaukee campus of the University of Wisconsin in November 1966 and May 1967. Only the papers by Comins, Cox, Naeseth, Ortopan, Talmadge, and Taylor have much that is pertinent. The information in these papers was most useful when originally given. Now, however, they have been generally superseded by revision or later publications. Refer to each of the cited names above for individual annotations. This collection is decidedly inferior to that of the University of Maryland Reclassification Conference held in 1968. (See Reference 22.) The concluding remarks by Samore should be contrasted to those of Phyllis Richmond in the publication: "The Use of the Library of Congress Classification." (See Reference 76.)

128. Satory, M. Max. "Class B—Philosophy and Religion of the Library of Congress Classification Schedules." *Library Journal* 62 (1937):450–453.

The purpose of this article is "neither to continue or expand upon . . . criticism" regarding the lack of instructions and explanatory notes in the LC schedules. It gives a rather detailed explanation of the B schedule structure, logic, etc., emphasizing negative as well as positive aspects. The article concludes that the LC schedules "seem to have gone a considerable way toward meeting those difficulties and especially that of correlation of material in these fields." The author makes no categorical judgment or comparison with other classifications. A valuable analysis of the structure of class B.

129. Sayers, William C. B. *A Manual of Classification for Librarians.* 4th ed. London: Andre Deutsch, 1967. (Library of Congress Classification, pp. 194–211.)

Sayers provides a historical introduction to the LC scheme. He briefly considers the main features of the system. He concludes that the scheme is fundamentally pragmatic, although its detailed structure may be a handicap for many libraries especially the smaller ones. However, Sayers is impressed by the system and counters some of the criticisms of Bliss. This is a basic introduction to the main features, class divisions, differences in class treatment, as well as a review of the classes for the LC scheme. Sayers presents a special chart to illustrate clearly the nature of the scheme. This is a traditional discussion of the LC Classification with no acknowledgment or discussion of any of the practical advantages of using LC such as the centralized cataloging functions, for example, L.C. cards with call number notations, etc. For a 1967 revision, the book demonstrates a curious ignorance of classification developments in the United States.

130. Schofield, E. B. "The Future of 'Dewey.'" *Library Association Record* 3 (1933):245–250.

This is a severe criticism of the DC 13: "the burying of new live topics in the narrow grave of a worm-eaten scheme." The author considers changes and enlargement of the DC for subjects like botany, which is hopelessly out-of-date in spite of revision and enlargement by the DC 13. Generally, an acrimonious analysis of the logic and organization of knowledge by the DC. Schofield also criticizes the LC scheme for being "thirty years out of date." Throughout the article, the term "museum" is a pejorative epithet thrown at DC, LC, British Museum catalog, etc. He supports the "tree-of-knowledge-as-a-living-organism" argument. This is a call for a classification scheme broad enough to always accommodate new and growing areas of information.

131. ——. "The Revision of Dewey." *Library Association Record* 1 (1934): 31–34.

This is a continued criticism of DC on the basis of inadequate major divisions of knowledge. "Why should any classification imprison itself in ten numerals when twenty-six letters are available which are as well known as the ABC?", Schofield asks, and goes on to observe that ". . . it is unreasonable to expect a scheme framed in the infancy of library classification to carry modern man safely and expeditiously through the fog-banks of current problems to the new Atlantis." In this regard, what was true in 1934 is all the more obvious today.

132. Schwartz, Mortimer. "Retrospective Application of Class KF at Davis." *Law Library Journal* 61 (1968):248–254.

This is a report on the retrospective application of the LC preliminary schedule KF to 37,000 titles. The project started on St. Patrick's Day 1967, and concluded, except for final revision, in November 1967. Schwartz provides information on the reasons for adopting the KF schedule rather than, for example, the LA County scheme. Problem areas of the KF schedule are discussed, such as what to do about international law (class JX). Interim policy decisions which grew out of these problems are outlined, as are general procedures used in the application of the KF schedule. Strangely, this process involved weekly or even daily visits to the Law Library at Berkeley (which uses the LA County K scheme) to verify or clarify class assignments in KF. Emphasis is placed on the uniform and standard application of the schedule by using all of the services of L.C.

133. Schwartz, Philip John. "Reclassification to LC: An Annotated Bibliography. *APLA Bulletin* 30 (1966):120–127.

A selected and annotated bibliography of 52 studies of reclassification projects which appeared to be most useful. The bibliography is preceded by general comments on DC and LC. The writer is in the "Dewey is dead" camp. Schwartz observes that there is "a dearth of detailed cost studies" available for the projects, as well as an obvious need for a procedure manual for the use of the LC Classification. Until the present time, this could be considered a highly useful list for any library considering a change to LC or even for just reevaluating its classification procedures.

134. Shaw, Ralph R. "Classification Systems." *Library Resources & Technical Services* 7 (1963):113–118.

Shaw distributed for classification more than 100 copies of documents that had been already classified by analysts of subject competence and experience. The same documents, in clean copy, were classified by the same analysts who had classified them previously, and not one case did a document get the same classification. Shaw makes a strong case for uniform, centralized, and standardized classification, and strongly impugns the validity of special local practices which so often exist in libraries on DC, and all too frequently in libraries on LC.

135. Shell, Elton E. "A Rationale for Using the Library of Congress System in Reclassification." In *Reclassification: Rationale and Problems; Proceedings,* edited by Jean M. Perreault, pp. 30–56. College Park, Md.: University of Maryland, School of Library & Information Services, 1968.

> This is one of the best arguments for the use of the LC Classification. Shell carefully discusses the major points in support of the use or adoption of LC, as well as properly dismissing some of the usually cited, but debatable, reasons for using LC. In his enthusiastic endorsement of LC, Shell ignores entirely the problems of LC serial classification, and too briefly dismisses the PZ 3 (omitting PZ 1 and 4) problem in literature. For a discussion of these two problem areas, refer to the text of this manual. Shell does not mention the potentially confusing, inconsistent, and admittedly (by LC) mistaken policy decisions in the application of the LC schedules in the above two areas. Obviously, as Shell cheerfully admits, LC is not perfect. However, one must be cautious in permitting the cost arguments to take precedence over all other considerations. With these two exceptions, Shell's rationale is a basic statement which should be read by anyone considering a change to, or the adoption of, the LC Classification system.

136. Shoemaker, Richard H., and Arginteanu, Selda. "Reclassifying the John Cotton Dana Library of the Newark Colleges of Rutgers University." *Journal of Cataloging & Classification* 5 (1949):19–23.

> After pointing out some of the serious (but transitory) disadvantages of reclassifying—such as the need to shift the book collection several times since extra stacks are generally not available, and the difficulty of predicting how various classes will grow—Shoemaker offers good reasons for reclassification from DC to LC. Some fringe benefits of reclassification, such as weeding, uniform public catalog, etc. are mentioned, with special emphasis on the benefits of uniformity and economy.

137. Slavens, Thomas P. "Classification Schemes for the Arrangement of the Literature of Protestant Denominations." *Library Resources & Technical Services* 9 (1965): 439–442.

> Slavens evaluates classification schemes that would be most useful in locating, in one place, materials of a given religious body. He covers DC, Decimale Universelle, Bliss, Colon, Rider, Union Theological Seminary, and LC. He concludes that the most detailed classification for bringing the literature together is Bliss. "Yet other factors tend to make [LC] a preferable scheme for a large collection." It can be expanded and adapted at points where it is inadequate. Since LC is a widely-used and up-to-date system, and is more easily applied than Bliss, Slavens favors LC.

138. Stouffer, Isabelle. "Princeton and the Library of Congress Schedule." In *Proceedings*, American Theological Library Association Conference, 7th Annual, 1953, pp. 21–23. Evanston, Ill.: The Association, 1954.

> This article has a very brief description of Princeton's involvement with LC, beginning in 1940. Their reclassification operated on such principles as "our method is to put new books in the old classification until all books on one subject can be reclassified into LC at one time." Stouffer deals specifically with the religion and philosophy areas, and describes how the reclassification proceeded. Subject problems and other difficulties are mentioned. In order to improve on LC, Princeton experimented with making its own schedule for general church history. While the desire is expressed to reclassify everything, they are reconciled to using two or three classification systems for many years to come! This is a telling account of how *not* to proceed.

139. Swann, Arthur W. "Remarks of . . . Comparing Dewey and L.C. Classifications." In *Proceedings*, American Theological Library Association Conference, 7th Annual, 1953, pp. 19–21. Evanston, Ill.: The Association, 1954.

> The standard arguments are presented for a change to LC. Incidental advantages, such as by-products of the reclassification process, are mentioned. Useful mainly for historical information.

140. "Symposium on Use of Main [medical] Classification Schemes." *Bulletin Medical Library Association* 41 (1953):333–360.

> The article on DC by Helen Wolter points out that DC is not the most suitable for medicine because it widely separates various aspects of an organ or a system. Wolter observes that if the primary function of a classification is to aid in locating a book, then any scheme will serve as well! Bertha Hallan, in her article on the LC Classification, indicates that it has served its purpose well because of its flexibility. The new third edition of Class R (Medicine) has provided the basic revisions required to make the scheme conform more closely with changes in medical knowledge. LC is definitely the favored of the two systems, on the basis of actual use in medical libraries.

141. Talmadge, Robert L. "One Library's Case against Conversion." In *Problems in Library Classification—Dewey 17 and Conversion*, edited by Theodore Samore, pp. 65–82. Milwaukee: University of Wisconsin, School of Library and Information Science; published in cooperation with R. R. Bowker, 1968.

> This paper deals only with the situation at the University of Illinois Library. With the special University of Illinois Automation Committee statement, "There was general consensus that if we were starting over again at the beginning we would choose LC rather than Dewey," the principal reasons for not reclassifying or classifying new acquisitions in a new system are presented. The basic reason is, naturally, the high cost of converting over four million volumes. Talmadge concludes that "LC is better than Dewey." One can only infer that Talmadge feels, for good or ill, that the University of

Illinois Library is stuck with Dewey. Admittedly the high cost of reclassification would give pause to any institution of this size. While there is no quibbling on this point, the argument is hardly a case against the use of LC. The possibility of maintaining two collections, one largely dormant, is mainly ignored.

142. Tauber, Maurice F. "Book Classification in University Libraries." In *University of Tennessee Library Lectures,* edited by Dale M. Bentz, no. 1 (1949), pp. 1–15. Knoxville: University of Tennessee, 1952.

Tauber reports on data gathered ten years ago concerning university faculty opinions about the Library of Congress Classification system. Centralized classification, which he has considered desirable, has not made much headway. "Moreover, a study of libraries which use the Library of Congress classification for arranging books reveals that in many instances the libraries fail to avail themselves of the numbers assigned by LC. Classification can only have some relation to suggestiveness in terms of library resources." Scholars feel that "a Classification to be satisfactory for scholarly purposes, must reflect the topical organization of the field as they view it." There may or may not be agreement for subject matter that constantly shifts. Tauber also reports the evaluations of the various scholarly disciplines on the LC Classification. "Classification schemes will not be satisfactory to the faculty member until he has been invited to participate in their creation, and until he has shown a genuine desire to contribute his knowledge to the growing problem of organizing library materials."

143. ———. "Cataloging and Classification." In *The State of the Library Art,* vol. 1, part 1, edited by Ralph R. Shaw, pp. 149–158. New Brunswick, N.J.: Rutgers University, Graduate School of Library Service, 1960.

This is a brief review of pertinent literature, with special reference to Thelma Eaton's survey article as well as a reclassification project by Ham. The Ham citation covers a change from Cutter to the DC. Ham's cost data seems of little use, although the listing of ten factors that influence the cost of reclassification is valuable for the project planning phase. The discussion of physical processing and card duplication is dated, since the project antedates Xerox machines (914, 720, etc.) and the Se-Lin labeler.

144. ———. "Classification of Books in College and University Libraries: Historical Aspects." *Library Quarterly* 12 (1942):706–724.

"Classification, it appears, has been a boiling-pot of controversy. . . ." This article is Tauber's report of a study of the recorded opinions of a few representatives from each of his five groupings, to illustrate the several lines of relationship between various individuals and classification systems in American libraries. The article reviews what Tauber feels to be important historical developments and influences on classification use. His comments are still useful for historical perspective.

145. ——— and Edith Wise. "Classification Systems." In *The State of the Library Art,* vol. 1, part 3, edited by Ralph R. Shaw, pp. 140–188. New Brunswick, N.J.: Rutgers University, Graduate School of Library Service, 1961.

This article presents a selective history of the LC scheme, dealing specifically with significant decisions in its formulation and development. The review also presents critical evaluations of the practical as well as the theoretical aspects of LC. There is a section on librarians' comments and evaluations of the LC Classification—critical as well as favorable. The paper concludes that most of the literature on LC has been basically descriptive. A useful, though brief, survey of the literature. Tauber and Wise give no considerations to cost factors in cataloging and tend to deal only with theoretical evaluations of the LC scheme. Little is made of the centralized cataloging potentialities of L.C.

146. ———. "Reclassification and Recataloging in College and University Libraries." Unpublished dissertation. Chicago: University of Chicago, 1941.

Although this dissertation is a basic work, it is dated in a number of obvious ways. Tauber's articles in *Library Quarterly* for July and October 1942; *College & Research Libraries,* 1942 and 1943; *The Acquisition and Cataloging of Books,* 1940; and Tauber's *Technical Services in Libraries,* 1954, taken together, contain the essentials of his dissertation research.

147. ———. "Reclassification and Recataloging of Materials in College and University Libraries." In *The Acquisition and Cataloging of Books,* edited by William M. Randall, pp. 187–219. Chicago: University of Chicago, 1940.

In this article, Tauber covers the following points: (1) a few definitions and the scope of the general problem, (2) the assumptions concerning reclassification and the methods of testing them, (3) the specific reasons for reclassification advanced by librarians, (4) problems of administration, and (5) evaluation of the processes. Sections three and four are especially recommended. "Most college and university libraries do not plan their reclassification and recataloging projects as effectively as they might." He notes the types of inefficiency on page 205. Tauber concludes that LC is the best and most economical system, and goes on to imply that this may not necessarily warrant a reclassification project. It is our opinion, however, that the developments of the last 20 years make it unmistakably clear that the LC Classification system should be used for current acquisitions—the prospect of a total reclassification can be considered later. This is an important article.

148. ———. "Reclassification and Recataloging in College and University Libraries: Reasons and Evaluations." *Library Quarterly* 12 (1942):827–845.

Tauber reports the results of a study of 60 libraries that changed to LC (based on his unpublished dissertation). Usually the librarian reclassifies and recatalogs "because he assumes they will increase the educational services of the library and/or reduce the costs of technical processing." The developments of the last 20 years have made it possible to practice centralized cataloging effectively and economically. L.C. has finally completed all of its schedules except K. It has gained sufficient financial support to begin to develop centralized cataloging projects on a national scale. Even though Tauber still counsels caution in considering reclassification, due to the tremendous costs, his article remains an important statement. Essential reading.

149. ———. "Reclassification of Special Collections in College and University Libraries Using the Library of Congress Classification." *Special Libraries* 35 (1944):111–115.

A survey and report on 23 libraries using LC. The three categories of classification problems are: "(1) classes of materials for which no LC schedules are available: law . . . ; (2) classes of materials which some claim are handled inadequately by the existing LC schedules; and (3) local collections . . . and other special collections. . . . Most college and university libraries have special collections which present difficulties during the reclassification process. Whether or not the collection is active should be the primary basis in the decision to reclassify. It should be remembered that it is cheaper and more efficient to reclassify and recatalog a collection during a general reorganization than it is to procrastinate and decide to change certain sections at a later time when special provisions for technical operations will have to be re-installed."

150. ———. "Reorganizing a Library Book Collection—Parts I and II." *College & Research Libraries* 6 (1945):341–345.

Tauber stresses the high costs involved in reorganization, and the necessity of establishing policies and procedures for work distribution. Valuable discussion of work organization in the categories of organization procedures, working quarters, mechanical aids, special collections, older and new materials, and the library user. The article is somewhat dated in its elementary discussion but is valuable for the attention given to the need for procedural planning and the development of standard routines. In Part II, he discusses the best ways to reclassify collections, e.g., most used whole classes, currency of materials, etc. He offers 11 suggestions to consider in recataloging. While acknowledging that the order of reclassification should rest on use, Tauber feels that new accessions should all go into the new scheme, even if the whole class is not under reclassification. Efficient and speedy procedures are the capstan of any reclassification project. Tauber concludes with an exhortation to reduce costs.

151. ———. "Special Problems in Reclassification and Recataloging." *College & Research Libraries* 4 (1942):49–56.

This paper deals with the problems that concern "(1) classification of special types of materials, (2) open-shelf collections, (3) letter classifications, (4) arrears in cataloged and classified materials, (5) experimentation in filing, (6) uses of films, (7) discarding and storage, and (8) union catalogs" in relation to the practices in a study of 60 college and university libraries "which have either completed reclassification or are still reclassifying by the Library of Congress system and in six other libraries which have always used the Library of Congress system." While the majority of the libraries surveyed have followed L.C. in most things, they more often than not prefer to arrange their fiction in English according to a national literature scheme, rather than in PZ 3. Other variations among the libraries were found to occur with the handling of textbooks, juvenile works, periodicals, and other materials. Tauber maintains that user satisfaction, and not cost, should be the primary consideration in adopting any special practices or modifications. Some discussion is given to the problems and procedures of a reclassification program. Stressing the absolute need for advanced planning prior to the commencement of a reclassification project, Tauber suggests that librarians examine the practice of introducing local modifications in the LC scheme and consider the possibility of giving better public service through economies and/or cooperative enterprises.

152. ———. "Subject Cataloging and Classification Approaching the Crossroads." *College & Research Libraries* 3 (1942):149–156.

A discussion of reforms proposed to achieve standardization in the areas of subject heading and classification. Tauber emphasizes that a large number of libraries do not, or are not able [read: won't] to, take full advantage of centralized cataloging. "Classification is primarily a librarian's device. As such, the acceptance of one system, preferably one based on a living collection of books, seems the effective procedure for the future. We cannot expect the program of cooperative and centralized cataloging and classification to be any more than empty words unless catalogers stop thinking of all sorts of reasons for not taking advantage of it." Three cheers! Did he really mean it?

153. ———. *Technical Services in Libraries.* New York: Columbia University, 1954. (pp. 261–283.)

Tauber very briefly reviews the characteristics of the LC system. Curiously (and inexplicably) he recommends that the LC class numbers on the printed L.C. cards not be accepted without examination because "these may not always fit the special needs or follow the established practice of the local library." Here the point seems to have been completely missed. He details the reasons for undertaking a reclassification program. Surprisingly, he appears to condone, rather than condemn, modifications of the LC scheme. Tauber also considers what is meant by, and involved in, reclassification. Various reasons for reclassification are enumerated: improvement of classification, improvement of library use, and improvement of library administration. Most of the material in this article is based on his dissertation. Specific policy suggestions are made. Tauber counsels a cautious approach to reclassification decisions, and feels that recataloging (to some degree) is unavoidable.

154. Taylor, Desmond. "Classification Trends in Junior College Libraries." *College & Research Libraries* 29 (1968):351–356.

A report of a survey of all (837) junior college libraries in the United States. Of the schools surveyed, 690, or 82 percent, responded. While the largest percentage use DC, there has been, since 1960, a slight trend toward LC. A statistical analysis of this trend with table data is provided. Twenty-one of the college libraries established since 1960 reclassified from DC to LC. The author concludes that little thought was given to the selection of a classification system. The decision was obviously based on user (and librarian) familiarity with a given system rather than the classificatory capabilities of the scheme or the economic implications of its application.

155. ———. "Is Dewey Dead?" *Library Journal* 91 (1966):4035–4037.

An epitaph written in the "God-is-dead" debate style. The author jeers at the inadequacies of the Dewey Decimal Classification and attempts to deflate the overblown reputation of Melvil Dewey. Useful, perhaps, for its enthusiasm.

156. ———. "Preparations for Reclassification." In *Problems in Library Classification—Dewey 17 and Conversion,* edited by Theodore Samore, pp. 112–128. Milwaukee: University of Wisconsin, School of Library and Information Science; published in cooperation with R. R. Bowker, 1968.

The first article in print that presents step-by-step procedures for reclassification, as well as describing the basic areas of concern in preparing for reclassification to LC. This paper is largely superseded by a later one given by Taylor at the University of Maryland Conference and, of course, by this manual. Only of academic interest now.

157. ———. "Reclassification: A Case for LC in the Academic Library." *PNLA Quarterly* 29 (1965):243–249.

An article based in part on one library's experiences. Taylor discusses reclassification problems, surveys, costs, advantages, and rationale. Although the cost figures presented apply only to the library discussed, they do support the case for LC's greater economy. The article strongly emphasizes the centralized cataloging benefits of using LC.

158. ———. "Reclassification to LC: Planning and Personnel." In *Reclassification: Rationale and Problems; Proceedings,* edited by Jean M. Perreault, pp. 97–112. College Park, Md.: University of Maryland, School of Library & Information Services, 1968.

This is a revised version of Taylor's original paper, published in *Problems in Library Classification—Dewey 17 and Conversion* and edited by Theodore Samore. Basic procedural information for an orderly and planned reclassification to LC is carefully presented in detailed steps. This was a useful guide which dealt with such topics as L.C. card reproduction, collection shifting, series and literature classification, and other such bothersome problems. This paper is superseded by this manual.

159. Thornton, John L. "Dewey Classification and the Special Library." *Library Journal* 58 (1933):789.

A very brief criticism of DC and a comparison with LC and the Brussels systems. Thornton concludes that DC is inappropriate for special library use—especially in the medical field. Only of historical interest.

160. Uhrich, Helen B. "Abridgement of the LC Schedules in Religion." In *Proceedings*, American Theological Library Association Conference, 7th Annual, 1953, pp. 24–27. Evanston, Ill.: The Association, 1954.

This is a report on Yale's study of L.C.'s BL–BX (Religion) schedules. The object of the study was to determine whether an abridged or condensed form of the schedule could be developed and adopted. This report is included only as a fantastic demonstration of egregious logic.

161. U.S. Library of Congress, Classification Division. *Author Notation in the Library of Congress,* by Anna Cantrell Laws. Washington, D.C.: GPO, 1917.

Laws offers a short explanation, with examples, of the use of the author notation in LC. ". . . the Cutter three-figure table is used as a basis in assigning numbers for books in fiction; the Cutter–Sanborn three–figure table for all other classes. Neither is strictly adhered to, and there are numerous exceptions." Laws provides a few general rules for the application of the author notation. A method of call number breakdown for spine marking and catalog cards is recommended (for a discussion of this subject see Section 3.1.4). The Laws booklet is largely superseded by a one-page explanation of the application of author numbers issued by the LC Subject Cataloging Division in 1962. Useful for historical and background information, but not for how to break the LC call number.

162. Van Hoven, William Davies. "User's Reactions to the Library of Congress Classification System in Two Academic Libraries in North Carolina." Thesis. Chapel Hill: University of North Carolina, School of Library Science, 1967.

With the usual references to Tauber and Hoage, this thesis presents a brief historical review of the best literature on user reaction to LC. Beyond this, Van Hoven reports on surveys of the patrons of two academic libraries— patrons who might be considered representative of most in this country—and concludes that if a book collection is well arranged and carefully marked, the classification system used means little. The thesis tells nothing that was not known before, namely that patrons are patrons and class systems are class systems, and only infrequently does one impinge upon the other.

163. Vann, Sarah K. "Toward the Seventeenth . . . Dewey." *Library Resources & Technical Services* 8 (1964):172–187.

A brief review of the application of later DC editions, especially the four-teenth, fifteenth, and sixteenth, in selected academic libraries. Vann covers the use of DC notes, DC numbers on L.C. cards, form divisions, relocations, and other problems. She reviews changes to be expected in the seventeenth edition. A typical DC exponent's view and review of DC relocations and changes, expressed in terms of the tacit-acceptance syndrome, as exemplified by Estragon and Vladimir in *Waiting for Godot*. No consideration is given to the costs of Dewey or the promises of centralized cataloging.

164. Veryha, Wasyl. "Problems in Classification on Slavic Books with Library of Congress Classification Schedules and Subject Headings." *College & Research Libraries* 28 (1967):277–282.

The author states that the LC schedules dealing with the Slavic world have not been updated and, in fact, do not reflect the real world of the last 50 years. The major inadequacies of LC in this area are illustrated, and a number of examples are provided to show that the schedules and subject headings are inconsistent and confused. Consequently, the arrangement for Slavic materials needs to be modified by L.C. A good definition of a problem area.

165. Voos, Henry. "Standard Times for Certain Clerical Activities in Technical Processing." Unpublished dissertation. New Brunswick, N.J.: Rutgers—The State University, 1965.

The Voos thesis is that too much attention has been paid to taking an entire process, adding together the costs of labor and materials, and concluding that this is the cost of cataloging a book. He offers a brief historical review of this argument. His premise is that identical repetitive processes in libraries can be timed. If the timing is of minute tasks, the increments which com-pose each particular library's operation can be collected to give some idea of how much time is spent on various portions of the tasks. He provides time and motion studies of such library activities as pasting book pockets, date due slips, and book plates, applying plastic covers, erasing, property marking, catalog card typing and related matters, lettering, etc. Voos has also provided a selective and annotated bibliography of items containing data appropriate to current technical processing. A few of his conclusions are obvious; others may enlighten. Generally, we feel the micromotion approach is strictly limited, in spite of Voos' enthusiasm. His table of summary data, and espe-cially his list of general recommendations, may be quite useful in evaluating some library procedures. (The summary data and conclusions are published in *LRTS*, 10 (1966):223–227.) Standard function times are listed, as are recommendations as to the cost limit of specific function times. It is useful to compare the survey of Hitchcock (see Reference 76) on average times for certain clerical activities in technical services with the average times of Voos. Some valuable cost data is reported.

166. Wall, Minnie. "From D.C. to L.C. at Auburn University." *Alabama Librarian* 14 (1963):6–7.

The eventual change to LC from DC was under serious consideration from 1949 until 1957 (!) when, finally, the decision to change was made. A very brief description of some of the general preparatory activities for the reclassification are noted. Reclassification, except for reference and a special collection, did not commence until 1960. A sterling example of administrative decision making and procedural genius.

167. Welsh, William J. "Considerations on the Adoption of the Library of Congress Classification." *Library Resources & Technical Services* 11 (1967):345–353. (Also in *Law Library Journal* 61 (1968):242–247.)

Welsh indulges in a cautious, almost political, exercise in equivocation. His observations on the problem areas of LC are, as far as they go, certainly valid. He discusses some of the reasons for adopting LC: LC class numbers are on L.C. printed cards, general use can be made of LC call numbers on L.C. printed cards, comparative costs of LC and DC original cataloging weigh in favor of LC, promises of automated centralized cataloging are real. Welsh avoids any controversial claim that the LC Classification system is superior. He presents the standard argument that L.C. does not recommend its classification for any other library, and further that the ". . . printed catalog cards does [sic] not enforce adoption of either the LC or DC . . . or of the LC subject heading list. Libraries have been and are free to make as much or as little use of the information on the catalog entries as they wish." While this is an essential official statement for any library considering for its own use the LC Classification system, it should be clearly recognized that a strong position on the several advantages of LC is *not* presented because L.C. has not yet been charged by law to assume the responsibilities of a national library operation. Until this is the case, L.C. will voice only cautious and/or noncommittal public positions.

168. Williams, Margaret. "Reclassification Program at Memorial University of Newfoundland." *APLA Bulletin* 29 (1965):99–104.

The author provides background information on the decision to reclassify to LC and briefly describes some of the methods used to achieve this objective. The reclassification involved 70,000 volumes in DC. Some modification of the LC schedules was instituted in the areas of Newfoundland history and Canadian literature. Otherwise, the general policy of accepting LC call numbers as given was established. She describes the use of the Xerox 914 in reproducing L.C. cards. Some procedures are outlined. It was estimated that the reclassification project would take ten years. All titles are not to be reclassified, and only those considered active will be handled. The remaining titles in DC will be consolidated and shelved in a special stack area. With only 8500 volumes reclassified in two years, the author reveals a remarkably inefficient plan for reclassification. The arguments offered for a change to

LC may be useful, but the information presented about the procedures of the change may be harmful.

169. Wolfert, Richard J. "Reference and Loan Library Converts to LC." *Wisconsin Library Bulletin* 62 (1966):106–107.

Wolfert describes a library which used the abridged edition of Dewey with no Cutter. He points out that in recent years, few multiple copies but many new titles were purchased, which complicated the cataloging and ordering processes. He considered a transfer to the unabridged DC, but because of the many and sometimes drastic changes in DC from edition to edition, and the tinkering required with the suggested DC numbers on L.C. cards (plus devising the Cutter number), reclassification to LC was decided. "The decision was based on a study of other libraries which have made this same change, reports appearing in various professional periodicals, and a study of the changes our cataloging staff had to make in call numbers for new titles added . . . while using the Dewey classification numbers given on LC cards." L.C. class numbers and subject headings are accepted as given. The list of L.C. subject headings is used instead of "see refs" and "see also refs" in the public catalog. "Mass production is the key in book manufacture and distribution. After a book is purchased the standardization procedure must continue. Books are written by individuals for the use of individuals; only the channel between the individual writers and readers is standardized. LC provides this service best. Problems will continue with any classification but they can be much better coped with" by using LC.

170. Wright, Wyllis. "How Little Cataloging Can Be Effective." *College & Research Libraries* 15 (1954):167–170.

Wright discusses cataloging shortcuts in regard to such items as shelflist information, ownership marks, collation information, subject headings, title cards, revising, etc. There are no specific remarks about the use of LC.

171. Wynar, Don et al. *Cost Analysis Study.* Technical Services Division, University of Denver Library. A project in technical processes seminar. Denver: University of Denver, Graduate School of Librarianship, 1965.

This is a project to determine the cost of placing a book on the shelves ready for use. The study is limited to procedures concerned with in-print, nonfiction books. It is probably one of the most detailed studies published. Cost data is especially useful for libraries on the LC system. Clerical help is used for precataloging, revising, and cataloging when L.C. cards are available. The major portion of recataloging and reclassification of the science collection into the LC system was done by clerical personnel. Wynar provides points of comparative reference on which to base other cost studies. There is considerable emphasis on the position that no academic library can afford technical processes which are inefficient and expensive. This is a detailed and up-to-date study of cataloging practices pertaining only to the University of

Denver Library. Although it deals exclusively with the activities of a single library, the techniques and practices are hopefully transferable. A useful study.

172. Zachert, Martha J. "Techniques for Reorganizing the Catalog of a Special Library." *Journal of Cataloging & Classification* 11 (1955):29–37.

A report on the reclassification and recataloging from Dewey to LC of a small (4000 volumes) pharmacological library. Zachert follows closely the suggested procedures of Tauber for reclassification. She gives a fairly detailed report of the steps and routines used. Since this library was so small, with only one professional librarian, it is unlikely that some of the solutions and procedures are adaptable to other projects. The author concludes that the theory of reclassification and recataloging, as stated in the literature (principally Tauber), was definitely helpful at every step of the planning and execution of this project.

Appendix A

STATEMENT ON TYPES OF CLASSIFICATION AVAILABLE TO NEW ACADEMIC LIBRARIES*

Introduction

NEW ACADEMIC LIBRARIES are faced with a rather important decision at their very beginning. What classification system will prove most adaptable and most durable over a long period of time? The Classification Committee, at the request of the Cataloging Policy and Research Committee, has studied this problem carefully. The statement embodying our conclusions does not consist of arbitrary recommendations for one scheme or another, but sets forth the characteristics of the major classifications as they apply to different situations. The question-and-answer method has been used for convenience in helping a library define its own situation. The Committee was extremely fortunate in having as a member, Miss Gertrude L. Oellrich of Alanar Book Processing Center, who is actually engaged in classifying with several schemes simultaneously and who, therefore, is in a good position to compare them.

Definition

The purpose of classification is defined in this statement as a systematic, subject-oriented arrangement for shelving, a location device for open or closed shelf collections of books, not for the classification of knowledge.

Statement

The field of study was narrowed to a survey of the comparative merits of the Dewey Decimal (DC) and Library of Congress (LC) Classifications. Both these systems are growing, are being kept up-to-date with quarterly revisions, and Dewey, at least, now has a users' guide to go with it.[1] One or the other of these two classifications is now used in the majority of academic libraries.

1. *Is it important to consider other classification systems in addition to the Dewey Decimal and Library of Congress schemes?*

There are several other classification schemes available, most being used in libraries somewhere in the world.

BLISS—This is used rather extensively in Australia. It is a good logical system, but is not being kept up-to-date for ease of usage. The manuscript version does not agree with the published version. Letter notation.

* Report of the Classification Committee, RTSD Cataloging and Classification Section, May 15, 1964. The Committee: Pauline Atherton, Joan Cusenza, Elva Krogh, Gertrude Oellrich, Elizabeth Overmyer, Annette Phinazee, Phyllis Richmond, Chairman.

RIDER—This is a new scheme quite similar to the Dewey Decimal Classification, but with a letter notation as in Bliss. There is no way of updating it except as individual libraries undertake the job.

READER INTEREST—This system is more suitable for a public library which must cater to constantly changing interests.

UNIVERSAL DECIMAL—This is a European adaptation of the Dewey Decimal Classification. It is greatly expanded in the science and technology sections to serve the purposes of scientific documentation. Except in occasional areas, the rest has scarcely more depth, and, in some cases, less modernity than Dewey. It is too lopsided for a general library, but would be suitable for special collections in scientific and technical subjects. A scientific-technical edition in English, with a good guide written by Jack Mills, is available.[2] This classification is updated periodically. If a new and centralized secretariat is established and the major revisions now under consideration are adopted, it may be of greater significance than it is now. A classification system to watch.

COLON—This system is used at various establishments in England and in India. The current (6th) edition schedules are rather limited in scope. It is very difficult to use because it necessitates an attitude of mind that is totally different from that employed in any other classification process. At present there is no good guide to its use. The explanatory portions in the 6th edition are extremely difficult reading and less than clear.

FACETED CLASSIFICATION—The schemes of this type developed so far are for specialized subjects. Until a general system is developed, this type of classification is not suitable for a generalized library.

2. *What characteristics influence the choice of a classification?*

COMPREHENSIVENESS—LC is much broader and more comprehensive than DC. It permits finer (closer) classification. The "P" schedules, in particular, are tremendous in size and, while hard to learn to use, have much "elbow room."

FLEXIBILITY—LC has the advantage of not being logical in exposition, as a rule, and while it is practically impossible to memorize, it is easy to expand without upsetting existing classified books. The advantage of a non-logical classification is apparent in dealing with rapidly advancing subjects, as the sciences, where a major change in thought can throw out a whole branch in a previous arrangement of knowledge. LC can interpolate where DC must compromise.

Dewey has to be expanded through further breakdown, sub-classification or re-naming and reassigning classes. LC can be expanded by interpolation because the whole system does not have to be logical but can, to a considerable degree, grow like Topsy without regard to its environment. It has been possible to abridge Dewey, but not LC.

LC permits variation in the treatment of specialized topics. Sayers[3] states that LC was the "first to recognize the necessity for variations of treatment as between the different classes, and it is this feature of the scheme which has found so much favor in academic libraries."

COMPLEXITY—The mixed notation of LC is more complex than the pure notation of DC. However, Gulledge[4] stated that the LC numbers are on the average shorter than DC.

INDEXING—LC has no combined index and this is considered a fault by users. The relative index of DC has been praised, although the index for the 16th edition is inferior to that of the 14th edition.

BROWSABILITY—DC has the advantage of providing browsability. In open stack libraries, this is important. It is practically impossible to browse with LC although people try it all the time.

NOTATION—Dewey's notation is positional, each position represents a classification level. LC notation is ordinal. Each class has a number of its own not necessarily related to preceding or following classes.

CLASSES—LC has three times as many classes as DC. Neither classification fits the college curriculum.

INTERPRETATION OF USE—DC seems to be superior in this because there is a Users' Manual for DC.

SYSTEMS OF SUBDIVISIONS—The system seems to be better-in LC, but the tables are difficult to use. Students have some difficulty learning to build numbers in DC, but once learned, the application is uniform throughout the system. However, if one uses LC cards there may be fewer instances when numbers have to be built.

REVISIONS—Both LC and DC are now being kept current with quarterly corrections.

Problem areas noted are fiction, translation, literature subdivisions, political subdivisions, and study and teaching. Both schemes have been criticized.

3. Is the choice of LC or DC a function of the size of the collection?

It seems to be an accepted fact in the literature on classification that the LC scheme, because it lacks general numbers for many areas, does not serve the small library needing broad classification.

The ceiling for the 15th edition of Dewey was for libraries of 200, 000, though this ceiling was lifted for the 16th edition to include libraries of whatever size. However, in a survey conducted by Thelma Eaton among college and university libraries, only in libraries of less than 200,000 volumes was the value of DC stressed.

The LC classification is used by 300 university, special, and governmental libraries in the United States and abroad. The scheme does not lend itself easily to abridgment for use in libraries with small collections, and serves best in libraries with large collections or special libraries which require minute subdivision of limited subjects.

The Committee recommends Dewey for libraries with general collections up to 200,000 volumes in size, and the Library of Congress system for those expected to be larger and for those small libraries with specialized collections in the social sciences and humanities.

4. *What local or existing factors must be considered in making a choice of a classification?*

Various questions were considered:
if the library is in a state system, what is the rest of the state doing?
should such factors as the use of fixed location (shelving by size), open or closed stacks, availability of a centralized catalog or even adoption of some special subject heading system be considered?
Apparently none of these factors had much to do with the choice of a classification system, since nothing could be found in the literature of librarianship relating to them.

5. *Is a divisional library vs. a central library a reason for preferring one classification or the other?*

In their description of the process of adapting the Dewey Classification for use in a college library, Ashton and Hansen note that "no system has been devised with the divisional plan as its basis." On the other hand, they do not recommend attempting to develop one. They modified the DC system to suit their needs with only 10% of the collection requiring reclassification. But their conclusion was that "Dewey, as it now stands, confuses the divisional library issue."[5] The LC system, having more classes, could be more easily adjusted to the divisional concept.

6. *Which classification, LC or DC, is more satisfactory for centralized cataloging?*

A. Library of Congress characteristics:
   (1) LC cards give class numbers plus LC-style Cutter numbers in the following proportion (barring law and lesser known languages): 85%.
   (2) There are fewer changes in LC class numbers than in DC. (see, for for example, literature periods between the 14th and 15th editions of Dewey).
   (3) LC will often serve specialized departments better than DC, and since a single system is easier for the whole college, the LC system becomes the chosen one where centralized cataloging is done.
B. Dewey Classification characteristics:
   (1) DC numbers appear on LC cards for about 35% of titles. This means that about 65% of cards purchased from LC have no DC number.
   (2) DC changes cause confusion when reprinted LC cards are used and require constant professional attention.
   (3) DC is too permissive. This is a boon to custom cataloging or to local cataloging preferences, but a Pandora's Box in centralized cataloging.
      e.g. *geography* and history combination.
         rearrangement of class to bring related classes together, such as philology and literature, 400 and 800.

biography in 920 or subject number.

bibliography in 016 or subject number.

extension of class numbers or *building* numbers beyond what is given on the LC card.

shortening of numbers when class number ends in .01, .08, etc. Requires common sense—one cannot stop at zero (821.0) if a general rule for no more than four numbers has been made.

7. *Should the classification numbers on the LC cards be accepted in preference to making local changes?*

The consensus in the literature is that catalogers should accept the Library of Congress classification choices in preference to making local changes. The reasons for this are:

(1) This practice makes the cataloging function easier and more economical.[6]

(2) Few, if any, libraries use *all* the numbers assigned by LC, but the majority indicate that they accept 90-99% of the numbers on cards and proof-sheets.[7]

(3) Dawson actually examined cards in a selected number of libraries and found only 84.45% of the numbers were accepted.[8]

Some of the reasons given for NOT accepting the numbers given on LC cards are:

(1) Changes in schedules since older cards were printed give obsolete numbers.

(2) Absence of numbers.

(3) Failure to accept wholly or apply consistently the various revisions of the classification systems.[9]

8. *What are the relative costs of using LC and DC?*

The comments below are based on daily observance of LC cards in a catalog department, a limited study of 500 LC cards as received, and a study of 500 LC entries in the National Union Catalog, excluding law and lesser known foreign languages.

Classification nos. on cards (excluding law & lesser known languages)

	Daily cards	500 cards	Nat. Union Cat. LC card entries
NO LC class number	10%	16%	15%
NO DC class number	50%	63%	70%

To supply class numbers where these are lacking on LC cards requires from 1 to 10 minutes per title by a person familiar with the LC and DC systems. Obviously, the DC is more costly in this respect, and only the advantages derived from its use can counterbalance this cost. It is said that fewer DC numbers will appear on LC cards in the future.

To this basic cost, which requires the employment of a professional cataloger for DC, must be added:

(1) variations due to edition changes on reprinted cards   10%
(2) extension of the DC number when libraries prefer close classification. Longer numbers are now being given on more recent cards   5%
(3) assignment of Cutter numbers for every title   100%
(4) assignment of fiction number (i.e. 813) if libraries do not use F or have no number for fiction   100%

The percentages here occurred in the 500 cards. A closer study might be useful.

Considering the LC classification, to the basic cost of supplying 15% of the numbers must be added the following:

(1) supply numbers for all subjects treated from the legal aspect   10% of the 500 cards
(2) supply literature numbers for PZ3   100%
(3) supply numbers for the papers, proceedings, etc., of universities, societies, etc., where LC has assigned an A class number (for the society) instead of a number for the subject in the paper
e.g. Riabov's *Rules of Motion of Artificial Celestial Bodies,*
     LC cards gives: 629.1388 (a case of
       AS36.U56 no. 1021   former DC number)
Some colleges want this material with the subject, so an LC number must be supplied for it.
In some cases only an LC A class number is assigned and no Dewey number, necessitating a new class number with either classification.

It is obvious that the LC system is less expensive even though some LC numbers are lacking and the problems of law, fiction, and series remain.

9. *Which classification would be easier to use for a mechanized system?*

Several factors have a bearing on which classification would be most easily mechanized.

STORAGE—Since the classification notation must be converted to Double Digit form, the storage space for each class number would be twice its length.

Storage units necessary would depend on the type of machine.

For example:

Decimal machine (IBM 7070 series) 10 digits to the field, allowing 5 letters or numbers per field.

Binary machine (IBM 7090 series) 18 digits to the field, allowing 9 letters or numbers per field.

Few LC numbers run higher than 10 digits (20 in the Double Digit form), which would take 2 fields in either machine.

For Dewey, if a maximum size were not predetermined, one would have to use the longest number in the library as base for determining how many fields were needed.

INPUT-OUTPUT PROCEDURES in compiler language—WRITE
TAPE or PRINT routines would be very simple for Dewey, but com-
plex for LC or UDC. The three statements below are written in
FØRTRAN for a number in each system:

FØRMAT (3H TK, F4.O, 1HM, I2)	LC (TK7872.M45 Masers)
FØRMAT (F9.6)	DC (629.134353 Rockets)
FØRMAT (F4.1,2H+, X,F4.1)	UDC (655.1+ 688.1 Print-ing and Binding)

Obviously Dewey is easier for the machine to handle on output since
there is less work to be performed internally. The same is true of
input statements, again using FØRTRAN as an example:

READ 5, K

5 FØRMAT (2A1, F4.O, A1, I2)	LC (TK7872.M45)
5 FØRMAT (F9.6)	DC (629.134353)
5 FØRMAT (F4.1,A1,F4.1)	UDC (655.1+ 688.1)

Some of the connectors in UDC could not be used in their present
form because they already have a meaning in FØRTRAN. (e.g. / =
start a separate line) Again, Dewey is easiest to handle as far as the
machine is concerned.

USE OF DC for storage and compiler—If DC were arbitrarily limited to
15 places after the decimal, it would require 2 fields for storage in a
binary machine of the 7090 type, or 3 in a decimal machine of the 7070
series. It would take the format (F18.15) in FØRTRAN for both input
and output.

The largest LC number would require the same field space in the
binary machine, but less in the decimal. It would take more machine
processing in FØRTRAN compiler language.

AN ALL LETTER NOTATION, with a decimal for subdivision, would
be even better than DC from a classification point of view, and no
worse from the machine point of view. Such notation does not now
exist.

IF A MECHANIZED SHELVING AND FETCHING SYSTEM is developed to replace stack men, classification as a shelf location code
could end. Books could be filed by accession number or some other
numerical system, or by size, etc. In such a case the dictionary catalog
might be replaced or supplemented by a classified catalog.

Classification itself could be more completely developed as an organizational system if it did not have to serve as a shelf location device.
Thus, relationships among concepts and structure could be described. Multiple generic relationship classifications could be made
by computer.[10]

REFERENCES

1. U. S. Library of Congress. Decimal Classification Office. *Guide to the Use of Dewey
Decimal Classification; Based on the Practice of the Decimal Classification Office
at the Library of Congress.* Lake Placid Club, Essex County, N. Y., Forest Press of
Lake Placid Club Education Foundation, 1962.

2. British Standards Institution. *Guide to the Universal Decimal Classification (UDC)*. London, British Standards Institution, 1963. (B.S. 1000C:1963).

3. Sayers, W. C. B. *A Manual of Classification for Librarians and Classifiers*. 3d ed. London, Grafton, 1955.

4. Gulledge, J. R. "LC vs. DC for College Libraries." *Library Journal*, 49:1027. 1924.

5. Ashton, J. R. and Hansen, O. B. "Adaptations of the Dewey Classification to a College Divisional Library." *Journal of Cataloging and Classification*, 10:86-91. April 1954.

6. Seely, Pauline A. "Dewey 16th edition." *Library Resources and Technical Services*, 6:179-183. Spring 1962.

7. Hoage, A. Annette L. *The Library of Congress Classification in the United States*. Unpublished D.L.S. dissertation, School of Library Science, Columbia University, 1961.

8. Dawson, John M. *The Acquisition and Cataloging of Research Libraries*. Unpublished Ph.D. dissertation, Graduate Library School, University of Chicago, 1956.

9. Scott, Edith. "Cooperation and Communication in Cataloging and Classification." *Southeastern Librarian*, 8:136. 1958.

10. Doyle, Lauren B. "Indexing and Abstracting by Association." *American Documentation*, 13:378-390. October 1962.

IN THE MAIL

The "Statement on Types of Classification Available to New Academic Libraries," a report of the Classification Committee of the Cataloging and Classification Section appearing in *Library Resources and Technical Services,* 9:104-111, Winter 1965, contains one statement so misleading that I cannot refrain from asking you to publish a correction.

In question 6, under "b. Dewey Classification characteristics," appears the following statement:

(1) DC numbers appear on LC cards for about 35% of titles. This means that about 65% of cards purchased from LC have no DC number.

While the first sentence of this statement is substantially correct, the second sentence does not follow from the first, and is contrary to fact. One statement refers to titles, the other to cards.

The situation is that, while DC numbers have, in recent years, appeared on LC cards for about 35% of the *titles* for which cards have been printed, this includes titles in all languages. Analysis of Card Division sales made during the last eight years or more indicate that over 93% of *cards* sold are for English language titles. Frequent spot analyses confirm this figure as approximately correct. We have analyzed in recent weeks sales of cards shipped to 136 libraries. For purposes of sampling, two separate combinations of small orders were chosen at random on two separate days. The results were as follows: in the first combination were 772 slips comprising orders from 100 libraries. Of these slips, 624 (80.8%) were for cards containing DC numbers. In the second there were 437 slips, comprising orders from 24 libraries. Of these slips 350 (80.1%) were for cards having DC numbers. The percentages of individual orders from different types of library subscribers in these two combinations were as follows: (1) college and university 50%; (2) public 20%; (3) high school 15%; and (4) special 15%.

In addition, separate orders from Columbia University, Long Island University, University of Nebraska, Princeton University, University of Rochester, and Tennessee Polytechnic College were analyzed. Out of a total of 627 orders filled, 72% or 450 had Dewey numbers and 28% or 177 did not. Likewise, individual orders from the following public libraries were analyzed: Boston, La Puente, Moline, Brookline, Tucson, and Little Rock. Out of a total of 967 individual orders, 80% or 750 had Dewey numbers and 20% or 217 did not.

We grant that it would be desirable if DC numbers could appear on even more than 80% of the LC cards that are sold, and, as reported in the Library of Congress *Information Bulletin,* 24:73, February 8, 1965, discussions are now being held on this very subject. I think we can safely (and happily) say that the statement under question 8 of the report ("It is said that fewer DC numbers will appear on LC cards in the future") can now be superseded by a more optimistic expectation.—*Benjamin A. Custer, Editor, Dewey Decimal Classification, The Library of Congress*

Appendix B

THE LIBRARY OF CONGRESS CATALOGS IN BOOK FORM

A Catalog of Books Represented by Library of Congress Printed Cards. (Cards issued from August 1898 through July 1942) Ann Arbor, Mich., Edwards Brothers, Inc., 1942–46. 167 volumes. Reprint edition available from Rowman and Littlefield, Inc.[1] $1500

———. *Supplement* (Cards issued from August 1942 through December 1947) Ann Arbor, Mich., J. W. Edwards, Inc., 1948. 42 volumes. Reprint edition available from Rowman and Littlefield, Inc.[1] $395

The Library of Congress Author Catalog, 1948–1952. Ann Arbor, Mich., J. W. Edwards, Inc., 1953. 24 volumes. Reprint edition available from Rowman and Littlefield, Inc.[1] $240

The National Union Catalog, 1952–1955 Imprints. Ann Arbor, Mich., J. W. Edwards, Inc.,[2] 1961. 30 volumes $420

The National Union Catalog, a Cumulative Author List, 1953–1957. Ann Arbor, Mich., J. W. Edwards, Inc., 1958. 28 volumes. Reprint edition available from Rowman and Littlefield, Inc.[1] $275

Also available separately from Rowman and Littlefield, Inc.[1]: vol. 27: *Music and Phonorecords*, $20.00; vol. 28: *Motion Pictures and Filmstrips*, $20.00.

The National Union Catalog, a Cumulative Author List, 1958–1962. New York, Rowman and Littlefield, Inc.,[1] 1963. 54 volumes $495

Available separately: vols. 51 and 52: *Music and Phonorecords*, $40.00; vols. 53 and 54: *Motion Pictures and Filmstrips*, $40.00.

The National Union Catalog, a Cumulative Author List, 1963–1967. Ann Arbor, Mich., J. W. Edwards, Inc.,[2] 1969. 72 volumes $670

Available separately: *Music and Photorecords*, 3 volumes, $75; *Motion Pictures and Filmstrips*, 2 volumes, $45.

---

[1] *Rowman and Littlefield, Inc., 84 Fifth Ave., New York, N.Y. 10011. (Prices quoted are f. o. b. Totowa, N.J.)*

[2] *J. W. Edwards, Publisher, Inc., Ann Arbor, Mich. 48106. (Prices quoted are f. o. b. Ann Arbor, Mich.)*

The National Union Catalog, a Cumulative Author List, 1968, 1969[5] $500
Monthly, with quarterly and annual cumulations.

The subscription price for *The National Union Catalog* includes its *Register of Additional Locations* and the following parts of *The Library of Congress Catalogs,* which are also available separately at the prices listed:
  Library of Congress—Motion Pictures and Filmstrips[5] $25.00
  Library of Congress Catalog—Music and Phonorecords[5] $20.00
  National Register of Microform Masters[5] $5.00

The National Union Catalog, Pre-1956 Imprints.

A comprehensive retrospective catalog in approximately 610 volumes to be published over several years beginning in 1968 by Mansell Information/ Publishing Ltd.[4]

Library of Congress Catalog—Books: Subjects, 1950–1954. Ann Arbor, Mich., J. W. Edwards, Inc., 1955. 20 volumes. Reprint edition available from Rowman and Littlefield, Inc.[1] $247.50
Library of Congress Catalog—Books: Subjects, 1955–1959. Paterson, N.J., Pageant Books, Inc., 1960. 22 volumes. Available from Rowman and Littlefield, Inc.[1] $247.50
Library of Congress Catalog—Books: Subjects, 1960–1964. Ann Arbor, Mich., J. W. Edwards, Inc.[2] [1965] 25 volumes $275.00
Library of Congress Catalog—Books: Subjects, 1965, 1966, 1967[5] $201.50
Library of Congress Catalog—Books: Subjects, 1968[5] $250.00
Library of Congress Catalog—Books: Subjects, 1969[5] $250.00
  Three quarterly issues.

The National Union Catalog of Manuscript Collections, 1959–1961. Ann Arbor, Mich., J. W. Edwards, Inc.,[2] 1962 $9.75
The National Union Catalog of Manuscript Collections, 1962. Hamden, Conn., The Shoe String Press, Inc.,[3] 1964 $13.50
The National Union Catalog of Manuscript Collections, 1963–1964[5] $10.00
The National Union Catalog of Manuscript Collections, 1965, 1966, 1967[5] $15.00

The National Union Catalog, a Cumulative Author List
L. C. card 56–60041

---

[3] *The Shoe String Press, Inc., 60 Connolly Parkway, Hamden, Conn. 06514.*

[4] *Particulars of prices, alternative subscription plans, and further information concerning this publication are available from Mansell, 360 North Michigan Ave., Chicago, Ill. 60601.*

[5] *These issues of the catalogs are sold by the Card Division, Library of Congress, Building No. 159, Navy Yard Annex, Washington, D.C. 20541. Their purchase may be charged against the accounts of subscribers to the card service; others must pay in advance by check or money order payable to the Chief, Card Division, Library of Congress. Payments from foreign countries for these publications may be made with UNESCO coupons. Prices quoted include postage.*

Index